MEDIA, POLICY AND INTERACTION

Also of Interest

Media Discourse and the Yugoslav Conflicts
Edited by Pål Kolstø
978 0 7546 7629 4

Discourse Power Address
The Politics of Public Communication
Stuart Price
978 0 7546 4818 5

The Future of Journalism in the Advanced Democracies
Edited by Peter J. Anderson and Geoff Ward
978 0 7546 4404 0

The Academic Presentation: Situated Talk in Action
Johanna Rendle-Short
978 0 7546 4597 9

Media, Policy and Interaction

Edited by

RICHARD FITZGERALD
University of Queensland, Australia

WILLIAM HOUSLEY
Cardiff University, UK

ASHGATE

Published by
Ashgate Publishing Limited
Wey Court East
Union Road
Farnham
Surrey, GU9 7PT
England

Ashgate Publishing Company
Suite 420
101 Cherry Street
Burlington
VT 05401-4405
USA

www.ashgate.com

British Library Cataloguing in Publication Data
Media, policy and interaction.
  1. Mass media--Political aspects. 2. Mass media and public
  opinion. 3. Mass media and language.
  I. Fitzgerald, Richard. II. Housley, William.
  302.2'3'014-dc22

Library of Congress Cataloging-in-Publication Data
Media, policy and interaction / edited by Richard Fitzgerald and William Housley.
    p. cm.
  Includes bibliographical references and index.
  ISBN 978-0-7546-7414-6 (hardback) -- ISBN 978-0-7546-9158-7 (ebook)
  1. Mass media--Political aspects. 2. Mass media--Social aspects. 3. Mass
media policy. 4. Communication in politics. 5. Discourse analysis. 6. Mass media--
Influence. I. Fitzgerald, Richard. II. Housley, William, 1970-. III. Title.

  P95.8M39335 2010
  302.23--dc22

2009026736

ISBN 9780754674146 (hbk)
ISBN 9780754691587 (ebk)

Mixed Sources
Product group from well-managed
forests and other controlled sources
www.fsc.org Cert no. SA-COC-1565
© 1996 Forest Stewardship Council
FSC

Printed and bound in Great Britain by
MPG Books Group, UK

Contents

List of Figures and Table

Notes on Contributors

Brendan Bartlett is a Gellibrand Scholar, UNICEF Fellow, King Mongkut Medallist and award holder of the Rotary International Certificate for Significant Achievement in Education. He is a professor in the Faculty of Education and Griffith Institute of Educational Research at Griffith University where he teaches graduate and undergraduate programs in teacher education. He researches how people identify the 'big ideas' in texts they create or read and in their everyday homeplace and workplace problems – and how they remember, make sense of, and deal with such ideas.

Alain Bovet currently works as a Postdoctoral Research Fellow at the Institut Marcel Mauss, EHESS (Paris, France) on a European project about assessment practices in talent shows on French and German television. He also teaches at the University of Fribourg (Switzerland). His research and teaching topics are focused on the sociological analysis of various communicative processes, from everyday conversation to public controversies. He approaches such processes through detailed empirical analysis, the relevance of which is not confined to micro studies of verbal interaction. Inspired by ethnomethodological conversation and categorization analysis, his PhD (University of Fribourg, Switzerland 2007) was devoted to the media coverage (press and television) of the Swiss public controversy about GMOs, with a focus on the constitution of political communities.

Susan Bridges has taught in mainstream and higher education for the past 25 years. Her research focuses on pedagogy, diversity and interaction and is informed by ethnographic traditions. She employs multi-method approaches to research design and has a particular interest in interactional analysis. She is currently an assistant professor with the Faculty of Dentistry, The University of Hong Kong working in curriculum development and e-learning. Prior to this, she was a research fellow with the Faculty of Education at Griffith University. She received the International Award for Excellence from the *International Journal of Diversity* in 2007 (Bridges and Poyatos Matas 2006); and was runner-up for the same award with the *Journal of the World Universities Forum* (Bridges and Bartlett 2008).

Baudouin Dupret is Senior Research Fellow at the French National Centre for Scientific Research (CNRS) and also guest lecturer in socio-legal studies at the University of Louvain (Belgium) and at the Institute for Advanced Studies in the Social Sciences (EHESS, France). He has published extensively in the field of the sociology and anthropology of law, legislation and media, especially in the

Middle East. His current work involves a praxiological approach to the production of truth in Arab contexts, including courts and parliaments, scientific expertise, the media, and religious education. Recently he has co-edited two issues (9 and 10) of *Ethnographic Studies* on the theme of 'media, wars and identities'.

Jean-Noël Ferrié is educated in Political Sciences. He is senior research fellow at the French National Centre for Scientific Research (CNRS), based in Grenoble, France, at the Institut d'Etudes Politiques (IEP, PACTE). He is the author of many articles on Middle Eastern politics and morals. He is the author of two books: *Le Régime de la civilité en Egypte. Public et réislamisation* (Paris, CNRS Editions 2004) and *La Religion de la vie quotidienne chez les Marocains musulmans. Rites, règles et routines* (Paris, Karthala 2004).

Richard Fitzgerald is a Senior Lecturer in the School of Journalism and Communication at the University of Queensland, Australia. His research and publications explore media interaction and language, particularly in the areas of news and public access radio discourse, and the development and application of the methodology of membership categorization analysis and conversation analysis for exploring the organization of cultural knowledge and identity in interaction. Currently, as well as continuing his collaborative work with William Housley, he is also preparing a book *Contemporary Media Language* (Edinburgh University Press) with Sue McKay.

Emo Gotsbachner has been teaching Discourse Analysis since 1998, at the Political Science Department of Vienna University, where he also received his PhD. Viewed broadly, his research has explored various aspects of the connections between social structures of meaning and the distribution of power and social control. Research projects have been on informal legal mechanisms and their interferences with state law; on normalised forms of xenophobia; and on discursive-rhetorical strategies of right-wing populist parties. Currently he is manager of a research project on interpretive frames and how audience groups of different social and political background make sense of televised political debates.

Christian Greiffenhagen is Simon Research Fellow at the University of Manchester, currently conducting ethnographic research on mathematical practice. His recent publications are 'Video analysis of mathematical practice? Different attempts to 'open up' mathematics for sociological investigation', *Forum: Qualitative Social Research*, 'Unpacking tasks: the fusion of new technology with instructional work', *Computer Supported Cooperative Work (CSCW)*, 'Visual repairables: analysing the work of repair in human-computer interaction', *Visual Communication* (with Rod Watson), and 'Where do the limits of experience lie? Abandoning the dualism of objectivity and subjectivity', *History of the Human Sciences* (with Wes Sharrock).

William Housley is currently Senior Lecturer in Sociology at the Cardiff School of Social Sciences, Cardiff University. He has published widely in a range of journals and is author of *Interaction in Multidisciplinary Teams* (Ashgate 2003) co-author (with Paul Atkinson) of *Interactionism: An Essay In Sociological Amnesia* (Sage 2003) and (with Paul Atkinson and Sara Delamont) *Contours of Culture: Complex Ethnography and the Ethnography of Complexity* (Alta Mira Press 2008). His research interests include culture, symbolic interaction, ethnomethodology, ethnography, studies of social organization, interaction, membership categorization, political communication, national identity, organizational decision making, subjectivity and innovation in qualitative methods.

Enrique Klaus is a PhD candidate in Political Sciences at the Institut d'Etudes Politiques (IEP, PACTE). His thesis is a praxiological study of moral scandals in the Egyptian political life. He has been living in Cairo for five years as a research assistant in a French research centre abroad (CEDEJ) and was co-editor of *Chroniques égyptiennes* 2006 (Cedej 2007). His research concerns are public space under authoritarian rule, media (press, satellite-TV, social networks and other Web2.0 applications) in the Arab World and Middle-East Studies.

Hanna Rautajoki works as a researcher and a teacher at the University of Tampere, Finland. Her background is in social psychology (MA) and she is currently writing a sociological dissertation on the formation of participation framework in Finnish socio-political television discussions. Her scholarly interests include moral discourse and cultural categorizations related to current affairs discussion programmes, televisual identity formation and participants' extra-situational orientations. The dissertation is supported by a graduate school within the Finnish Doctoral Programme in Social Sciences (directed by Anssi Peräkylä) and it has enjoyed guidance and supervision from Jörg Bergmann, Ilkka Arminen, Mikko Lehtonen and Johanna Ruusuvuori.

Johanna Rendle-Short is Senior Lecturer in Linguistics and Applied Linguistics at the Australian National University. Her main research interest is conversation analysis, talk-in-interaction, and embodied discourse. She is the author of *The Academic Presentation: Situated Talk in Action*, in the Directions in Ethnomethodology and Conversation Analysis Series (Ashgate 2006). She analyses Australian political news interviews and the interaction of children with communication disorders. She is currently interested in the use of address terms, including terms such as 'mate', 'love' and 'darl'.

Marián Sloboda graduated from Charles University, Prague, Czech Republic (MA in Linguistics, Phonetics and Slavonic Studies), where he currently works as Researcher at the Department of Linguistics. His interests lie in ethnomethodologically informed sociolinguistics and discourse analysis. His most recent research has dealt with language management in Belarus, European multilingualism and the relationship between language and economy.

Sue Thomas is a Senior Lecturer in the Faculty of Education at Griffith University. Her research investigates the interrelationships between education policy and other institutions, such as the media, systems, schooling practices and professional identities. Her research into these interrelationships focuses on the language of policy, i.e. the discursive nature of policy. Sue uses Critical Discourse Analysis to analyse the discursive analysis of current policies on teacher quality as well as the discursive construction of professional identities of both teachers and educational leaders. Publications include *Education Policy in the Media: Public Discourses on Education* (Post Pressed 2006) and *Rethinking Leadership in Global Policy Contexts* (Springer forthcoming).

Patrick Watson is a PhD candidate at the University of Manchester, completing his doctoral research on the use of performance measurements by elected and bureaucratic officials. His main research interests lie in the role of ethnographic studies in political science as well as the impact of technological innovations on politics. He is currently Research Associate at Middlesex University (London) on the project 'Isis: Protecting Children in Online Social Networks'.

Acknowledgements

The authors would like to thank the editors for their guidance, their respective departments for their support and the ORF (Austrian Public Broadcasting Corporation) for permission to use material analysed in this book.

Transcript Conventions[1]

hello.	falling intonation
hello,	slight rising intonation
hello¿	rising intonation, weaker than that indicated by a question mark
hello?	strongly rising intonation
hel-	talk is cut off
>hello<	talk is faster than surrounding talk
<hello>	talk is slower than surrounding talk
HELLO	talk is louder than surrounding talk
°hello°	talk is quieter than surrounding talk
↑ or ↓	marked rising or falling shifts in pitch
he::llo	lengthening of a sound or syllable
<u>he</u>llo	emphasis
(1.0), (0.3)	timed intervals (silence), in seconds and tenths of seconds
(.)	short untimed pause, less than 0.2 of a second
.hh	audible inhalations
hh	audible exhalations
*	creaky voice
=	latched talk – talk following previous talk with no gap
[ ]	simultaneous/overlapping talk
(ook)	transcriber uncertainty

---

1 Common conversation analysis transcription conventions used in this volume. (See for example, Lerner, G. 2004 (ed.) *Conversation Analysis: Studies from the First Generation.* Amsterdam and Philadelphia: John Benjamins. Rendle-Short (this volume)).

Chapter 1

Media, Policy and Interaction: Introduction

Richard Fitzgerald and William Housley

The rise and prominence of studies of discourse reflects the importance now being given to understanding communication practices as part of and in relation to a range of social processes. One of the crucial institutions central to societal communication that lies betwixt and between the state, the market and the individual is the news media. And one of the central activities of the news media within democratic social forms is to hold elected officials and government to account. As a consequence of this conceptualization of the public sub-constitutional role of the news media social scientists, and discourse analysts in particular, have focused on the news media as a means of exploring the relations between language, policy communication, political accountability and public(s) (cf Chilton and Schäffner 2002).[1]

At one level the study of the social through language, or discourse, has developed an acute sensitivity to the political dimensions of language and power and the way language represents and shapes understandings of the world (Fairclough 1995, 2003, Van Dijk 1988, Wodak 2009). At another level an attention to the detailed methods participants use in order to conduct their talk-in-interaction has contributed to a reconsideration of traditional socio-political categories such as race, class, gender and social identity as members' phenomena irredeemably embedded in social action and language use (Sacks 1974, 1995, Garfinkel 1967, 2002, Button 1991, Hester and Housley 2002). A concern with members' practices and the accomplishment, use and display of socio-political categories within talk-in-interaction is of increasing interest to those pursuing ethnomethodological and related forms of analysis. The analysis of media practices in relation to policy debate, situated mediated political practices and communication provides an avenue of enquiry along which this increasing interest has found empirical resonance. The chapters in this collection represent cutting edge analyses of mediated socio-political practices built, as they are, upon members' methods of practical reasoning and interaction. The focus on language and talk-in-interaction provides a lens through which the relationship between members' methods and mediated political performance and practice can be understood.

Analyses of politics and the 'public sphere' in relation to rationality and communication are connected with Habermasian conceptualizations of the

---

1 See also the journals *Discourse and Society*, *Discourse Studies*, *Discourse and Communication*, *Language and Politics*, and *Text and Talk*.

social. It is fair to say many of the concerns with politics and the public sphere are framed within notions of communicative rationality, ideal speech situations and distorted communication (Habermas 1989). In recent years these ideas have informed debates surrounding the public sphere and the media as its relationship with political processes has grown more distinct to the point that it has become an integral feature of political process and communication in developed and developing societies. It is also of relevance where matters pertaining to the truth, policy debate and accountability are routine concerns for the emerging mediated public sphere. In this collection we have aimed to gather and present work by an internationally diverse set of scholars who respecify these concerns through the examination of language as social action.

Analysing Language, Media and Political Debate

The chapters in this collection represent an examination of the discursive relationship between the public and policy articulated in and through mediated forms of public space. In a general sense the analyses that follow explore the organization and presentation of policy in the public sphere and in particular the language, interaction and discourse practices of policy makers, politicians and other 'public agents' when engaged in explanation, defence or promotion of 'public matters' within and through the media. In this the collection represents a departure from treating the analysis of public policy at the level of government programs by focusing on the situated practices of policy presentation and discussion as part of a *mediated* public sphere. The focus, then, is on examining the lived negotiated detail of policy work within a communicative domain which increasingly makes use of a range of 'access' technologies (e.g. open letters, interactive TV debates, phone-ins, e-mail, blogs and social networking sites) in constituting public debate in relation to policy and news management.

As suggested earlier, at the heart of this collection is an interest in language use within the mediated political realm. This interest can be found at the core of all the chapters in this collection, although the particular direction this takes in each differs according to various analytic traditions and the social political context(s) of data. In exploring the relationship between language, discourse and policy, the authors select various methodological frames through which to trace the interconnected levels of relevance for both immediate participants and overhearing or temporally related audiences. For some, the level of analysis focuses on the interactional process by exploring the intersection of media language and public policy, whilst at the other end of the spectrum the level of analysis explores the ideological role of the media in framing and generating public attention in relation to government policy. Between these two analytic foci the papers frame and explore different levels of analysis that, whilst grounded in the interactional details of the media event, reveal and connect different levels of the socio-political and ideological contexts in which the policy exists and of which the policy is inexorably a part.

The focus on the interactional details of mediated events where policy debate or communication is salient means that many of the papers begin their analysis by drawing on ethnomethodologically informed methods such as conversation analysis (CA) and membership categorization analysis (MCA). These two methods can be understood as providing a way to explore the *in situ* orientation of the participants to the local contingencies of interaction whilst at the same time anchoring the socio-political levels of analysis within a particular mediated version of the interaction order. Through these locally focused approaches the analysis of further levels of discourse are then grounded within the management of the interaction as a negotiated accomplishment of the 'policy work' (e.g. communication, explanation, presentation and discussion of proposals/effects) in which the participants are engaged. In this way attention to the detail of language use *in situ*, and particularly the way language is hearably designed for an audience, underpins the connection between language and the wider social and political environment in which it is cast. Given the centrality of the methodologies of conversation analysis and membership category analysis for many of the chapters presented in this collection it is useful to provide an introduction to these methods.

Conversation Analysis and Membership Categorization Analysis

Both CA and MCA derive from Harvey Sacks' (1974, 1995) groundbreaking work examining everyday language and talk. Both of these approaches are grounded in the lived interactional detail of talk and interaction with the focus of CA on the sequential unfolding of interaction and the focus of MCA on the way people display their understanding of the social world around them. Since Sacks' early work CA has gone on to develop a prominent place within the analysis of language use, particularly in the analysis of institutional interaction (cf Arminen 2005). Prominent among these studies are those that have used CA as a means of highlighting the fine-grained sequential management of turn taking, the allocation of speech rights and topic change within broadcast contexts (Greatbatch 1988, 2001, Clayman and Heritage 2002, Hutchby 2006). MCA, whilst for many years a neglected area of Sacks' work, has recently developed a growing body of research and interest and is now an established ethnomethodological approach for examining practical methods of socio-cultural categorization work in relation to the local accomplishment of social organization and social order (Garfinkel 2002). The methodological approach first discussed by Sacks (1974, 1995), and developed by subsequent authors (Jayyusi 1984, Watson 1997, Hester and Eglin 1997, Housley and Fitzgerald 2002, 2009, Fitzgerald and Housley 2002, Housley 2000, 2002), provides a fine-grained analytic method for exploring the way members accomplish their interaction and display their knowledge of the world through the complex but methodical organization of social categories, devices and predicates mapped onto categories.

Whilst these two methodologies developed at different paces, and have at times been seen as separate enterprises, work to bring the two methods back together has increased through recognition that sequential and categorial work are mutually and inextricably entwined features within the ongoing flow of interaction. The combinational analysis of category work as part of the unfolding sequential management of interaction has since provided a rich seam of empirical observation through which to understand multiple layers of interaction (Fitzgerald and Housley 2002, Housley and Fitzgerald 2002, 2009, Benwell and Stokoe 2006, Fitzgerald, Housley and Butler 2009).

The routine mutual work of social knowledge in sequence is highlighted by Sacks's (1974) now famous example of the child's story 'The baby cried. The mummy picked it up'. The power of the descriptive apparatus upon which Sacks embarks is grounded in the basic idea that we have no problem making sense of the story as being about a mummy picking up her baby in response to her baby crying. Sacks locates the understanding of the story through the hearer recognising the social categories 'baby' and 'mummy' as related or tied to each other through the organizational device 'family'. Through this commonsense recognition procedure a set of expectable attributes (predicates) may be associated with the categories (that is, babies cry, mothers comfort their children) and linked together within the organizational device 'family'. This constitutes the actions as not only expected but also directed at each other, that is, *this* baby's crying is for *its* mother and the mummy's action is *expected* because the baby is crying. Thus, the way we hear this story is that it is the mother of the baby who picks up the baby and she does so because her baby is crying, when in fact no such necessary connection is explicit in the sentences. That is to say, we make sense of the sequence of the actions in the story through applying our commonsense knowledge about the way social categories act and interact to render the story intelligible. Thus this basic frame of members' categorization practices, together with a number of commonsense rules of application, work as practical registers that reinforce the observed or described actions of social categories where such categories are collected within occasioned organizational devices and which form a major part of the commonsensical framework of members' methods and recognizable capacities of practical sense-making.

Analysing Interaction, Policy and Debate

Whilst the analysis of media and political interaction through CA work has had significant impact on understanding the way political interviews and debates are managed through various media, only recently has attention turned to the topic of politics as a focus of analysis. In these initial studies, and continued in this volume, the focus is shifted to examining the use of sequential, categorial and discursive devices and practices in the presentation of policy and political debate within the media/political sphere as well as public/citizen engagement though public access media formats (Fitzgerald and Housley 2006, Housley and Fitzgerald 2001, 2003a,b, 2007, Leudar and Nekvapil 2000, 2007, Ekström and Johansson 2008).

For many of the authors in this collection a combination of MCA/CA together with other methodological approaches are utilized as a way of relating the fine-tuned analysis of the local interactional detail with an approach that addresses wider social knowledge. The combination of methods allows the authors to explore the detailed workings of social categorization as a mediated aspect of the wider political discourse and socio-political environment of which it is part and which it addresses. Indeed, as the chapters in this collection make clear, the discussion of public policy and the organization of political debate within democratic contexts trade on identifying and appealing to categories of population for support or appeal.

The strength of the analytic frames adopted are revealed in the way the deployment of social categories and category use in the immediate contingencies of persuasion are negotiated through a matter of timing, opportunity and relevance. In this way the actual content of 'politicized' devices organized around national, religious and ethical/moral 'logics' are seen as indexical to the particular circumstances and context of their use. For it is in the construction of these devices on the ground through methods of inclusion and exclusion of various categories that the political argument is made, heard and reported. These devices are always created *in situ* as the work of assembling the categories, and the work to which these categories and devices are put, are managed within the immediate and local context of their use. This indexicality of language use is central to the analytic detail within this collection but with an appreciation that the local work of categorization is *designed* for a wider political environment. As such, whilst garnering support or advocating for or against a particular policy, debating a future action or stirring up trouble is irredeemably achieved through local action, this action is not isolated or private but, as knowingly public, reveals a wider strategic purpose which is both observable through the local dynamics of the situation, the media event in which it exists and the wider political context in which it operates.

The Contributions in this Collection

The strength of this collection is in bringing together different political contexts, public policy issues and media practice but where the problem is in many respects the same – exploring the actual detail of political and media interaction and its relation to the wider media political and social environment. With this context in mind we now turn our attention to the contributions to this collection.

In Chapter 2, the editors William Housley and Richard Fitzgerald examine the way identity categories, predicates and configurations are used in accomplishing policy debate in participatory frameworks. Through this discussion a focus on the immediate and micro-character of activities, such as those found in a radio phone-in and political interview, are seen to provide a powerful apparatus through which senses of democratic exchange and the promotion of specific views and contested issues can be realized. Using MCA and CA the authors argue that the display of popular opinions as found in callers' comments on radio phone-ins, or the questioning of an interviewer on behalf of the electorate, public, or people 'out there' often use the form of personalized categorial encounters which provide a powerful moral ordering of the topic and local debate. In this way Housley and Fitzgerald demonstrate how interviews, phone-ins and the like represent a form of interactional and discursive machinery through which accountability is popularly heard to be enacted and realized and policy debate organized, managed and displayed.

In the next chapter Alain Bovet explores an aspect of participatory democracy in Switzerland where citizens have the right to initiate or modify public policy by raising enough signatures to trigger a national vote. However, as Bovet demonstrates in his analysis of televised debates prior to a vote taking place, the media orientation to 'for' and 'against' positions serves to create an over simplified prism around the debate through which subtle issues and positions are not available. Through an analysis that combines MCA and CA Bovet initially highlights the work that on screen captions do in creating a binary frame through which panel members are allocated to either 'side' of debate. This not only serves to allocate positions to those involved in the debate but also through use of biographical information prior to the debate provides a categorial frame by which topic identity drawn upon is predicated with credibility within the debate. However, rather than this being a result of media influence or preference, Bovet demonstrates that it is the very structuring of the issue around a 'for' or 'against' vote that shapes the media debate, and the way the debate is conducted. Thus, any subtlety or sophistication of the argument and the possible positions or opinions available around an issue are instead constrained by the two meta-categories of an omni-relevant reductive relational device; namely 'for' or 'against'. What the discussion highlights, and which is further fleshed out in other discussions in the collection, is the way category work is both essential to political and policy discussions but also how this constrains and influences the workings of political processes.

In the next chapter Emo Gotsbachner examines a political debate in Austria using MCA and CA to detail interactive moves and identity work that enables the speakers to position themselves within and as part of an interpretive frame from which to conduct their argument. By examining interpretive frames through their communicative structure Gotsbachner highlights the production and comprehension of discourse through its 'recognizability', through the routine standardized deployment of words, phrases, sentences and stereotyped images, sources of information that when used provide thematically reinforcing clusters of facts or judgements. Within this interpretive frame the work of identity is seen as crucial as it provides access, legitimation and credibility to the speaker. Whilst initially highlighting the interactional work of establishing a credible identity through self categorization it is the categorization of others which is shown to be a key element in establishing, maintaining and defending a credible position within an adversarial debate. In this Gotsbachner reveals a high degree of dexterity by which speakers are able to interpret local interactional events as representative of the presence or absence of predicates of political value such as trust, honesty and credibility.

Using a similar set of methodological tools Hanna Rautajoki develops an analysis of the closings of two Finnish TV debates dedicated to discussing the possible use of military force by the US against Afghanistan following the 9/11 attacks. The analysis focuses on the closing round of answers by panel members as they are invited by the hosts to consider the implications of future action. Rautajoki's analysis highlights the way the closing question serves to bring together and draw a line under the preceding debate and move to the 'future' through considered speculation of possible action and consequences. Rautajoki highlights the way the panellists orientate to the creation of a moral device 'us'. This moral device draws upon an 'omni-relevant' device of national membership, to which the audience are assumed members of and through which taken for granted predicates are expressed through notions of recognizable 'national' characteristics as a way of navigating and constituting stances towards particular political and foreign policy matters. As becomes evident throughout this collection the relationship engendered between social categories and their related predicates serves an important function in political debate which is no more evident than through the various appeals to the collective 'we' device through which particular rights and responsibilities are predicated. The power of an inclusive 'we' allows the speaker to envelop or include themselves within the 'we' group and thus be able to claim speaking rights on behalf of the category. In Rautajoki's discussion the invocation of 'shared values' is used to predicate shared moral opinions and assumptions about how *future* events are to be interpreted.

In the next chapter Johanna Rendle-Short examines the use of shared values and inclusive predicates through the work that goes into categorizing sections of the population through appeals to national 'mythic' predicates. Using CA and drawing from a number of Australian radio and TV interviews the discussion explores the way Australian politicians use media interviews to advance their argument through the creation of, invocation of and appeal to 'communities' invoked around audience and population. Whilst dividing an 'audience' for political purpose is a theme throughout this collection the analysis highlights the way those appeals are made through an interpretive frame of 'mateship' and 'a fair go'. For Rendle-Short the appeal to various political constituencies is operationalized through the generation of a sense of community that possesses certain predicates through which the political spokesperson then aligns themselves to. The preference for radio talkback programmes and radio interviews has been a mainstay of Australian politics, finding its zenith during John Howard's premiership for its direct and intimate address to particular audiences. However, rather than this being a one-way process the analysis demonstrates the mutual dependency of the politician and host through the possessive reference of the listeners (through descriptions such as '*your* listeners', '*your* audience', 'voters who are listening to *you*'), though pointing out that the host addresses an audience whilst the politician addresses a constituency.

In the next chapter Patrick Watson and Christian Greiffenhagen shift the focus from media debates to the process of policy news gathering by press gallery journalists. Through an ethnomethodologically informed ethnography combined with CA and MCA Watson and Greiffenhagen examine the 'press scrum' in which short exchanges of question and answer sequences provide the raw material for later broadcast or publication. Examining the information gathering process prior to broadcast the authors reveal the collaborative work by journalists; where rather than the encounter being a competitive free for all with journalists competing for scoops or exclusives there is a high degree of collaboration throughout the event. This is manifest in a number of ways such as questions being collaboratively managed and answers treated as being 'for everyone', as well as an orientation to local technological considerations and medium-specific materials. As the authors point out, the collaborative work engaged in by and within the press scrum where policy is questioned is not for an overhearing audience – rather this process stands prior to any particular medium (e.g. TV or Radio) or the political leanings of the specific news organ.

The way events are framed and policies presented through such framing is central to the discussion by Marián Sloboda in his examination of Belarus news where he highlights the work of categorizing a national population in support of a national policy. In this case, rather than the political and media discourse creating opposing sides around a policy by drawing on omni-relevant predicates of national characteristics as explored by Rautajoki (this volume), Sloboda explores how category work serves to create the 'other side' of the debate as being outside the country and in opposition to national policy. Using MCA and CA methods of analysis the author explores the way in which the news presenter introduces various interviewees who appear 'on cue' as relevant categories in support for government action. Thus, rather than the interviewees representing or offering contrasting positions around a topic or issue with the host acting as mediator, as discussed in many of the chapters examining political debates in this collection, the outside reports create a position from which the opposing or counter argument is located outside of the national 'community', and with vested interests to do so. In highlighting the idealized yet ambiguous democratic accountable role of the media in Belarus and other countries Sloboda's analysis raises some interesting questions around the wider processes within and through which policy is addressed through the media. Whilst the role of the media as facilitating democratic accountability is shown as a rhetorical device in Sloboda's chapter it is not of course confined to his case study. Rather, the media in this and other countries is shown to use various techniques by which to present opinions – or the context from which those opinions are presented – from within or as part of a particular (moral) frame.

An examination of moral accountability in politics is explored by Baudouin Dupret, Enrique Klaus and Jean-Noël Ferrié through following the progress of a political scandal arising initially from a comment by the Egyptian Minister of

Culture in a newspaper article suggesting the headscarf worn by some women was 'regressive'. The authors construct a dialogic network (Nekvapil and Leudar 2002) by which to trace the evolution of the scandal through its interconnected manifestations published in media and parliament discussions. The evolution of the story is explored through different levels of analysis beginning with an examination of the way the scandal is initially constructed within parliament, through the generalizing process by which the Minister's personal life is then brought to bear on his public role, to the wider political context in which 'reputation' is then judged against competence and fitness to carry out public service. Through tracing the scandal through its dialogic network of mutual interdependence of media and politics the authors highlight the trajectory of the scandal and in doing so relate this to understanding the anatomy of scandals.

Susan Bridges and Brendan Bartlett continue with the theme of education policy as well as the technique of invoking a moral device of 'good' and 'bad' teachers in their analysis of a policy by the Hong Kong Government to improve professional standards of teachers. Focusing on an open letter to all teachers the discussion explores the policy data through three levels of analysis; the social and historical context of the document, the language and organization of the content of the document, and finally the ideological power revealed through lexical choice. In doing this the authors explore the way membership category work is used within the letter to invoke a moral imperative to accept the ideas behind the policy and act accordingly.

Sue Thomas's chapter also draws from the Australian media to examine the construction of a 'problem' by the media and allocation of 'responsibility' for that problem prior to government policy formation. Using Critical Discourse Analysis (CDA) Thomas highlights the way policies around teaching and education exist in a highly politicized policy arena where the categories of 'good' and 'bad' teaching and teachers are infused with morally inflected ideology. In her discussion, Thomas examines a series of newspaper articles and commentary leading up to and against a background of proposed government policy concerning the need to equip teachers through on going development of professional standards. Focusing on one particular Australian newspaper, *The Australian*, Thomas traces the discussion of and around education policy and the proliferation of news articles on education policy in the run up to a government policy conference. Through this the discussion highlights the way the media created a discursive context by which policy discussions could be framed. In some ways the analysis resembles a number of discussions within the collection that highlight the creation of simplified binary opposition through which the opposing position is to be interpreted as ideologically informed (as opposed to the newspaper and its readers' position) and thus any objection can be dismissed as reactionary and obstructionist in relation to the future discussion of education policy.

What becomes clear from the varied discussions in this collection is that whilst the studies draw from different types of analysis a concern with language practices and categorization, albeit within sequential, dialogical, moral and ideological frames, is central to understanding media, interaction, policy and debate. While polls may be invoked, or statistics relayed and discussed, the primary means through which policy debate and talk is accomplished and presented are grounded in mundane methods of lay reasoning. This collection demonstrates the way in which such reasoning is articulated and presented in political discourse and the mutually constitutive relationship between culture, discourse and interaction as a dynamic and fluid entity through which categorizations of self, identity, claims-making and normative assessments are routinely employed during, and as an essential resource for, policy debate.

References

Arminen, I. 2005. *Institutional Interaction: Studies of Talk at Work*. Aldershot: Ashgate.

Benwell, B. and Stokoe, L. 2006. *Discourse and Identity*. Edinburgh: Edinburgh University Press.

Button, G. 1991. (ed.) *Ethnomethodology and the Human Sciences*. Cambridge: Cambridge University Press.

Chilton, A. and Schäffner, C. 2002. *Politics as Text and Talk: Analytic Approaches to Political Discourse*. Amsterdam and Philadelphia, PA: John Benjamins.

Clayman, S. and Heritage, J. 2002. *The News Interview: Journalists and Public Figures on the Air*. Cambridge: Cambridge University Press.

Ekström, M. and Johansson, B. 2008. Talk scandals. *Media, Culture and Society*, 30 (1), 61-79.

Fairclough, N. 1995. *Media Discourse*. London: Arnold.

Fairclough, N. 2003. *Analysing Discourse Textual Analysis for Social Research*. London: Routledge.

Fitzgerald, R. and Housley, W. 2002. Identity, categorization and sequential organization: the sequential and categorial flow of identity in a radio phone-in. *Discourse and Society*, 13 (5), 579-602.

Fitzgerald, R. and Housley, W. 2006. Categorisation, accounts and motives: 'letters-to-the-editor' and devolution in Wales, in *Devolution and Identity*, edited by J. Wilson and K. Stapleton. Aldershot: Ashgate, 111-126.

Fitzgerald, R., Housley, W. and Butler, C. 2009. Omnirelevance and Interactional Context. *Australian Journal of Communication* (in press).

Garfinkel, H. 1967. *Studies in Ethnomethodology*. Oxford: Polity.

Garfinkel, H. 2002. *Ethnomethodology's Program: Working out Durkheim's Aphorism*. Lanham, MD: Rowman & Littlefield Publishers.

Greatbatch, D. 1988. A turn-taking system for British news interviews. *Language in Society*, 17 (3), 401-430.

Greatbatch, D. 2001. Conversation analysis: neutralism in British news interviews, in *Approaches to Media Discourse*, edited by A. Bell and P. Garrett. Oxford: Blackwell, 163-185.

Habermass, J. 1989. *The Structural Transformation of the Public Sphere: An Inquiry into a Category of Bourgeois Society*. Cambridge, MA: MIT Press.

Hester, S. and Eglin, P. 1997. *Culture in Action: Studies in Membership Categorisation Analysis*. Washington, DC: University Press of America.

Hester, S. and Housley, W. 2002 (eds). *Language, Interaction and National Identity*. Aldershot: Ashgate.

Housley, W. 2000. Category work and knowledgeability within multidisciplinary team meetings. *TEXT*, 20 (1), 83-107.

Housley, W. 2002. Moral discrepancy and 'fudging the issue' in a radio news interview. *Sociology*, 36 (1), 5-23.

Housley, W. and Fitzgerald, R. 2001. Categorisation, narrative and devolution in Wales. *Sociological Research Online*, 6 (2).

Housley, W. Fitzgerald, R. 2002. The reconsidered model of membership categorisation. *Qualitative Research*, 2 (1), 59-74.

Housley, W. and Fitzgerald, R. 2003a. National identity, categorisation and debate, in *Language, Interaction and National Identity*, edited by S. Hester and W. Housley. Cardiff Papers in Qualitative Research. Aldershot: Ashgate, 38-59.

Housley, W. and Fitzgerald R. 2003b. Moral discrepancy and political discourse: accountability and the allocation of blame in a political news interview. *Sociological Research Online*, 8 (2).

Housley, W. and Fitzgerald, R. 2007. Media, categorisation, policy and debate. *Critical Discourse Studies*, 4 (2), 187-206.

Housley, W. and Fitzgerald, R. 2009. Membership categorization, culture and norms in action. *Discourse and Society*, 20 (3), 345-362.

Hutchby, I. 2006. *Media Talk. Conversation Analysis and the Study of Broadcasting*. Maidenhead: Open University Press.

Jayyusi, L. 1984. *Categorisation and Moral Order*. London: Routledge and Keegan Paul.

Leudar, I. and Nekvapil, J. 2000. Presentations of Romanies in the Czech media: on category work in television debates. *Discourse and Society*, 11 (4), 488-513.

Leudar, I. and Nekvapil, J. 2007. The war on terror and Muslim Britons safety: a week in the life of a dialogical network. *Ethnographic Studies*, 9, 44-62.

Nekvapil, J. and Leudar, I. 2002. On dialogical networks: arguments about the migration law in Czech mass media in 1993, in *Language Interaction and National Identity*, edited by S. Hester and W. Housley. Aldershot: Ashgate, 60-101.

Sacks, H. 1974. On the analyzability of stories by children, in *Ethnomethodology*, edited by R. Turner. Harmondsworth: Penguin, 216-232.

Sacks, H. 1995. *Lectures in Conversation*, edited by Gail Jefferson. Vol. 1 and 2. Oxford: Blackwell.

Van Dijk, T. 1988. *News as Discourse*. London: Lawrence Erlbaum Associates.

Watson, D.R. 1997. Some general reflections of 'categorisation' and 'sequence' in the analysis of conversation, in *Culture in Action, Studies in Membership*

Categorisation Analysis, edited by S. Hester and P. Eglin. Lanham, MD: University Press of America and International Institute for Ethnomethodology and Conversation.

Wodak, R. 2009. *'Politics as Usual': The Discursive Constructions and Representation of Politics in Action*. Basingstoke: Palgrave.

Chapter 2

Membership Category Work in Policy Debate[1]

William Housley and Richard Fitzgerald

Introduction

In this chapter the themes of public accountability, government policy and interaction are examined through empirical instances of media discourse as a means of exploring the use of identity categories, predicates and configurations in accomplishing policy debate in participatory media frameworks. The discussion respecifies and explores the situated character of media settings as a means of documenting, describing and illustrating the interactional methods associated with policy debate, public participation/representation and democracy-in-action.

Broadcast news and related media formats not only report 'facts' but are also used as a resource for the breaking of government initiatives and policy to the wider voting public (Boorstin 1973). Furthermore, the media is seen to represent an area where 'accountability' and other forms of democratic checks and balances are performed (Fairclough 1995) and where debates concerning government policy have been articulated and re-examined within the ever-expanding space of influence that is occupied by media institutions and programmes. These developments are often linked to the supposed developing role of the media in public engagement (Thomas, Cushion and Jewell 2004).

Despite new forms of media/citizen participation emerging, political communication remains overwhelmingly channelled through mass media with public participation programmes, such as panel debates, letters to the editor and radio phone-ins, familiar forums of public deliberation and engagement (Wahl-Jorgensen 2002). The appeal of public access programmes lies in the opportunity to contribute to public debate and confront established power through the lived experience of ordinary people, articulated through personal stories and testimony which connect their personal experiences with larger political issues and contribute to an 'emancipatory public sphere' (Livingstone and Lunt 1994: 160). Indeed McNair, Hibberd and Schlesinger (2002: 109) note that the movement from elite to mass representation in public participation broadcasting, including the shift from deference to an interrogative style of media political interaction, has contributed

---

1   This chapter is an edited and revised version of a paper first published in *Critical Discourse Studies* (2007).

substantially to the development of a culture of mediated public access in political debate (Clayman and Heritage 2002). A critical dimension of participation, therefore, involves the contours of interaction enabled and constrained by mediated forms of public access to public debate. It is this dimension of public participation that this chapter will focus upon through a consideration of empirical examples.

Analysing political talk-in-interaction

Traditional conceptualizations of the public sphere, accountability, and democracy often gloss over the micro-sociological dimensions of democratic practice, opinion management and democratic accountability. However in this chapter we highlight the interactional machinery of policy debate within media settings and demonstrate that the interactional practices within these settings can be understood to organize and present activities associated with the dissemination of information, public scrutiny and accountability within democratic social forms. By drawing upon the methods of membership categorization analysis (MCA) in combination with conversation analysis (CA) (Housley and Fitzgerald 2002a, 2009, Fitzgerald and Housley 2002, Butler 2008, Stokoe 2009) we illustrate how an analysis of the interactional and social organization of media settings can formulate an understanding of democratic life as an interactional accomplishment that is located within specific discursive spaces, moments and sedimentations.

The analysis of broadcast language through CA has revealed some of the participatory methods through which media talk is organized, as part of the wider environment of interaction, but also contributed to understanding how media interaction is organized as mediated interaction. Prominent among these studies are those that have adopted CA as a means of exploring turn taking, the allocation of speech rights, topic change and recipient design within broadcast contexts (Hutchby 1996, 2001, Thornborrow 2001, Thornborrow and Fitzgerald 2002). While CA has provided a powerful and important understanding of the social/sequential organization of media talk-in-interaction, the development of membership categorization analysis (for example, Sacks 1995, Hester and Eglin 1997, Watson 1997, Fitzgerald and Housley 2002, 2006, Housley and Fitzgerald 2002a, 2003, 2009) and other forms of enquiry have provided a methodological means of analysing not only the social organization of the situated character of media discourse but also the accomplishment and constitution of opinions, claims-making, the moral constitution of accountability, and the situated articulation and promotion of world views or government policies. The immediate and micro-character of activities associated with public access programmes such as radio phone-ins or political interviews thus provides a powerful apparatus through which senses of democratic exchange and the promotion of specific views and contested issues can be realized. For example, interaction between an interviewer and a member of the government, or exchanges between host and a member of the public, can be framed and utilized as resources for doing accountability in a democratic society in a manner that preserves a sense of immediacy and is tied to a clearly defined frame of subjectivity. The display of popular opinions in the radio phone-in or the questioning of an interviewer on behalf of the electorate, public, or people 'out there' form powerful interactional events that can be relayed to large numbers of listeners in the form of a personalized encounter (Scannell 2000). Indeed, within the USA and Australia, the power of talk-radio, with its characteristic use of phone-ins, interviews, and, sometimes, vitriolic abuse of opinions that differ from those favoured by the programme host, has been marshalled as a resource for a number of single issue campaigns and the pursuit of party politics. Whilst within the United Kingdom this trend is not as evident, the format does provide space for exchanges of opinion and the promotion of certain world views and perspectives of citizens in relation to government policy as a topical matter.

Methodological approach

As indicated above, in the analysis below we draw on the two interrelated approaches to the analysis of talk-in-interaction, CA and MCA. We approach the sequential organization of media debate within the frame of turn-generated utterances in which the categorical features and sequential flow of question/ answer formats are crucial to understanding interaction and, by extension, forms of mediated interaction (Sacks 1995, Watson 1997, Fitzgerald and Housley 2002). An additional consideration here involves the normative and moral characteristics of categories and categorization. While the display of categories and devices are situated events, they also display members' moral work and normative assessments as a practical and occasioned matter (Jayyusi 1984, 1991, Housley and Fitzgerald 2009). Thus, a central methodological characteristic of this form of analysis is a concern with the categorical and sequential dimensions of talk-in-interaction that is grounded in terms of the normative descriptive apparatus of 'culture-in-action' (Hester and Eglin 1997). In situating the broader dimensions of broadcast talk in relation to the interactional production of participatory discourse, opinion management and display of accountability we explore two interrelated aspects. Firstly, we explore how models of categorization and identification are utilized as a means of accomplishing and resisting patterns of inclusion/exclusion, warrantability and unwarrantability in relation to plans for Welsh and Scottish devolution in the United Kingdom prior to the referendum on the matter. Secondly we explore the role of moral categories and devices as a means of assessing the trustworthiness of political collectives and accomplishing accountability through specific interactional methods within the context of the 2001 Bovine Spongiform Encephalopathy (BSE) crisis in the UK.

Geography, identity and warrantability

Radio phone-ins or talkback are seen to hold a unique place as an important venue for 'populist deliberation', through which citizens and politicians can bypass mainstream news and journalistic formats to get their message or opinion across in what is often seen as a 'genuine public sphere' (Ross 2004: 787, see also Hutchby 1996, Thornborrow 2001, Hutchby 2001, Housley and Fitzgerald 2002b, Fitzgerald and Housley 2007, Rendle-Short this volume). In the example below we explore the categorical work employed within a political phone-in through the way identity and geography may be tied to a notion of 'warrantability' to speak on a topic. The topic here is the 1997 UK government proposals for the devolution of Wales. This type of participatory format often promotes debate along the lines of, and is organized around, the positions of either 'for' or 'against' an issue (see also Bovet this volume). Within this organization the caller will, and is expected to (Hutchby 1996), offer opinions that implicitly, or more often explicitly, allocate a position on the issue at hand and in so doing cast him or her into a topic opinion category (Fitzgerald and Housley 2002). Whilst in this case the caller does indeed offer an opinion, of particular interest here is the further suggestion by the caller that her opinion may not be legitimate due to her category membership, and subsequently the way the host configures the caller's category in relation to the topic. In this way, the local categorical membership and predicates of the caller become a political issue approached by the host through configuring hierarchies of category membership.

Extract 1: Election Call, UK BBC Radio 4 and BBC 1

```
68 H:Double four our next caller is Betty Lawson from Norfolk
69 C:I think Wales should vote no(.) and the reason, I live in
70   Norfolk so Perhaps they think I shouldn't have a say, but they
71   already have too many quangos and if you have a secretary of
72   state for Wales who is a member of the Cabinet and without such
73   a big majority would be accountable to the House of Commons in
74   debate they will know what's going on this way they will not know
75   what's going on and if you get little clans of people people like
76   you've got in these various quangos now they are simply ur ur
77   feeding their own interests and it would be a state where Scotland
78   would be on its own Wales [would be on its own]
79 H:                        [well let's just just ]
80   Let me ask you Betty Lawson just ur r ur ask you why you think
81   that as someone from Norfolk you should have a say in the
82   [way that Wales ] is governed
83 C:[because I think]
84   whether you like(.) well if you look at the Balkans and that's
85   the example I would make they had all these Serbs,
86   Cro[ats and Muslims]
```

```
87 H:   [but that doesn't] that doesn't quite address
88      [the point of wh]y you as as somebody from England should have
89 C:   [it's the same thing]
90 H:   say ur in the affairs of Wales
91 C:   well how much money has Scotland and Wales had from England?
92 H:   well let let me put that to…
```

Having given her opinion at line 69 the caller then begins to offer an account for why she holds this particular view. However, before finishing the first point upon which she has embarked she shifts focus and suggests that 'they' (we suggest that 'they' refers primarily to the two guests but also to their supporters and possibly, in the broadest sense, all those in Wales) might question the legitimacy of her having an opinion on this topic because of her geographical location (from *Norfolk*). Thus, despite the caller having telephoned the programme, got on air, and offered an opinion, she nonetheless suggests that her opinion may be seen as *unwarrantable* because of her category membership. That is to say, she suggests that for some people she may not occupy a topic relevant category to be afforded a relevant topic opinion category of either 'for' or 'against'. Thus for the caller the political question 'should Wales vote yes or no' on which the media debate is organized also has within it the possibilities of warranted and unwarranted opinions. This is so despite the media debate she is entering encompassing the whole of the UK and despite the fact that callers from different parts of the UK have previously called in and given their opinions. For this caller there is a moral ordering of opinions into those that 'should' and 'should not' be treated as warrantable organized around geographic category membership. After making this point the caller then moves onto another point. However the host, at line 79, picks up on the point about geography and the caller's warrantability to have an opinion on this topic. As discussed elsewhere (Fitzgerald and Housley 2002) the topic opinion category 'against' not only operates as a predicate of 'caller' but may also be utilized by the host in the next turn position to adopt the opposite category member for this device and thus generate debate.

In this case, although the caller has provided some footing concerning possible characterizations of her opinion of Welsh devolution, the host's question seeks out the grounds of her own account which questions her legitimacy to speak due to her self-professed 'problematic' geographical category membership. In formulating the question the host shifts the reference from the caller's personal geographical location '*I live in Norfolk*' to the broader device in which the caller is then collected as a member of the category '*all those* who live in Norfolk'. Thus, for the host, the caller's self proposed problematic location (i.e., *Betty Lawson in Norfolk*) is treated not as a matter peculiar to the caller as an individual, but in terms of the caller as a member of the category 'those who live in Norfolk'. The reformulated category 'people from Norfolk' subsumes the caller's individual location as part of a category in relation to the device '*this* media debate on Welsh devolution' and from which the caller and host orientate to the relevance of a category's opinion on the topic.

Despite the host's question concerning the caller's topic category membership the caller begins to offer further observations about devolution. Thus at line 87 the host again seeks to clarify the relation and relevance of the caller to the topical device, though now the host changes the category descriptor from '*Norfolk*' to '*England*'. The shift by the host from Norfolk to England reformulates the issue of warrantability as the category 'people from Norfolk' becomes part of the device 'people from England', and through consistency these are category members of the device 'areas outside Wales'. Indeed further use of the consistency rule would suggest that as these geographical categories are part of the United Kingdom but are not Wales, they could also include the categories of Scotland and Northern Ireland. It is not then that Norfolk is in a problematic relationship in having a say on Welsh devolution, but that Norfolk is a category within the device England and England is a category within the device 'not in Wales'. The issue then is about the status of opinions on Welsh devolution from category members of the device 'not in Wales'.

Here then the topic of warrantability is configured around category membership of political and geographical devices where the relevance of a category to a topic can be understood in terms of warrantability and claims-making. In this case the negotiation of categories of identification (i.e., national identity, place and geographical location) has a powerful influence on the character of debate and the ability to advance claims on specific policy – such as devolution. This process, however, is not merely confined to issues of national identity. In terms of radio talk and public participation such interactional work provides an apparatus for normative configurations of inclusion and exclusion, not only of callers or guests but also of the collectives and groups generated via debate that provide possible loci of identification for listeners. This use of categorization work and related methods is also evident in the next extract, in which remote identities and configurations of public membership are invoked and mobilized alongside explicitly moral devices in a political interview format.

Moral discrepancy and allocating blame: personalized categories and collective accountability

In the next example, from a BBC television current affairs programme *On the Record*, the interviewer makes use of various forms of moral categorization in attempting to make the political guest accountable in relation to a specific moral device, blame *requires* punishment. These forms of moral device are not necessarily tied to persons or actions *a priori*, although they may be ascribed during the course of interaction. Rather, the ascription of moral devices is a product of unfolding interaction and the availability of cultural categories and predicates through negotiated parameters of inference *in situ*. These moral devices may include trust, competence and honesty, and their associated predicates. As the extract demonstrates, the ascription or non-ascription of such moral devices is achieved through the exploration of a form of category-invoked moral calculus in which certain (relational) predicates of moral attributes are displayed. In the extract below the interviewer begins to question the guest about the public inquiry into the BSE crisis, and suggests that the current government will be using the previous government's handling of the BSE crisis as a resource during the upcoming election campaign.

Extract 2: On the Record, BBC 1, February 11, 2001

```
1.I: You're going to be using it (.) as I understand it (.) the BSE crisis
2. and the way the(.)Tories handled it (.) to attack them during the
3. election campaign when it arrives (.) but you have a problem here
4. don't you (.) because you don't seem to think anybody is to blame (.)
5. that is to say (.) nobody is being punished for it (.) therefore we
6. can assume can we not (.) that nobody is to blame (.) Why isn't
7. anybody being punished? It's a question an awful lot of people want
8. answered.
9.G: Look (.) firstly I think the electorate made their mind up on the
10. Conservatives' handling of the BSE tragedy at the last general
11. election (.) The whole purpose of the government's interim response to
12. Phillips is to look forward (.) not to look backwards (.) and to make
13. sure we put arrangements in place so that something like this never
14. happens again (.) or at least we've taken every step we possibly can
15. to avoid it.
16.I: But I think if I were a farmer whose livelihood had been destroyed (.)
17. or even more (.) much more (.) if I were the parent of a child who has
18. died (.) I would say fine (.)that's a perfectly good politician's
19. answer (.) but I want somebody's neck on the block for this (.) I want
20. somebody to be punished for it (.) it's a completely human response
21. isn't it?
```

Here the interviewer starts off by noting that the potential (suggested) strategy of the government (of which the interviewee is a member) in the next election presents a problem as their response to the inquiry into the outbreak and handling of the crisis is that no one is to blame. The interviewer suggests that this response represents a 'problem' because the response does not constitute a clear allocation of blame. This is qualified through the elicitation of a further (non) action, namely that 'nobody is being punished for it' (line 5). The categories of blame and punishment can be understood to form a moral device that can be heard to constitute a relational and procedural normative pairing, namely blame → punishment. This relational pairing is reiterated through the way in which the interviewer affirms the moral device being introduced: 'nobody is being punished for it, therefore we can assume can we not, that nobody is to blame' (lines 5 and 6). The suggestion is then closed with an affirmation of the second part of the pairing (lines 6, 7): 'Why isn't anyone being punished?'. The introduction of the moral device is characterized by an elicitation of the first part in line 6, by asking why nobody is being blamed or punished, and characterizes such a question as one that is of interest to a 'lot of people' (line 7). Organized in a specific way the device begins with the first part of the moral equation (blame), then relates the second half of the equation in terms of a relational and procedural pair (blame and punishment), and ends with a question that affirms and displays the second half of the moral equation (why nobody is being punished for the BSE crisis). In this way the moral device of blame → punishment can be introduced by the interviewer within the question/ answer format of the political interview.

Furthermore, the closing question provides ground for establishing a procedure for ascribing a discrepancy between blame and punishment within the context of the BSE crisis. In this case, a possible discrepancy being ascribed to the government – the (non) allocation of blame (not) resulting in some form of punishment – is one that can be used as a resource for generating potentially damaging characterizations of the government to which the guest belongs. However, in this instance, while the guest has the option to deal with such moral-device-oriented questioning, the option of not even recognizing the device also remains a possibility. This may well be a morally dangerous strategy, as non-recognition of the moral principle can provide a further resource for the interviewer's work of generating accountable responses or characterizing government policy and action in an unfavourable manner. The guest's response at line 9 exhibits a standard method for dealing with questions that generate potential spaces within which moral discrepancy or a moral vacuum may be ascribed to the collectivity that the guest represents. In terms of 'answer management', the guest utilizes some methods associated with providing a fudged response to morally searching question formats (Housley 2002). The guest does respond to the category-bound topic of 'people' by pointing toward the 'electorate', which can be understood as a relevant co-category of the device 'population'. However, the issue of the allocation of blame and punishment is not referred to. The guest refers to the previous government's handling of the BSE crisis – reflected, it is suggested, in the election result in 1997. This is followed by a description of the government's 'interim' response to the Phillips report in the BSE crisis, which is characterized as looking forward and 'not to look backwards' (line 12) and to ensure that policies or 'arrangements' are put in place in order that 'something like this never happens again'. This category display represents a form of fudged response that utilizes topical complexity as a means of responding to the moral device introduced by the interviewer in the account/question format. As has been discussed previously (Housley 2002), topical complexity can be understood as a manoeuvre that facilitates multiple local rationalities, hearings and histories of the exchange. As such, a design feature of broadcast settings is that the talk is available for recording, and segments may be replayed and discussed and different claims made about what has been meant within different news contexts. The use of topical complexity may also generate topical incoherence, as opposed to the coherence characterizing informal talk-in-interaction. Such incoherence provides material for fudging the response in terms of a number of alternate category connections that are not directly related to the question (although they may represent preferred topics for those being questioned, and provide a way to give preferred answers in political news interviews) – in this case questions about the allocation of blame and punishment.

At line 16 the interviewer responds to this fudged response to the question and moral device being pursued. The response takes the form of two condensed story formats that ground the moral device of BSE, blame → punishment, in terms of specific membership categories and predicates of topical affect: a farmer whose livelihood had been destroyed and a parent 'of a child who had died' (line 17, 18). The interviewer suggests that members of these categories would be entitled to blame someone and that it would be reasonable to expect punishment of those blamed (line 18) – that is, they would be oriented to the moral device set up, described, and initiated at the beginning of the interview by the interviewer and which the guest has, so far, not recognized or chosen to refer to. The device, in this instance, is expressed in terms of wanting 'somebody's neck on the block for this'. The account is again closed with a question, asking for confirmation that orientation to the moral device of blame → punishment is a normative 'human response'. The duplicative organization of categorization and devices (Watson 1997) enables a drawing of the moral device blame → punishment within the context of the BSE crisis as one that is both personally realized and topically relevant (the 'farmer', the 'parent') and universally recognizable and understandable ('human response'). This pitches the device not merely as one that is locally specific or particular, but as one that is also universal. This is, in one sense, a reflexive synecdoche, in which particular circumstances (as represented in the condensed stories of the farmer and the parent) are mapped onto universal categories – in this case, normative human responses – and which serves to re-set the original moral device as a means of generating further questions and making discrepancies in thinking and action available for inspection by the overhearing audiences. Furthermore, these devices represent forms of moral reasoning that are presented as universals but also connected to particular topic-relevant identities. Thus, the moral device does not merely represent a powerful means for evaluating the ethicality of action; it also ascribes action, thoughts, feelings and reasoning to members of the population as 'topic relevant categories' via the invocation of powerful predicates couched in terms of emotive accounts. Thus, the process of making politicians accountable and the questioning of government intentions can be seen to rely on appeals to identity categories and moral predication. Moreover, as opposed to the participatory framework of the radio phone-in, in political interviews members of the public are not directly visible or hearable. However, despite this apparent absence, the public and associated membership categories – normative forms of personal and social identity configuration – are routinely mobilized and used as a resource in accomplishing accountability. Thus whilst not physically present the pervasion of identity work in media spaces reveals the way the public and other interested parties are appropriated, 'represented' and constituted.

Conclusion

The analysis of participatory frameworks (radio-phone-ins, panel debates), political news interviews, and so forth in the manner outlined and demonstrated in this chapter affords a number of insights and empirical observations into the social organization of such media formats. Of notable interest here is the manner in which micro-forms of interaction provide for a systematic production of an apparatus that frames public participation, the elicitation of views, and/or the interrogation of politicians in terms of a personalized, human-scale encounter. While polls may be invoked, or statistics relayed and discussed, the primary means through which policy debate and talk is accomplished and presented in the formats explored above (and in the chapters in this volume) is grounded in mundane methods of lay reasoning and, though formalized, the organization of sequential interaction. The power of the personalized encounter and micro-interactional formats as a means of reproducing a sense of 'propinquity' within the mass media represents an enduring dialectic between the mass character of media communication and the micro-character of much media political programming, such as face-to-face interviews or individual caller-to-host encounters. This includes not only turn taking but also the observable manner through which debate is generated in terms of actor-level cultural resources, knowledge and attributes in the form of topic-relevant categories, practical moral reasoning and lay processes of inclusion and exclusion in assessing the warrantability of displayed opinions concerning government initiatives, actions and policy. In some respects this process has affinity with Sharrock's concept of 'owning' knowledge (1974), where 'opinion' relies on specific forms of category work that often specify identity and associated predicates as the 'knowledgeable' basis from which such opinions can be advanced.

Whilst public debates represent a powerful means of generating programming and maintaining popular participatory formats it also represents a discursive framework in which a particular sense of how the world works is displayed. This is a world in which the invitation to public participation and opinion is mediated by a filtering requirement that ascribes warrantability and the legitimacy of claims in terms of experience and the selection of a suitable topic relevant personal category (person from Norfolk, farmer, parent). In some respects this mirrors Beck's (1992) observation concerning biographical solutions to systemic contradictions. In other words, collective modes of action are increasingly being substituted by increasingly individuated forms of narrative and practice in relation to wider social problems, uncertainty and risk. In the political interview, such forms of public concern are represented and displayed through moral devices and, in the case explored here, emotive accounts that feature and relate certain forms of membership and topic-relevant events. This provides an interesting social universe in which participation and opinion is both invited (enabled) and allocated (constrained) in terms of resources and reasoning that can, at one level, be understood in terms of lay reasoning and the current fashion for identity-based politics and individuated modes of experience, explanation and consumption.

Finally the approach adopted and pursued in this chapter and others in this volume represents a radical departure from traditional conceptualizations of media, policy and debate. The concern here is to examine how methods of social organization and situated machinery for invoking and processing members' knowledge are used to represent, explore and promote specific world views and configure the manner in which the public is given voice in relation to government policy. This form of life, this interactional milieu, is suffused with practical methods of reasoning. The format of the interview, phone-in, and so forth makes use of the base line of members' interactional resources (for example, turn taking or the provision of accounts), moral understandings and principles (blame → punishment) and categories of cultural knowledge and their associated predicates.

This format generates interest and debate, but is also appropriated as a means of presenting a particular hierarchy of discourse within which, in the case of radio phone-ins, the invited public accounts are processed or, in the case of interviews, represented. It is our contention that an empirical understanding of these processes and forms of representative work is vital to a sociological understanding of the media that seeks to explore the representation and accomplishment of the interface between the public sphere, media and government policy. Furthermore, in terms of wider debates concerning democracy, accountability and the public sphere within the media, an understanding of how such formats operate provides a vital resource for developing innovative modes of wider public representation and participation in an information and media-dominated age. The process through which such voices are organized is thus an essential but under-researched topic of inquiry. A reconsideration of membership categorization practices in relation to interaction within participatory media settings provides a means of appreciating the manner in which culture and categorization are utilized as a means of configuring and constituting senses of accountability. Furthermore, this chapter demonstrates the way in which a concern with such practices makes visible the way(s) in which political discourse is not merely a scenic backdrop upon which interaction is inscribed. Rather, a consideration of the mutually constitutive relationship between culture, discourse and interaction enables a respecification of the political field as a dynamic and fluid entity through which categorizations of self, identity, claims-making and normative assessments are routinely employed during the course of 'public debate'. To this extent this chapter displays a Sacksian commitment to categorization and interaction, while at the same time demonstrating how liquid modernity and fluid identities (Bauman 2000) might operate in practice.

References

Bauman, Z. 2000. *Liquid Modernity*. Cambridge: Polity Press.

Beck, U. 1992. *The Risk Society*. London: Sage.

Boorstin, D.J. 1973. *The Image*. New York, NY: Athenaeum.

Butler, C. 2008. *Talk and Social Interaction in the Playground*. Aldershot: Ashgate.

Clayman, S. and Heritage, J. 2002. *The News Interview: Journalists and Public Figures on Air*. Cambridge: Cambridge University Press.

Fairclough, N. 1995. *Media Discourse*. London and New York: Arnold.

Fitzgerald, R. and Housley, W. 2002. Identity, categorisation, and sequential organisation: the sequential and categorical flow of identity in a radio phone-in. *Discourse Studies*, 13 (5), 579-602.

Fitzgerald, R. and Housley, W. 2006. Category, motive and accounts: devolution in Wales, in *Devolution and Identity*, edited by J. Wilson and K. Stapleton. Ashgate: Aldershot, 111-126.

Fitzgerald, R. and Housley, W. 2007. Talkback, community and the public sphere. *Media International Australia Incorporating Cultural Policy*, 122, 150-163.

Hester, S. and Eglin, P. 1997. *Culture in Action: Atudies in Membership Categorization Analysis*. Washington, DC: International Institute for Ethnomethodology and Conversation Analysis and University Press of America.

Housley, W. 2002. Moral discrepancy and 'fudging the issue' in a radio news interview. *Sociology*, 36 (1), 5-21.

Housley, W. and Fitzgerald, R. 2002a. The reconsidered model of membership categorisation analysis. *Qualitative Research*, 2 (1), 59-74.

Housley, W. and Fitzgerald, R. 2002b. National identity, categorisation and debate, in *Language, Interaction and National Identity*, edited by S. Hester and W. Housley. Aldershot: Ashgate, 38-59.

Housley, W. and Fitzgerald, R. 2003. Moral discrepancy and political discourse: accountability and the allocation of blame in a political news interview. *Sociological Research Online*. Available at http://www.socresonline.org.uk/8/2/housley.html.

Housley, W. and Fitzgerald, R. 2007. Categorization, interaction, policy and debate. *Critical Discourse Studies*, 4 (2), 187-206.

Housley, W. and Fitzgerald, R. 2009. Membership categorization, culture and norms in action. *Discourse and Society*, 20 (3), 345-362.

Hutchby, I. 1996. *Confrontation Talk: Arguments, Asymmetries, and Power on Talk Radio*. London: Lawrence Erlbaum Associates.

Hutchby, I. 2001. 'Witnessing': the use of first-hand knowledge in legitimating lay opinions on talk radio. *Discourse Studies*, 3 (4), 481-497.

Jayyusi, L. 1984. *Categorisation and the Moral Order*. London: Routledge & Kegan Paul.

Jayyusi, L. 1991. Values and moral judgement: communicative praxis as moral order, in *Ethnomethodology and the Human Sciences*, edited by G. Button. Cambridge: Cambridge University Press, 227-251.

Ross, K. 2004. Political talk radio and democratic participation: caller perspectives on Election Call. *Media, Culture and Society*, 26 (6), 785-802.

Livingstone, S. and Lunt, P. 1994. *Talk on Television: Audience Participation and Public Debate*. London: Routledge.

McNair, B., Hibberd, M. and Schlesinger, P. 2002. Public access broadcasting and democratic participation in the age of mediated politics. *Journalism Studies*, 3 (3), 407-422.

Sacks, H. 1995. *Lectures on conversation,* Vols. 1 and 2, edited by G. Jefferson. London: Blackwell.

Scannell, P. 2000. For-anyone-as-someone structures. *Media, Culture and Society*, 22 (1), 5-24.

Sharrock, W. 1974. On owning knowledge, in *Ethnomethodology: Selected Readings*, edited by R. Turner, Harmondsworth: Penguin, 45-53.

Stokoe, L. 2009. Doing actions with identity categories: complaints and denials in neighbor disputes. *Text and Talk*, 29 (1), 75-97.

Thomas, J., Cushion, S. and Jewell, J. 2004. Stirring up apathy? Political disengagement and the media in the 2003 Welsh Assembly elections. *Journal of Public Affairs*, 4 (4), 355-364.

Wahl-Jorgensen, K. 2002. The normative-economic justification for public discourse: letters to the editor as a 'wide open' forum. *Journalism and Mass Communication Quarterly*, 79 (1), 121-133.

Thornborrow, J. 2001. Authenticating talk: Building public identities in audience participation broadcasting. *Discourse Studies*, 3 (4), 459-479.

Thornborrow. J. and Fitzgerald, R. 2002. From problematic object to routine add-on: dealing with e-mails in radio phone-ins. *Discourse Studies*, 4 (2), 201-222.

Watson, R. 1997. Some general reflections on 'categorization' and 'sequence' in the analysis of conversation, in *Culture in Action*, edited by S. Hester and P. Eglin. Lanham, MD: University Press of America, 49-76.

Chapter 3

Configuring a Television Debate: Categorisation, Questions and Answers

Alain Bovet

Introduction

Much of the growing literature devoted to media interaction is focused on the sequential organisation of interviews or panel discussions (Schegloff 1988/1989, Relieu and Brock 1995, Clayman and Heritage 2002, Hutchby 1996, 2006). Whilst this body of research highlights an important area in the analysis of turn construction and turn taking practices, it tends to neglect some important aspects of the ordinary accountability of such occasions. As regards the analysis of television debates, one neglected aspect concerns the internal relationship between the categorisation of invited parties and the manner in which they are invited to speak by the host.[1] In the case of political debates, this question cannot be separated from the ongoing broader controversy that reflexively defines what the particular television programme is about and what is deemed to be at stake. Taking those dimensions into account contributes to an appropriate understanding of how the occasion is produced, not merely as another issue of the programme, but as this specific programme about that particular theme with these co-present panellists. In short, the analysis is expected to exhibit how the specificity of a single political television debate is constituted. However, this analytic focus does not imply neglecting the sequential organisation of the examined occasion. Quite the contrary, it is through the sequential accomplishment of an ordered debate that it is made accountable as a specific political occasion. The principal aim, then, is to maintain a praxiological approach while dealing with public and political processes of a wider scope.

The outlined approach will be exemplified through the analysis of some aspects of a television debate, broadcast on the French-speaking channel of Swiss television. The debate concerned a referendum that proposed to tighten the regulation on genetic engineering. This political issue occasioned a long and animated controversy in Switzerland. The analysis focuses on the configuration of the debate that is at the same time strictly bipolar and distinctively asymmetrical.

---

1   The following studies are exceptions to this neglect: Barthélémy 2008, Bovet and Terzi 2007, Broth 2008, Cuff 1993, Fitzgerald and Housley 2002, Hester and Fitzgerald 1999, Housley and Fitzgerald 2007.

The distinction between supporters and opponents of the referendum is made relevant not only in the way the panellists are categorized but also in the way they are asked questions. The analysis first examines the 'on-screen captions' that appear on the TV image and provide categorial information on the currently speaking panellist. The on-screen captions exhibit systematic differences between the panellists of both camps. The analysis focuses on the 'scientific' panellists of both camps. The supporters of the initiative appear as partisan experts, whereas the opponents of the initiative appear as 'pure' scientists. The second analysis is devoted to the categorisation procedures through which the host introduces two panellists and asks them a question. This analysis shows a systematic relation between the categorisation of the next speaker and the question she/he is asked. The final analysis briefly examines the answers given by the two panellists to see how they treat the categorisation that was used in and through the question.

The categorical order can thus be shown to be oriented to, in and through turn taking practices of the most familiar kind (Watson 1994, 1997, Psathas 1999, Widmer 2001). The endogenous articulation of categorial and sequential phenomena was first demonstrated through Sacks' seminal lectures (Sacks 1992), but has been largely neglected by conversation analysis, and its focus on the sequential organisation. According to Hester and Francis (2000), this criticism of conversation analysis does not imply that the categorial dimension should be given a theoretical priority. In line with Garfinkel's ethnomethodology, the accountability of a setting is an accomplished phenomenon, which has to be discovered and described by the analyst. It would not make sense to reduce the accountability of a setting to a limited set of features (categorisation, sequence, gestures, etc.). My focus in this chapter on the categorical and sequential dimensions of a setting is then not theoretically grounded. I will rather attempt to justify this focus on empirical bases.

In sum, the proposed analysis makes a contribution to an understanding of media and political culture that is based on actual and documented practices rather than theoretical constructs. Before launching the analysis I will bring some explanations on the Swiss political system and on the issue at hand, the initiative 'for genetic protection'.

The Swiss '(Semi-)direct' Democracy

The Swiss political system is referred to as 'direct' or 'semi-direct' democracy. One of its main instruments is the popular initiative: at any time, Swiss citizens can collect signatures on a project aimed at a modification of the Federal Constitution. If they are able to gather 100,000 signatures, their project is submitted to a national vote. Before the vote, it is debated in the Parliament. The vote of the Parliament is then sent to every Swiss voter as a recommendation for the decisive national vote.

The Parliament can either accept or refuse the project. In the latter case, the Parliament may propose a counter-project on which the citizens will also vote. In some cases the group that launched the initiative withdraws it in favour of the counter-project. Whatever the Parliament decides, the Swiss citizens have to vote: on the initiative, on the counter-project, or on both. This happens three to four times a year, with usually several projects for the same voting day.

Another important procedure is called the 'referendum'. It allows citizens (provided they have gathered 50,000 signatures) to oppose a law voted by the Parliament. The initiative and the referendum make Switzerland one of the most participative democracy in the western world. One interesting and possibly surprising outcome of this system is a quite conservative policy. Only one out of ten initiatives is accepted by the citizens. This fact is usually explained by a presumed orientation of the Swiss culture toward consensus and compromise. The Government for example is not composed according to a majority/opposition logic but is made up of members of the four main political parties. When the Parliament rejects an initiative and sends it to the vote without counter-project, it is assumed that the initiative is quite radical and most of the time it is rejected by the voters.

This specific feature of the Swiss political system has been widely discussed in social, historical and political science literature (e.g. Kloeti et al. 2004). What is typically missing from this literature is a detailed description of the practices through which an initiative can be made to appear as radical. My purpose in this chapter is to propose some observations on practices that contributed to make an initiative accountably radical in the Swiss public sphere.

I will deal with a media event that is a kind of democratic ritual. Two or three weeks before the vote, every important Swiss TV channel devotes a special broadcast to the objects of the vote. My data is taken from a TV debate that the public French speaking channel devoted in May 1998 to the initiative 'for genetic protection'.

The initiative 'for genetic protection'

There has been a long and intense debate on genetic engineering and GMOs in Switzerland during the last 15 years (Bonfadelli et al. 2002, Bovet 2007a). The climax of the debate was the long and intense campaign that prepared a national vote on the initiative 'for genetic protection' in June 1998. This initiative proposed to write in the Constitution the interdiction of genetically modified (GM) animal productions, of GM plants disseminations and of the patents on GM products. The Parliament and the Government recommended rejecting the initiative without proposing a counter-project. The campaign began in 1996 and was increasingly intense until the vote in June 1998, when the initiative was eventually rejected by 71 percent of the voters. A daily newspaper described it as the 'vote of the century'. Ten years later, such a description might probably be considered much exaggerated. It nevertheless indicates the importance of this initiative at the time it was debated.

Of course my purpose is not to offer a causal explanation of this clear rejection. I will rather attempt to describe how this initiative has been accounted for, by various and opposite parties in the practical course of a TV debate.

Pre-categorising the Panellists: 'On-screen Captions' and the Configuration of the Debate

A first idea of the logic through which the panellists are categorised can be drawn from the 'on-screen captions'. The on-screen captions are the brief written information about one panellist that appear on the bottom of the screen, usually during her/his first turn at talk and sometimes during some of her/his subsequent turns. While the introduction of the on-screen captions during the debate is contingent on the course of the speech exchange,[2] their content is not. All the on-screen captions were written before the beginning of the debate. A resource for their writing lies in the configuration of the controversy that is available when the TV debate is prepared. Of course this configuration is reproduced and possibly redefined through the situated use of the on-screen captions during the TV debate.

Before analysing some of the on-screen captions, another aspect of the pre-categorisation of the panellists must be introduced. The spatial organisation of the debate is strongly bipolar. The panellists are distributed into two camps: the supporters and the opponents of the initiative. This bipolarity is exhaustive and exclusive. This means that, except for the host, there is no possibility of participating in the debate if one does not sit in one of the two camps. Interestingly the same holds for the public in the studio, which is separated into two distinct terraces. As I will show later, this bipolar configuration is also produced *in situ* by the host, who makes sure that any turn at talk be intelligible as a supporter's or an opponent's turn.

From the beginning, the TV debate is presented by the host as aiming at helping the viewer to form his/her opinion about the initiative 'for genetic protection'. With such a goal, the broadcast is expected to be not only impartial but also to provide the viewer with reasons to choose one camp over the other. In other words, each camp should be given equal treatment while at the same time be clearly distinguished from the other.

The on-screen captions offer some solutions to this delicate task. I will focus first on the on-screen captions of the panellists whose categorisation implies some form of scientific expertise. Whilst they can be found on each camp, synthesizers 1 to 5 below refer only to the 'scientific experts' who support the

---

2   See Bovet 2007b for a detailed analysis of the sequential placement of the on-screen captions.

initiative, listed in order of appearance in the debate.[3] The on-screen captions are all made up of two lines. The third line in italics is my literal English translation, with full formulations of Swiss acronyms or abbreviations.

On-screen captions 1-5

1   Elisabetta RIATSCH DAMI
Pharmacienne, Comité Oui, GE
Pharmacist, Yes Committee, Geneva

2   Walter VETTERLI
Ing. Agronome, WWF Suisse
Agronomist engineer, WWF Switzerland

3   Josette FERNEX
Biologiste, Mouv. écologiste, Jura
Biologist, Environmental movement, Jura

4   Dr François CHOFFAT
Homéopathe, FR
Homeopath, Fribourg

5   Prof. Samuel DEBROT
Protection des animaux, VD
Protection of animals, Vaud

The first line of each on-screen caption gives the name of the panellist. On-screen captions 4[4] and 5 complete the name with an abbreviated title, 'doctor' and 'professor'. The second line adds various elements of categorisation of the panellists. On-screen captions 1 to 4 ascribe to the panellist an occupation that implies, to various degrees, a scientific training.[5] Another element is present in on-screen captions 1, 2, 3 and 5. This element can be glossed as 'membership in

---

3   Such a synoptical presentation is entirely artefactual, since never more than one on-screen caption appears on screen. The same holds for this specific collection under the auspices of scientific expertise. In other words this arrangement of data is not natural, at least less natural than textual transcripts of situated action.

4   In the rest of the chapter, I will use these numbers to refer to the on-screen captions.

5   The scientific expertise of the fifth panellist might be doubted, since, contrary to the other four, no scientific occupation is mentioned. The 'professor' title suggests his membership in an academic discipline, though one could still imagine a non scientific discipline, such as literature. As the host makes it clear when she introduces him later in the debate, Samuel Debrot is a *retired* professor of animal medicine, which explains that no occupation is mentioned in the on-screen caption.

a political movement'. In the first case, 'Yes Committee', is specifically related to the initiative. In the on-screen captions 2, 3 and 5, the panellists are affiliated to environmental or animal rights movements. On-screen caption 4 does not affiliate the panellist to a political movement. I will come back later to this special case.

Though an affiliation to a political movement does not explicitly specify a position on the initiative, it has a special relevance here. The initiative has been launched and supported by such movements. At the beginning of the debate, the host recalled this fact when she described the initiative. Something is thus predicated through the categorisation about those panellists and their motivation for being in this programme. In sections 3 and 4 below I will show what practical use can be made of such category predicate. It should be noticed here that this first brief look suggests, at least for four of the supporters of the initiative who are explicitly ascribed some form of scientific expertise, that another collection is considered worth mentioning, which is the membership of a political movement. In this respect, the on-screen captions of the scientists of the opposite camp clearly differ, as on-screen captions 6-9 reveal.

On-screen captions 6-9

6 Dr Heidi DIGGELMANN
Fonds nat. recherche scientifique
National science foundation

7 Prof. Jean-Pierre ZRYD
Biologie végétale, UNI LSNE
Plant biology, University of Lausanne

8 Prof. Suzanne SUTTER
Pédiatre, Chercheur, UNI GE
Pediatrician, Researcher, University of Geneva

9 Prof. Jacques DIEZI
Toxicologie, UNI LSNE
Toxicology, University of Lausanne

According to on-screen caption 6, the panellist speaks on behalf of the Swiss scientific authorities. The title of 'doctor' appended to her name indicates that she holds a PhD, even though the discipline is not specified. On-screen captions 7, 8 and 9 are quite similar: all three panellists are presented as professors in Swiss universities, and their discipline is specified. On-screen caption 8 indicates further that the panellist is at the same time a professor, a researcher and a (child) therapist.

There are two strong contrasts between these four on-screen captions and the five on-screen captions of the scientific panellists of the opposite camp that were examined above. The first contrast concerns the scientific expertise. On-screen captions 6 to 9 present top researchers who hold prestigious positions and a top manager of the main Swiss research institution. On-screen captions 1 to 5 present rather ordinary scientists and/or scientifically trained panellists. As mentioned before, these panellists are systematically also affiliated with a political movement. This last collection is specifically absent from on-screen captions 6 to 9. Whatever their political affiliation,[6] it was not considered relevant for the on-screen caption.

Two of these nine on-screen captions (4 and 8) present panellists as medical doctors. Here again the contrast is very strong. On-screen caption 4 indicates the title, 'doctor', a specialisation, 'homeopathy', whose scientific status is controversial and a rather rural region. On-screen caption 8 on the contrary provides all the possible indicators of scientific legitimacy.

This brief examination of the content of some of the on-screen captions used in this TV debate serves to highlight an important aspect of the configuration of the controversy, accomplished within this specific part of the debate and the production and use of such on-screen captions during its course. The controversy is configured as opposing political movements on the one side and scientists on the other side. This configuration seems consequential for the production of the on-screen captions. While it seems relevant to indicate the scientific expertise of the supporters of the initiative, the same does not hold for the possible political affiliations of the opponents of the initiative. In other words, the opponents appear as only scientists, though prominent ones. The supporters appear as (ordinary) scientists, but also environmental activists.

It is necessary to go beyond the analysis of the content of the on-screen captions, in order to see, for example, how the two collections' 'occupations' and 'political affiliations' are used and made relevant *in situ* in the speech exchanges. Before turning to this second part of the analysis, it might be interesting to have a brief look at some of the other on-screen captions. I want to focus here on the on-screen captions that emphasize the political identity of the panellists. Contrary to on-screen captions 1, 2, 3 and 5, the following ones use descriptive resources that are exclusively taken from political devices.[7]

On-screen captions 10-12

    10   Pascal COUCHEPIN
    Conseiller fédéral
    Federal counselor

---

6   During the debate, Jacques Diezi's membership in the Socialist party is orally 'revealed' by the host.

7   A 'Federal counselor' is one of the seven members of the Swiss government. A 'national counselor' is a member of the low chamber of the Swiss parliament.

11   Christian GROBET
Conseiller national, All. de Gauche
National counselor, Left Wing Alliance

12   Véronique PÜRRO
Femmes socialistes suisses
Swiss socialist women

The panellist presented by on-screen caption 10 is against the initiative, while the panellists presented by on-screen captions 11 and 12 support it. What these three panellists share in common, as opposed to the ones discussed so far, is a more general categorial relevance to the debate. Their legitimacy in such a debate is not related to the specific issue at hand, but to the political collectivities they're part of, i.e. the 'Federal council', the 'Left Wing Alliance' and the 'Swiss socialist women'. As such, they can participate in other similar debates, which is not the case for the panellists we have seen before.

This said, an important difference remains to be noticed between on-screen caption 10 and on-screen captions 11 and 12. This difference lies in the fact that the camp of the initiative is related to the left. The membership of Christian Grobet in a left wing party is considered relevant and worth mentioning. In the case of Véronique Pürro, such a membership is even the only element of categorisation that is added to the name in on-screen caption 12. This again is an aspect of the configuration of the controversy. Besides being described as launched by environmental movements, the initiative has been largely presented as supported by the left. Interestingly, the opposition to the initiative has not been described as a right-wing position. This feature is observable in on-screen caption 10 where the panellist is described only through his membership of the Federal council. His membership of a right-wing party is not mentioned.

This is certainly an ordinary 'footing' feature in Swiss public discourse, where the Federal counsellors are normatively required to speak on behalf of the collegial government and not on behalf of their party. My point then is not that the right wing political orientation of the Federal counsellor should have appeared on the on-screen caption. This would amount to an ironical position towards the journalists who wrote the on-screen captions. Rather what is notable here is that on-screen captions 10, 11 and 12 are perfectly adequate descriptions of the panellists, in that they provide the viewer with relevant categorial information for all practical purposes. The interesting aspect of that adequacy is the asymmetry between the two camps, where one is associated to the left while the other is not associated to the right.

A similar asymmetry has been observed before about the on-screen captions devoted to the 'scientific' panellists. While the opponents of the initiative were presented as 'pure scientists', the scientists of the opposite camp were systematically associated with an (environmental) political movement. The categorial work accomplished by the on-screen captions results then in an asymmetrical presentation of the two camps. The supporters of the initiative appear as activists in environmental and left-wing movements and parties. The opponents of the initiative appear as top scientists and member of the government. To the extent that the on-screen captions present the panellist as an accountably legitimate participant of the debate, they can be seen as providing the viewers with reasons for the presence of the various panellists in the debate. In this perspective, the categorial work just described can be seen as witnessing and at the same time 'locally' accomplishing a configuration of the controversy in a debate. In this configuration, the categorial work provides the viewers with motives and explanations. The initiative appears then as grounded on ideological activist positions, while the opposition to the initiative appears as the business of scientific and political authorities.

The previous analysis was based exclusively on the on-screen captions. Such data show that the controversy is considered relevant and oriented to by the TV crew in the preparation of the broadcast. I want now to turn to the use of categorial resources in the situated course of the debate.

Categorising the Panellists through Questions

The sequence I will focus on is located at the beginning of the broadcast. It consists of the first round of interventions by some of the panellists, two from each camp. After greeting the TV audience and the panellists, the host recalled the existing regulation on genetic engineering in Switzerland. The initiative was then presented as having been launched by various movements who had judged this regulation insufficient. Then the host announced a short document describing the state of the art in genetic engineering. After the document, the host presented the initiative through the three interdictions of dissemination, animal production and patents on GMOs. She then asks the first question to one of the panellists.

Transcript 1[8]

```
Mod: (…) voilà les interdictions que souhaite l'initiative
     pour la protection/ génétique\ alors madame . madame
     elisabetta riatsch dami/ vous êtes pharmacienne de
     formation/ vous avez une formation scientifique/ vous êtes
     par ailleurs co-présidente du euh comité genevois oui/
     euh: à la protection génétique/ euh vous êtes partisane/
     de cette initiative/ et donc de ces interdictions qu'on
     vient de citer/ . jusqu'à quel point va votre rejet du
```

---

8   The transcripts are based on the usual, conversation analytic transcription conventions, except for the transcription of intonation, where / indicates a rising intonation and \ a falling one.

```
        génie génétique\ en tant que tel et globalement\ parlant\
Riats:tout d'abord je ne rejette pas/ le génie génétique\ . ce
        que: (…)
```

English translation:

```
Host:(…) these are the interdictions that the initiative for
      genetic/ protection\ wants now mrs mrs elisabetta riatsch
      dami/ you were trained as a pharmacist/ you received a
      scientific education/ moreover you are co-president of the
      geneva committee yes/ to genetic protection/ you support/
      this initiative/ and hence the interdictions that were
      just mentioned/ . to what extent do you reject genetic
      engineering\ as such and globally\ speaking\
Riats:first of all I do not reject/ genetic engineering\ . what
      I (…)
```

Let me introduce some brief remarks on the organisation of the activity, before examining this sequence. No one other than the host has spoken before Riatsch does in this extract. It means that the host takes a very extended turn at talking before the first speaker transition despite many places where a transition could have occurred. This shows that all the participants of the debate cooperate to produce an accountable debate, where the host takes and is given the first and extended turn, and the panellists speak only when asked to by the host. This collective behaviour should not be described as caused by the specific speech exchange system of the TV debate. It should rather be said that the participants exhibit an orientation to its local and sustainable relevance, through, among other aspects, not speaking unless asked to by the host (Clayman and Heritage 2002, Schegloff 1988, 1989).

After briefly presenting the interdictions wanted by the initiative, the host addresses one of the panellists through her name. The panellist is then presented through some descriptions. She is first attributed a scientific education through the mention of a training in pharmacology. A second characterisation is more directly related to the initiative. Her involvement in a committee is not only relevant to the debate itself but more precisely to what took place just before, that is the presentation of the interdictions wanted by the initiative, as the host explicitly states ('the interdictions that were just mentioned'). After a brief pause, which is accountably a pause since no question has been asked so far, the host asks a question ('to what extent do you reject genetic engineering?').

The task of answering such a question, what Clayman and Heritage (2002: 196-203) call the agenda of the question, requires the respondent to give an assessment of the extent or the degree of her own rejection of genetic engineering. The agenda is not taking a stand for or against genetic engineering. In other words the question is not 'do you reject genetic engineering?' but '*to what extent do you reject it ?*'. The fact that Riatsch rejects genetic engineering is not what the question is about but a presupposition embedded in the question.

The design of the question is an indication of the relevance of the categorial elements that were introduced before. That Riatsch is co-president of the committee 'Yes' to genetic protection is certainly a relevant ground for asking about the extent of her rejection of genetic engineering. However her training in pharmacology is denied any relevance. She might for instance properly answer with pharmacological arguments, but the relevance of this categorial aspect is not made relevant by the question.

Before dealing with Riatsch's answer, I want to see and compare this question to the question that is asked to the fourth panellist. Let me first explain this selection in the data. The first four questions asked by the host make up a sequence that is clearly and explicitly distinguished from the rest of the debate. As the host later explains, this first sequence is expected to elicit 'principled positions'. In order to achieve this, the host asks one question to two members of each camp. In doing this she concretely uses the bipolar configuration, as she asks the same question to the two supporters and the same holds for the opponents. This means that the same question is asked to the second supporter solicited in this sequence. As we will see in the following transcript, it also means that the second opponent solicited is asked the same question as the first opponent, who is a Federal counsellor. The host explicitly mentions the recycling of the question, indicating thereby the systematic relevance of the bipolarity in the conduct of the debate. Let's now turn to the fourth question of this sequence.

Transcript 2

```
Mod:(…) face au génie génétique/ professeur heidi diggelmann
     . vous êtes euh présidente du conseil du fonds national
     de la recherche scientifique/ vous êtes vous euh contre
     cette initiative/ vous êtes dev- vous êtes professeur
     de microbiologie à l'université de lausanne/ donc vous
     travaillez vous-même avec le génie génétique/ . et
     alors même question que tout à l'heure pour monsieur
     le conseiller fédéral/ est-ce vous trouvez vous qu'il
     y a qu'on peut y aller qu'il y a pas de précautions
     particulières à f- à prendre que le génie génétique ne
     présente aucun danger\
Digg:euh non euh je crois que j'ai une euh position beaucoup
     plus dif+férenciée/ .
```

English translation:

```
Host:(…) towards genetic engineering/ professor heidi
     diggelmann . you are president of the national science
```

```
    foundation council/ you are against this initiative/
    you are a microbiology professor at the university of
    lausanne/ so you work with genetic engineering/ yourself
    . and so same question as before to mister federal
    counselor/ do you think that we can go that there are no
    particular precautions to take that genetic engineering
    does not present any danger\
Digg:uh no I think that I have a much more qualified position/
    . (…)
```

As was the case for the first question, the panellist is presented through a lot of categorial work before being asked the question. The first aspect is her scientific expertise. She is presented as the head of the national science foundation board. She is also described as a University professor, working in the field of genetic engineering. A second aspect is her opposition to the initiative. Contrary to the pharmacological training that was attributed to the first panellist, there is no question here about the relevance of Diggelmann's scientific expertise since it is focused on genetic engineering. Both aspects of her categorisation by the host seem equivalently relevant for the question that is asked. I would like now to briefly discuss the formulation of the question through a comparison with the first question.

The question consists here in asking whether the panellist rejects any regulation of genetic engineering. The two questions have obvious similarities and strong, if less obvious, differences. They are similar in their 'provocativeness'. Both questions rely upon a relation between a camp and a somewhat radical position. As we have seen, the first question presupposes that supporting the initiative implies the radical fundamentalist position of rejecting genetic engineering. The agenda of the question consists for the respondent in giving an assessment of the extent or the degree of her own rejection of genetic engineering. The second question is similar since it concerns the radical over liberal position of rejecting any regulation on genetic engineering. The 'provocativeness' of both questions then relies on the implication between a particular camp in the debate and a radical position on the topic, absolute rejection on the one hand and absolute trust on the other hand. As the host explicitly indicates it, there is a systematicity that is articulated to the bipolar configuration: the same 'provocative' question is asked to members of the same camp.

Yet, this similarity in 'provocativeness' should not obscure an important difference. This difference is oriented to by the distinct answers that each question receives. The following transcript corresponds to the first part of Riatsch's answer.

Transcript 3

```
Mod:(…) jusqu'à  quel point va votre rejet du génie génétique\
    en tant que tel et globalement\ parlant\
Riats:tout d'abord je ne rejette pas/ le génie génétique\ .
    ce que: ce que je rejette/ c'est le fait qu'on veuille
    appliquer une technologie/ à la hâte\ . à tout prix/ .
    sous des pressions commerciales/ des gens ont investi des
    sommes colossales/ et attendent maintenant des bénéfices/
    . or il n'y a aucune urgence\ . je rejette donc les
    applications du génie génétique\ . et cela pour deux
    raisons/ . la première (…)
```

English translation:

```
Host:(…) to what extent do you reject genetic engineering\ as
    such and globally\ speaking\
Riats:first of all I do not reject/ genetic engineering\ .
    what I reject/  is the fact that one wants `to apply a
    technology/ hastily\ . at all costs/ . under commercial
    pressures people have invested colossal amounts and now
    expect profits/ . yet it's not at all urgent\ . therefore I
    reject the applications of genetic engineering\ . for two
    reasons/ . the first (…)
```

Riatsch's answer clearly shows an orientation to the presupposition embedded in the question. She does not treat the agenda of the question but begins by coming back to one of its presuppositions in order to negate it with emphasis and then specifies that she does not reject genetic engineering itself but its applications. There is then a long expansion which is prospectively announced by Riatsch as the 'two reasons' that ground her rejections of these applications. I will come back later to this expansion. Notice that Riatsch's turn so far has provided many transition relevance places, notably just before announcing the 'two reasons', where there's a falling intonation and a pause after an utterance that concludes what has been said so far. The host does not use this opportunity, which indicates that the panellist is given an extended floor and the possibility to develop reasons and arguments. It also indicates that the work accomplished by the respondent on the question is not sanctioned as incorrect or improper.

This work consists in escaping the agenda of the question in order to disaffiliate with a radical position that was presupposed by and embedded in the question. Such a work is not necessary for doing the same job with the other question that we have seen before. This is showed by Diggelmann's answer.

Transcript 4

```
Mod: (…) et alors même question que tout à l'heure pour
      monsieur le conseiller fédéral/ est-ce vous trouvez vous
      qu'il y a qu'on peut y aller qu'il y a pas de précautions
      particulières à f- à prendre que le génie génétique ne
      présente aucun danger\
Digg:euh non euh je crois que j'ai une euh position beaucoup
      plus différenciée/ . il faut aussi dire/ que le génie
      génétique/ c'est pas une technique tout à fait nouvelle/
      (…)
```

English translation:

```
Host:(…) and so same question as before to mister federal
      counselor/ do you think that we can go that there are no
      particular precautions to take that genetic engineering
      does not present any danger\
Digg:uh no I think that I have a much more qualified position/
      . it must also be said/ that genetic engineering/ is not
      so much of a new technology (…)
```

The agenda of the question consists here in affiliating or disaffiliating with the radical position of rejecting any form of regulation. Diggelmann does it in a very explicit and straightforward way, before expanding her answer. This means that the reply to the provocation, which is likely to be expected by the host,[9] can be accomplished through answering the question, from within the agenda. Diggelmann has then dispensed with the work upon the question that Riatsch had to accomplish. In Riatsch's case, the moderate position must be conquered against the question, whereas in the second case, the question is an invitation to occupy the moderate position.

These observations indicate an 'asymmetry of imputation'[10] in the different questions that are asked to the supporters and to the opponents of the initiative. The formulation of the question imputes a radical position to the supporters of the initiative. This does not mean that the supporters of the initiative are denied the opportunity to disaffiliate from such a radical position. It rather indicates that they have to devote a preliminary part of their answer to this job. On the contrary, the opponents 'only' answer the question.

---

9   A 'provocative' question is a routine way to launch a debate. In other words, the first question asked to a panellist is almost never of a general and docile kind such as 'what do you think of …'.

10   This expression was suggested by Rod Watson.

I take these sequential features to indicate that the configuration I have delineated before is relevant to the parties involved and consequential for the course of the examined activity. These are the two criteria that Schegloff (1991: 128), drawing from Sacks' work (Sacks 1992), established as warranting the analytical invocation of dimensions of the context. We have seen before that the supporters of the initiative were systematically described as associated with left-wing and environmental movements. The opponents were on the contrary presented as top scientists and a Federal counselor, without any mentionable relations with political movements. Through her (different) questions, the host imputes a radical position to the camp of the initiative while she asks the opponents to take a stance about such an imputation.

This differential treatment relates back to what was observed about the on-screen captions earlier in the chapter. On-screen caption and question designs exhibit the congruency of the configuration of the debate. Sacks dealt with a similar phenomenon when he said that 'characters appear on cue' (Sacks 1992, I:182-187, 410-416). An ongoing narrative designs a slot for a new character, whose appearance does not have to be accounted for. For example, when teenage kids talk about drag racing, the character 'cop' appears on cue. The narrator does not need to explain what a 'cop' is doing in a story of speed driving. A similar slot in a configuration can be given to actions.[11] In the examples above, it is 'on cue' to impute a radical position to panellists that are (verbally and visually) categorised as activist or at least as members of political movements. It is also 'on cue' to ascribe such an imputation to the panellists themselves if they have not been affiliated to any political movement. According to Sacks, 'if an explanation is available, then it's *that* explanation that is *the* explanation, and formulates what it is that's happened' (Sacks 1992. I: 412). In the case examined above, *that* categorisation work provides *the* relevant basis for the interrogation of the panellists.

Two remarks are in order here. First these observations should not be taken as a criticism of the host's action. On the contrary, the formulation of the question can be seen as a competent solution to a complex problem. As said before, the host must at the same time be impartial and provide the viewer with reasons to vote yes or no about the initiative. Her questioning is at the same time provocative for both sides, and differential, and in this respect coherent with the configuration assembled by the whole broadcast. The second remark has to do with the collaborative nature of the activity. Polemical as it might be, a TV debate requires that various parties agree on a large number of dimensions of the activity. Though some aspects of the broadcast may be explicitly discussed and agreed to before it begins, most of the arrangement is accomplished in the contingencies of its course. It then requires a strong collaboration between the

---

11   'What you have to do is build in characterizations of the way a set of institutions operate, the way sets of persons know what anybody else knows, and the like. Just to provide for a quite ordinary segment of conversation' (Sacks 1992. I: 185).

panellists and the host. This holds even if the host is submitted to a rather sharp criticism during the debate, which was the case in this broadcast. Before the conclusion, I want to briefly further this last remark and see how, in their answers, the two panellists contribute to the accountability of the configuration.

Answers, Categories and Configuration

I noted in the previous section that Riatsch was categorised both as a pharmacologist and as deeply involved in the campaign for the initiative. The question she was asked after this description was certainly relevant to the second categorisation. Though it was not excluded, the relevance of her occupation as pharmacologist was not necessarily relevant to the question she was asked. Let us see now how she handles this categorial dimension in and through the answer she provides.

Transcript 5

```
Riats:tout d'abord je ne rejette pas/ le génie génétique\ .
     ce que: ce que je rejette/ c'est le fait qu'on veuille
     appliquer une technologie/ à la hâte\ . à tout prix/ .
     sous des pressions commerciales/ des gens ont investi des
     sommes colossales/ et attendent maintenant des bénéfices/
     . or il n'y a aucune urgence\ . je rejette donc les
     applications du génie génétique\ . et cela pour deux
     raisons/ . la première est de l'ordre des conséquences\
     . on n'a: pas suffisamment  évalué les risques . à moyen
     terme\ encore moins à long terme\ . les risques au niveau
     de la santé/ . avec l'introduction de nouveaux allergènes/
     . avec les nouvelles substances qui seront à notre
     portée/ .. risques écologiques/ . avec la possibilité de
     transfert de gènes entre les cult- des cultures pardon
     à notre flore sauvage/ ou aux: microorganismes de la te:
     rre/ . sans compter toutes les surprises/ les effets
     secondaires/ euh qu'on a déjà observés à l'application du
     génie génétique/ j'espère qu'on pourra y revenir/=
Mod: =bien sûr/
Riats:la deuxième raison fondamentale . pour laquelle je: je je
     milite/ .. c'est une raison de principe/ . je . je pense/
     qu'on ne peut pas/ euh regarder le: genre euh le . tous/
     les êtres vivants comme un lego de gènes\ . je pense/ que
     tous les êtres vivants sur terre ont une raison d'exister
     . l'homme chat chien . poireau euh coccinelle que chacun/
     a une raison propre et que la vie dépend de l'équilibre/
     entre tous les partenaires de la création\ . entre tous
```

```
les écosystèmes\ et transgresser les barrières naturelles
comme on le fait par des manipulations génétiques/ ne peut
qu'engendrer des déséquilibres\ déséquilibres au niveau
de l'alimentation\ . mondiale/ . des déséquilibres au
niveau des écosystèmes\ . au niveau de la biodiversité\
. et enfin/ au niveau de notre santé/ et de la santé des
générations futures\
```

English translation:

```
Riats:first of all I do not reject/ genetic engineering\ .
     what I reject/ is the fact that one wants to apply a
     technology/ hastily\ . at all costs/ . under commercial
     pressures people have invested colossal amounts and now
     expect profits/ . yet it's not at all urgent\ . therefore
     I reject the applications of genetic engineering\ . for
     two reasons/ . the first one has to do with consequences .
     we have not sufficiently assessed the mid-term risks\ and
     even less the long-term risks\ . health risks/ . with the
     introduction of new allergens/ . with the new substances
     that will be available/ .. environmental risks/ . with the
     possibility of gene transfer between cultures sorry from
     cultures to our wild flora/ or to earth micro-organisms/ .
     not to mention all the surprises/ secondary effects/ that
     were already observed with applied genetic engineering/ I
     hope we can get back to this later/=
Host:=of course/
Riats:the second fundamental reason . for which I militate/
     .. is a reason of principle/ . I . I think/  that the
     genre/ uh all/ living cannot be seen as a gene lego\ . I
     think/ that all being on earth has a reason to exist .
     man cat dog leek ladybird each/ has a proper reason and
     life depends on the balance/ between all the partners
     of the creation\ . between all the ecosystems\ and
     trespassing natural barriers as it is done through genetic
     manipulations/ can only engender imbalance\ imbalance in
     world\ food/ . imbalance in ecosystems\ . in biodiversity\
     and finally in our/ and future generations' health\
```

I will not propose a detailed analysis of this quite long answer. I only want to notice that Riatsch does not utter this answer *qua* pharmacologist. Some of her arguments, in particular those that concern risks, may perfectly well derive from her pharmacological expertise, but it is not a 'footing' that she is claiming or assuming. She appears through her answer as a supporter of the initiative, possibly with pharmacological knowledge, but certainly not as a pharmacist who would happen to support the initiative. In other words, the formulation of her answer indicates that the configuration that has been described before, and its categorial aspects, is recognised and produced by Riatsch also. Her answer exhibits a strong environmental involvement in a political issue, and only possibly and secondarily a scientific expertise. One striking aspect of her intervention is the strong personal footing that she takes, especially when she exposes her second reason. On all of these features, the answer provided by Diggelmann is deeply different.

Transcript 6

```
Digg: euh non euh je crois que j'ai une euh position beaucoup
      plus différenciée/ . il faut aussi dire/ que le génie
      génétique/ c'est pas une technique tout à fait nouvelle/
      . les chercheurs/ ont vingt-cinq ans/ d'expérience .
      dans le domaine/ euh du génie génétique/ et jusqu'à
      maintenant/ aucun accident/ mettant en danger l'homme/ ou
      l'environnement a été/ enregistré\ . jusqu'à ce jour\ .
      les chercheurs/ eux/ ils veulent des règles\ . et ce sont
      d'ailleurs eux/ qui ont pris l'initiative/ il y a déjà
      vingt ans/ . d'émettre/ et d'élaborer des règles pour
      l'application responsable/ de cette euh technologie/ . et
      . c'est aussi les chercheurs/ et les académies/ qui ont
      au fond créé une commission de sécurité en biologie en
      suisse/ il y a déjà vingt ans/ et qui ont enregistré et
      surveillé toute l'activité dans ce domaine depuis vingt
      ans alors/ . depuis qu'on a l'article constitutionnel/ on
      l'a déjà dit/ on a aussi/ des garde-fous euh·au niveau
      légal et comme on a dit au fond euh la manipulation
      de l'embryon humain/ le clonage de l'humain/ ou des
      interventions/ sur les cellules comme les ovules/ ou
      les spermatozoïdes/ sont interdites/ alors/ euh . les
      chercheurs/ ils ne sont pas du tout contre des garde-
      fous/ ils sont pour les garde-fous/ mais ils sont tout
      à fait contre les interdictions/ qui mettraient au fond
      hors-jeu/ la science suisse dans un domaine/ où on est
      particulièrement performant\
```

English translation:

```
Digg: uh no I think that I have a much more qualified position/
      . it must also be said/ that genetic engineering/ is
      not so much of a new technology . researchers/ have
      twenty-five years/ of experience in the field/ of genetic
```

```
engineering/ and so far/ no accident/ endangering man/
or environment has been/ recorded\ . up to this day\ .
the researchers/ they/ want rules\ . and they/ took the
initiative/ twenty years ago already/ . in establishing/
and elaborating rules for a responsible application/ of
that technology/ . and . it is also researchers/ and
academies/ who basically created a biological security
commission in Switzerland/ twenty years ago already/
and who have recorded and watched all the activity in
this field for twenty years so/ . since we have the
constitutional article/ it has already been said/ we
also have/ safeguards at the legal level and as it
was said basically human embryo manipulation/ human
cloning/ or interventions/ in cells such as ovules/ or
spermatozoids/ are forbidden/ so/ . researchers/ are not
at all against safeguards/ they support safeguards/ but
they are absolutely against interdictions/ that would
basically rule Swiss science out of the running/ in a
domain/ where we are particularly efficient\
```

I will only stress the salient features of Diggelmann's intervention. The main answer consists in a reply to the provocative question: far from refusing any regulation, the genetic engineering researchers pioneered in establishing rules for their own practices. Through this argument, Diggelmann displays her knowledge of the history of the field as well as of the current practices and their legal framework. The conclusion is of particular interest. Diggelmann establishes a distinction between 'safeguards', which the researchers support, and interdictions, 'that would [...] rule Swiss science out of the running'. With such a conclusion, Diggelmann adopts a very broad footing. She not only claims knowledge of the field, but speaks on behalf of the Swiss scientific community. In her perspective, one can hardly imagine how a scientist might support the initiative and its 'interdictions'. In and through such an answer, Diggelmann claims and endorses her double categorisation of expert in genetic engineering and of head of the Swiss science. Beyond that combination of footing and categorisation, she aligns with and even strengthens the configuration of the debate.

Conclusion

The accountability of a TV debate consists of a lot of heterogeneous elements that compose a texture of relevance in and as the practical circumstances of its collaborative production. The analyses proposed in this chapter cannot treat each of these aspects.[12] For this reason, I focused on the categorial organisation of the activity and its articulation to some sequential properties. I accounted for this articulation through the idea of a configuration that at the same time pre-exists in the public sphere and is reproduced and redefined in this particular debate.[13]

I tried to show, on the basis of a categorisation analysis of the content of some on-screen captions, that, although there are scientists in both camps, they are not the same scientists. While the supporters of the initiative appear as environmental activists with various forms of scientific expertise, the opponents of the initiative are prominent scientists, and their possible political affiliations are not considered relevant or worth mentioning. I showed a similar aspect in the categorisation of the 'political panellists'. For the supporters of the initiative, their left-wing affiliation is mentioned, contrary to the right-wing affiliation of the Federal counselor who is opposed to the initiative. There is then a general politicisation of the supporters of the initiative and an equivalent 'depoliticisation' of the opponents.

The second and third part of the analysis attempted to show, through a brief analysis of two pairs of question and answer, that this configuration was relevant to the parties and consequential for the activity. The formulation of the question demonstrated an asymmetry of imputation that was congruent with the configuration. Interestingly, the analysis of the answers given by two 'scientific' panellists of each camp suggested their alignment on the configuration, the supporter adopting a rather environmental activist footing, and the opponent speaking on behalf of the Swiss scientific community. The categorisation work, and the motivations that can or cannot be predicated upon it, appears then to bear a programmatic relevance for the actual conduct of the activity examined in this chapter.

Several elements of my analysis relied on procedures of commonsense reasoning that were not as such submitted to a praxiological analysis. For instance I took for granted that imputing a radical position through a question was related to a logic of categorisation emphasising the membership in a environmental movement. The purpose of my chapter was to suggest the interest of targeting phenomena that can probably only be approached through such incomplete praxiological analyses. The configuration of a controversy and its situated incarnation in a TV debate is such a phenomenon. Working with the articulation of sequential practices and categorisation procedures is a way to begin to apprehend it. The analysis of the sequential organisation of media interaction has generated a remarkably rigorous corpus of empirical studies, however a focus on the sequential aspects of interaction risks missing a central dimension of the accountability of these media practices. In particular what makes them political rather than *just* interactional.

---

12   For a less allusive account of the accountability of this TV debate, see my PhD (Bovet 2007a), though it has to be clear that it is not primarily a matter of number of pages. A 90 minute TV debate cannot be exhaustively analysed, whatever the number of pages available.

13   This idea is close to the notion of 'master narrative' developed by Lynch and Bogen (1996) in their study of the Iran-Contra hearings.

References

Barthélémy, M. 2008. Reception-in-action in a panel interview: the interactional production of several kinds of 'Public in relation with a problem'. *Ethnographic Studies*, 10 (2), 89-105.

Bonfadelli, H. and Dahinden, U. (eds). 2002. *Gentechnologie in der öffentlichen Kontroverse*. Zürich: Seismo.

Bovet, A. 2007a. *La mise en question du génie génétique dans l'espace public suisse. Analyse des pratiques médiatiques de mise en forme et de mise en œuvre du débat public*. Ethesis, University of Fribourg (Switzerland).(http://ethesis.unifr.ch/theses/index.php#SES)

Bovet, A. 2007b. Donner à voir le débat politique. Le montage en direct d'un débat télévisé. *Bulletin Suisse de Linguistique Appliquée*, 85, 181-202.

Bovet, A. and Terzi, C. 2007. Vers une définition positive de la publicité des interactions médiatiques, in *Le français parlé des médias. Actes du colloque de Stockholm 8-12 juin 2005*, edited by M. Broth et al. Stockholm: Acta Universitatis Stockholmiensis, 49-61.

Broth, M. 2008. The 'listening shot' as a collaborative practice for categorizing studio participants in a live TV-production. *Ethnographic Studiesi*, 10 (2), 69-88.

Clayman, S. and Heritage, J. 2002. *The News Interview: Journalists and Public Figures on the Air*. Cambridge: Cambridge University Press.

Cuff, E.C. 1993. *Problems of Versions in Everyday Situations*. Washington, DC: University Press of America.

Fitzgerald, R. and Housley, W. 2002. Identity, categorisation and sequential organisation: the sequential and categorial flow of identity in a radio phone-in. *Discourse and Society*, 13 (5), 579-602.

Hester, S. and Fitzgerald, R. 1999. Category, predicate and contrast: some organizational features in a radio talk show, in *Media Studies: Ethnomethodological Approaches* edited by P.L. Jalbert. Lanham, MD: University Press of America, 171-194.

Hester, S. and Francis, D. 2000. Ethnomethodology, conversation analysis and 'Institutional Talk'. *Text*, 20, 373-396.

Housley, W. and Fitzgerald, R. 2007. Categorisation, interaction, policy and debate. *Critical Discourse Studies*, 4 (2), 187-206.

Hutchby, I. 1996. *Confrontation Talk. Argument, Asymetries and Power on Talk Radio*. Mahwah, NJ: Lawrence Erlbaum Associates.

Hutchby, I. 2006. *Media Talk: Conversation Analysis and the Study of Broadcasting*. Maidenhead: Open University Press.

Kloeti, U. et al. 2004. *Handbook of Swiss Politics*. Zurich: NZZ Publishing.

Lynch, M. and Bogen, D. 1996. *The Spectacle of History. Speech, Text and Memory at the Iran-contra Hearings*. Durham and London: Duke University Press.

Psathas, G. 1999. Studying the organization in action: membership categorization and interaction. *Human Studies*, 22,139-162.

Relieu, M. and Brock, F. 1995. L'infrastructure conversationnelle de la parole publique: l'analyse des réunions politiques et des interviews télédiffusées. *Politix*, 31, 77-112.

Sacks, H. 1992. *Lectures on Conversation*. 2 vols. Oxford: Basil Blackwell.

Schegloff, E. 1988/1989. From interview to confrontation: observations on the Bush/Rather encounter. *Research on Language and Social Interaction*, 22, 215-240.

Schegloff, E. 1991. Reflections on talk and social structure, in *Talk and Social Structure: Studies in Ethnomethodology and Conversation Analysis* edited by D. Boden and D. Zimmerman. Cambridge: Polity Press, 44-71.

Watson, R. 1994. Catégorie, séquentialité et ordre social, in *L'enquête sur les catégories* edited by B. Fradin, L. Quéré and J. Widmer. Paris: Editions de l'Ecole des Hautes Etudes en Sciences Sociales, 151-184.

Watson, R. 1997. Some general reflections on 'categorization' and 'sequence' in the analysis of conversation, in *Culture in Action: Studies in Membership Categorization Analysis* edited by S. Hester and P. Eglin. Washington, DC: University Press of America, 49-76.

Widmer, J. 2001. Catégorisation, tour de parole et sociologie, in *L'ethnométhodologie: une sociologie radicale* edited by M. de Fornel, A. Ogien, L. Quéré. Paris: La Découverte, 207-238.

Chapter 4

Asserting Interpretive Frames of Political Events: Panel Discussions on Television News

Emo Gotsbachner

Introduction

The evocation of social and political interpretations that legitimise a certain policy position is a basic strategy for generating support in a democratic system, which can become crucial for people's experience of political events (Fischer 2003: 55). This chapter explores how political actors try to establish their interpretive frames of current problems and developments in debates with political opponents on TV. Live discussions on political issues in news programs like the ones on Austrian public television (ORF) are broadly valued for their 'authenticity' because they are expected to reveal participants' supposedly 'original' political motivations more openly than interactively less demanding press conferences or interviews. Unlike the prearranged choreography of similar events e.g. on American TV, these debates are open in their setting and proceeding. Nonetheless, impressions of authenticity can be fundamentally misleading, because rhetorically trained politicians – when successful – may produce calculated effects by deliberate formulations and patterns of behaviour, which become evident through close linguistic and interactional analysis.

Conceptually I will build on the basic insight of studies in political communication and mass media that interpretive frames make up the very core and influence of political messages (Iyengar 1991, Gamson 1992, Schön and Rein 1994). While trying to compensate for conceptual/methodological shortcomings of these mostly social-psychological studies (Scheufele 1999), I will take up their pivotal point about one function of 'frames': A dominant frame can 'determine what counts as a fact and what arguments are taken to be relevant and compelling' (Schön and Rein 1994: 23), and therefore also set the terms of interpretation for competing frames. Consequently, the political struggle for dominance has an intrinsically interactionistic side to it: political positioning is always oriented to and directed towards other, competing political interpretations in the struggle for public support. So the methodological/conceptual approach of my analyses presented here may in turn have some exemplary value for other, less openly competitive, discursive events, where political actors use *heteroglot* speech forms (Bakhtin 1998) to influence politically and socially heterogeneous audiences.

In this chapter I will sketch a methodological approach for analysing the complex discursive practices used in televised panel discussions (see Gotsbachner 2008) by inspecting a range of examples from Austrian news programs. Most difficult to grasp in any description and assessment of rhetorical devices is the interweaving of semantic and activity patterns. In order to demonstrate and explore their interrelations I differentiate three planes in the constitution of meaning: the planes of activity structure, political 'narrative' and social knowledge. Identifying the essential elements necessary for interactively establishing an interpretive frame on these three interrelated planes, and trying to systematize the discursive means used in such events will be the main task here.

Interpretive Frames

To begin, I will briefly explain how interpretive frames work, before going on to outline how to analyse them in televised political debates. The sociological concept of frames goes back to work by Erving Goffman (1974) and Gregory Bateson (1972), addressing a fundamental problem of communication: as most utterances in our ordinary day-to-day conversations are – and have to be – incomplete, allusive or otherwise truncated, whatever speakers leave out as taken for granted has to be added in the minds of receptive listeners. Consequently, vital to an efficient communication and to all understanding are referential frames, which organise this process of 'filling in' knowledge (Donati 1992, Entman 1993, Gamson 1992, Goffman 1974, Gotsbachner 2008, Minsky 1975, Schön and Rein 1994). 'Bateson demonstrated that no communicative move, verbal or nonverbal, could be understood without reference to a metacommunicative message or metamessage, about what is going on – that is, what frame of interpretation applies to a move'. (Tannen 1993: 3). Like other common mechanisms of understanding this can be used for tactical manipulation by political actors. Interpretive frames are important communicative devices guiding recipients' interpretations; a) by their interactive, procedural function in local, situated communication and b) as semantic clusters of meaning and 'social knowledge'. This double function is what makes a frame paradigm fruitful in spanning gaps between interactionistic approaches and those concerned with ideology and social knowledge.

From the latter perspective frames of interpretation are culturally and socially available and individually acquired 'data structures for representing a stereotyped situation' (Minsky 1975: 212), organising all sorts of social knowledge about social roles, settings and situations. The communicative function of frames in the production and comprehension of discourse is based on their *recognisability* 'by the presence or absence of certain keywords, stock phrases, stereotyped images, sources of information and sentences that provide thematically reinforcing clusters of facts or judgements' (Entman 1992: 52). Particular frames contain a series of more or less variable standard elements, or '*slots*', including roles of involved persons, key situations, defining figures, processes, problem solutions etc. When recognizing a certain frame, audiences will expect these specifications to be verbalized during the talk and – while listening – actively look for them, because they are known as important parts of this frame. If in the talk or text no elements or implicit hints occur offering themselves to fill the slots, recipients will draw on the frame they reproduce from their memory and reconstruct fitting elements by default assignments (Minsky 1975: 213).

> ... once a frame is elicited to define a perceptive input, data or elements, which are difficult to fit, will be 'adapted' or selectively dropped out, while gaps will be filled by adding the missing elements to complete the 're-cognised' pattern. Since a frame is a known structure, the elements that are constitutive of it are implicitly considered as 'naturally' tied together. The consequence is that mentioning some elements – sometimes even one – is usually enough to recall the whole set (Donati 1992: 141).

The use of frames thus enables recipients, while listening to talk or reading a text, to consider pieces of information which (probably) are implied, but not actually being given, and continuously build up projections about what is going on and what should come next, as continually assigned and revised hypothetical assumptions.

The interactional side of establishing an interpretive frame is more delicate and has been explored only recently (Tannen 1993, Gotsbachner 2008), although there are numerous studies illuminating certain aspects in the interactional constitution of meaning. The detailed processes in the negotiation of identities are a prominent example. In fact, how Harvey Sacks (1992) describes the working of membership categorisation devices (MCDs) can also be taken as paradigmatic for the constitution of a certain frame in an unfolding interaction. Like other elements making up for the 'slots' in interpretive frames, MCDs are 'inference-rich' utterances that other participants expect to contain crucial information: the implicit positioning and (self-)description of a speaker, or of a person referred to. Like other key elements they are designed for recognisability by specific recipients (Sacks 1992: 239-259; Housley 1999; Introduction, this volume). And like other key elements of opening up an interpretive frame, they occur and are expected to occur in certain places of an exchange, usually first self-references in an encounter or after formally marked frame-switches (see Müller 1984: 80f.). Once introduced – however implicitly – an identity needs to be maintained subsequently by further actions.

> The sort of greeting exchanged, the sort of description offered, the sort of biographical details exhibited, (...) but also the kind of humour tendered, the style of authenticity enacted, and the degree of interactional grace commanded provide varieties of resources for negotiating identities. (Schenkein 1978: 61f.).

If and how the other participants ratify this implicit positioning or offer contesting representations will have consequences for the distribution of roles, the modes of participation and the further development of an encounter (Kallmeyer and Schmitt 1996, Gotsbachner 1999, 2001).

Let us turn to political panel discussions on television. As in all arguments, the negotiation of identities is crucial to the assertion (and also challenging) of interpretive frames in televised confrontations with political opponents. The implicitly maintained positioning of identity claims determines, who is ascribed the competence, credibility and suitable political position to talk about what types of issues, deciding about rights of definition and burden of proof. On the other side, revealing the antagonist's 'ideological' distortions and political motivations through assignment of an ascribed identity can 'tilt' the assessment and perception of his or her whole framing.

What I am addressing here on identity claims is what I have mentioned above and what I will exemplify further on: that establishing an interpretive frame against similar, but adversarial efforts of other politicians is a complex business which requires actors to adjust their rhetorical moves on different levels. In order to be asserted successfully, self-identity-claims on the narrative level (introducing one's role according to one's definition of a social/political situation or problem) need to be enacted authentically through this actors' speech activities. Demonstrating a certain stance and behaviour, proposing certain moves etc, is important because this always carries implications for positioning – for example Transcript 5 will show a politician forgoing his advantage of being addressed as a university professor by departing from the restrained manner expected for this position. Finally, participant roles and identity claims must also correspond with what a politician stands for in public debate, the specific political positioning established on the level of common socio-political knowledge.

Methodologically this means that in examining the complex mechanisms of establishing an interpretive frame in political panel discussions we need to integrate at least three interrelated dimensions of analysis. Along with how claims and propositions are made and ratified (the first level of inquiry, the pragmatic level of speech activities) we need to consider, how they relate to frames on the second level, the level of creating a 'political narrative' or 'storyline' out of ambivalent social 'facts'. And then how these two levels relate to the third, the level of established social knowledge commonly available to broader communities of interpretation. My differentiation of levels in the 'constitution of meaning' here builds on a 'Gesprächsanalyse' in the vein of Werner Kallmeyer and Fritz Schütze (1976, 1977, also Bergmann 1994, Deppermann 2005) which in turn builds on a Conversation-Analysis-kind of 'analytic mentality' (Schenkein 1978). The German 'Gesprächsanalyse' expanded CA's basic orientation to member's 'communicative problems' – which participants have to face and can be shown to orient to themselves, in turn taking, 'doing formulations' etc., – to more specific communicative problems or requirements constitutive for certain discursive genres (like the negotiation of credibility in informal court proceedings,

Gotsbachner 1999), and made this orientation their baseline of analytic inquiry (Kallmeyer 1988: 1104, Deppermann 2005: 50). Schenkein's analysis (1978) had, for instance, anticipated this step by working out different ways of treatment all contributing to the same form of identity negotiation (official vs. unofficial identities) specific to an insurance-selling-event, but without using the description of the communicative problem for explicating some constitutive characteristics of the particular event they were observed in.

My aim is to identify the 'constitutive communicative problems' of participants in televised political debates on the three levels of activity structure, political 'narrative' and social knowledge, and use them to systematize the discursive requirements crucial for interactively asserting an interpretive frame. Condensed to one sentence these 'constitutive communicative problems' could be formulated as something like: political actors try to construct a consistent 'story line' from inherently ambivalent political 'facts' while simultaneously reacting to adverse questions of the moderator and multiple challenges from opponents, and they do so conscious of performing in front of a heterogeneous audience.

Gaining Control over the Local Distribution of Talking Rights

Among the crucial discursive requirements for asserting an interpretive frame is that discussants defend or even expand their range of self-determination. Different moves of discussants imposing demands on their opponents and escaping those directed at themselves have been systematically conceptualised in the fruitful analytical model of 'enforcement' (Kallmeyer/Schmitt 1996). This model refines basic conversation-analytic concepts like 'conditional relevance' into complex realms of tactical discursive manoeuvring on the levels of speaking opportunities, utterance meanings, factual representations, discursive actions and social relationships. Losses and gains within debates are dependent on the struggle for dominance on these interdependent levels of activity structure and constitution of meaning. 'Dominance' can be observed to a certain degree empirically in participants' ability to increase demands (by controversial assertions, accusations, calls for legitimation or explanation etc.) on their opponents so that they cannot meet them satisfactorily within a limited timeframe. This ability is dependent on gaining control over the local distribution of talking rights. The empirical examples I will discuss show the close connection of participant roles and participants' leeway in interaction in the contest over talking opportunities.

My first example is from a panel discussion from 2001 on a referendum by the populist-right Austrian Freedom Party (FPÖ), which proposed blocking the Czech Republic's entry into the European Union by stating conditions concerning the atomic reactor Temelin. In this discussion the FPÖ party secretary Westenthaler is asked by the moderator about the possible diplomatic damage of an Austrian veto to the EU enlargement. Westenthaler postpones answering the question by claiming to react to a misrepresentation of his opponent. We will see that a constitutive problem inherent to first statements in political panel discussions is that discussants need to open up their interpretive frames on the narrative level while simultaneously demonstrating their commitment to the discussion by answering the question of the moderator. Westenthaler's 'Let-me-firstly….'-preface is a typical minimal solution to this dilemma. The conflict I document in the transcript occurs when Westenthaler, after consuming as much time as his opponent had for his opening statement, still doesn't prepare to answer the question

Transcript 1: ZiB-16-11-2001-Temelin

```
W:    … and when this reactor joins the grid as it is .hhh we will
      interpose our veto
M:    Even if [Austria would be internationally isolated]
W:           [This is-]                    Well this is always the
      question. You know, France and Great Britain use vetoes all
      the time and neither France nor Great Britain are isolated
      when [they veto/]                              [When]=
M:         [But not against- not] not against the EU-en[largement]
W:    =it (.) Could I once finish speaking? Thanks Mister
      Adrowitzer. When it concerns vital …
```

Technically the moderator's two objections are made for thematical steering, not for taking over the speaking opportunity. When Westenthaler insists on his right to 'finish speaking', he had already regained the floor, so his insisting is dysfunctional here, a typical 'enforcing' move. Westenthaler treats the objections as repeated illegitimate interruptions, an interpretation which implicitly challenges the moderator's right to ensure that his questions are answered, and thereby also the moderators role to control talking opportunities. The moderator, in turn,

Figure 4.1   ZiB2 Studio Discussion 2001

fails to rebuff this implicit challenge. His gestured answer instead demonstrates withdrawal (see Figure 4.1).

What is at stake in this simple, but inferentially loaded 'Could I once finish speaking?' can be shown in the further development of the interaction, where we find not only participant's own manifest interpretations of what is happening, but also the emergence of the local interactional order (Bergmann 1994; Kallmeyer and Schmitt 1996). It can be revealed only in close attention to the pragmatic/ thematical context, where we need an understanding of turn taking mechanisms and organisation, and the implicit negotiation of participant roles. The moderator's implicit, involuntary ratification of Westenthaler's tactical claim – and accordingly the damage to his institutionalised role – have determining effects on the further discussion. Westenthaler is then able to continue his opening statement to double the length of what his opponent had been allotted, an imbalance which subsequently influences total talking time and mirrors the moderator's loss of control over speaking opportunities. Westenthaler keeps interrupting his opponents' statements with disturbing remarks and finally delivers an undisguised propaganda speech for the FPÖ-referendum even after the moderator had signalled the end of the discussion.

Using complex CA-models we could register that the moderator's objections fail to renew the 'footing shift' (Clayman 1992) of his initial question, where he had said: 'EU-commission-president Prodi has warned in tomorrow's press that Austria .hh a veto to the enlargement could harm Austria very much'. In the excerpt above we see that when the moderator renews the gist of his question he makes himself vulnerable by leaving his neutralistic stance, formulating his objections not as citation from an important political player but as his own undistanciated, opinionated statements.

But panel discussions in Austrian television from that time show that the rules concerning 'footing shift renewals' were usually not treated as strictly as in Clayman's model (1992: 170f.). More important seems the fact that attacks on news moderators were a recurring discursive tactic of Westenthaler and other FPÖ-politicians in TV-interviews, accusing the broadcasting corporation ORF generally of acting against them in a partisan manner. Drawing on the development of the FPÖ Gotsbachner (2003; forthcoming) analyses how this rhetorical tactic became a recurring interactional resource and part of the FPÖ's long term political strategy – to claim for themselves rebel status against the political/media system, attracting an increasing electorate of protest voices.

Focusing on our baseline of developing the participants' requirements for meeting the 'constitutive communicative problems' in a televised panel discussion and in determining these challenges on the pragmatic level we can see how important enforcing moves are for discussants to expand their range of self-determination. However enforcing moves are also risky, because in the struggle over talking rights they can be reverted, as I will demonstrate with an example of another discussion. This panel discussion (below) was about charges of corruption the Green Party delegate Pilz had raised against Social Democrat politicians, among them his opponent in this discussion, Mayr. When Pilz starts his first statement – asked by the moderator to present evidence for his charges – Mayr interrupts him after only three sentences. Mayr accuses Pilz of lying deliberately and, after getting no adequate reaction, enrages himself into an emotional outbreak, personally and loudly attacking his opponent for deliberate abuses and undemocratic behaviour (see Gotsbachner 2008). According to Kallmeyer and Schmitt's concept of enforcement we can say that the problem with this sudden outburst was its break with the 'ladder of escalation' (1996: 95ff), where personal insults of this strong kind usually occur and can be claimed to be legitimate only after an extended sequence of mutual escalation, which is absent here.

However in the data below we can see how the attacked Green delegate Pilz profited from this outburst. Pilz contrasted Mayr's shouting by responding very slowly and calmly and, after having been interrupted for the seventh time in his attempts to regain the floor, responded:

Transcript 2: ZiB-14-10-1998-Construction-scandal

```
P:    Are you, Mister Mayr,=
M:    YOU HAVE CAU- THAT'S WHAT YOU HAVE CAUSED!
P:    Mister Mayr, are you ready (0.6) in a discussion=
M:    I am completely ready [but I am not ready-]
P:                          =[in a democracy (.)] to listen for
      just a few minutes?
M:    I am ready to listen for many minutes but I am not ready
      for this humiliating politics- why did you give this press
      conference in Carinthia? (0.4) Maybe because of upcoming
      elections …
```

Pilz returns the accusations of undemocratic behaviour by asking Mayr to comply with 'democratic' discussion discipline, but Mayr interrupts again and continues his attacks. The discussion normalises only after the moderator intervenes for a second time and urges Mayr to allow his opponent to answer the question. Pilz then uses this first opportunity to talk again by turning to the moderator, explaining: 'But, but you can imagine roughly how pretty lively things were in the Vienna city council during the time of the absolute majority of the Socialists. This was just a brief impression'.

This comment, concluding Pilz' diligent handling of the opening sequence, contains a sublime, inference rich characterisation of Mayr's identity. Pilz had contrasted his opponents' behaviour by systematically slowing down his responses, and not joining or responding to Mayr's escalation, making him even wilder and making this behaviour visible for the audience at the same time. Pilz' metadiscursive question in Transcript 2 forced Mayr into discrediting himself as a politician not 'ready' to democratic discussion. Pilz immediately builds his next remark on this 'impression', alleging the notoriousness of Mayr's behaviour which he just had made visible. Summing up a complex analysis (Gotsbachner 2008) we can say that Pilz succeeds in turning Mayr's fierce endeavours of enforcement against himself, and his *bonmot* about the state of politics during socialist rule becomes widely cited in the next day's press. Mayr was depicted as somebody not used to oppositional critique and its controlling function.

But in this *bonmot* Pilz not only succeeds to define his opponent's identity in a way relevant to his charges of corruption, he also succeeds in discrediting the important first representation of his opponents' interpretive frame ('ungrounded attacks seeking political profit').

Later, towards the end of the discussion, Pilz is able to realize the interactive implications of his first victory for a second time.

Transcript 3: ZiB-14-10-1998-Construction-scandal

```
M:  … instead of keeping employment in [our own country]
P:                                     [These are the usual]
    tactics, [the (?…)]
M:        [These are - Your tactics] Your tactics Mister Pilz are
    to create a stir and wait until like in CIA-methods you will be
    passed [documents. ]
P:        [Don't start], now please don't start shouting again
    Mister Mayr.
M:  No I don't   °(I do not)°-
P:  Mister Mayr (0.8) we have to accept that the year-long looking-
    away of politicians has created an unbearable situation…
```

When Pilz, now himself interrupting his opponent, objects that the Social Democrat's appeal to securing employment was a foul, tactical argument (which he had explained just before – and which I will come back to later), Mayr replies by starting to characterise Pilz's own 'tactics'. These charges could have been dangerous to Pilz, who had admitted in another press-interview being passed secret documents leaked from political bureaucracy, but he neutralizes them by again switching to the metadiscursive level. Pilz warns Mayr not to start shouting again, and although in fact Mayr doesn't (he only speaks more vivid and pronounced), he implicitly ratifies this interpretation by retracting and becoming silent.

There are some general conclusions to be drawn from these examples. Firstly, they show how an interactional order emerges from turn to turn, binding back the participants by supplying negotiated reference points and orientations they can be shown to adhere to themselves – in Transcript 3 Mayr shows himself aware of his previous 'defeat', as does the moderator Adrowitzer for the rest of the other discussion. Secondly, the examples show how this order is tactically influenced by 'enforcing' moves which succeed to win the at least implicit ratification of the opponent. The risk of enforcing moves is in their interactional success, because, as demonstrated in Transcripts 2 and 3, they can be turned around. So, the rhetorical assessment of interactional roles and the evaluation of talking behaviour itself (what counts as an 'interruption', or as 'shouting'), is subject to the interactional constitution of meaning (Kallmeyer and Schmitt 1996: 33). Even institutionalised roles (like the moderator's) are subject to this negotiation process, so that televised discussions become a primary forum for the placement and initial stabilisation of claims in the socio-political renegotiation of established positions. Losses and gains on the pragmatic level of a panel discussion not only influence the negotiation of participant roles and identities, but simultaneously also the validity of positions in the interactive constitution of meaning (Kallmeyer and Schmitt 1996: 25).

Enforcing moves on the pragmatic level of establishing an interpretive frame are essential to the negotiation process. But they also create points of increased attention for the opponents' answer in the following turn, which opponents can use to place their own representations. Beside first statements such points are preferred moments to place inference rich utterances which can become key elements of participants' interpretive frames on the narrative level. How important the placement of remarks is for establishing one's frame can be demonstrated via how Pilz's *bonmot* was taken over by the press (Gotsbachner 2008) while Mayr's accusation of Pilz's seeking political profit in Transcript 2 doesn't gain any influence, neither in the discussion nor elsewhere.

In political panel discussions enforcing moves of a thematically provocative kind (more transparent in the next transcripts) are essential for any actor to translate their political agenda and purposes into the very tasks of the discussion, thereby influencing the overall theme of what all the talking is heard to be about and what is regarded to be part of (or distracting from) the discussed topics. So, generally, it is on the pragmatic, activity level that thematical initiatives with all their inferential import on relevancy-, identity- and credibility-claims become interactionally focused objects, engaging the attention of the participants (Müller 1984: 63) and also guiding audiences' interpretations of this interactional negotiation of meaning.

Pilz' behaviour during his interrupted opening statement, and later in his compact disposal of Mayr's critical objection in Extract 3 also demonstrates that for establishing one's interpretive frame it is not so important to talk as much and as long as possible. Rather what is important is to secure one's control over talking rights in such a way that one is able and legitimated to intervene at the right point and in sufficient detail for an effective involvement in an interaction (Kallmeyer amd Schmitt 1996: 47).

Framing and Reframing Political Events

I have already mentioned that in first statements (or answers) discussants have to provide a short characterisation of the 'punch line' of their position, opening their interpretive frame on the narrative level and provisionally setting expectations for what their whole talking activity will lead to. On this narrative level the overall task for discussants is to introduce different thematical aspects connected to their version of the social or political problems discussed, and to arrange them into a complex, conclusive story line. After presenting an example of framing and reframing I will show that crucial to these efforts is building up a more or less consistent network of tacit, paralogical references between single statements.

The discussion in my fourth example is from 2005. The finance-minister of the then conservative Austrian government, Grasser (ex-FPÖ), is criticised for his budget by Green Party leader Van der Bellen.

Transcript 4: ZiB-2-3-2005-Budget-speech

```
vdB:(…) .hhh My criticism is essentially this .hhh Minister
     of Finance Grasser has succeeded during these years .hh
     to turn, from a generally appreciated (.) uuhm member
     of  government (.) into a minister (0.3) who (1.5)
     assiduously, strongly and energetically works – during all
     these years – at undermining his credibility. And I'll
     give you two examples, one (0.3) dating back and a current
     one. .hh (1.0) ((clears his throat)) It is not so long ago
     that you tried, in your budget-speech .hhh uuhm to make us
     believe that the budget for education and science would be
     raised for 700 million Euros per year (.) I needed some
     hours to find out, that these were simple double-countings
     (.) .hh in the course of autonomizing the universities ...
```

In this extract Van der Bellen uses an assumption of the minister's identity to frame his critique of budgetary cuts in education and science, starting his characterisation with 'assiduously, strongly and energetically'. These three words are Grasser's own preferred ones to characterise his own politics, and the camera catches him listening with a radiant smile. However Van der Bellen then concludes by actually formulating that 'Grasser undermines his own credibility' – and here the camera shows Grasser's freezing face. Van der Bellen gives an example of the minister's 'creative accounting' – admitting that he himself (having been introduced as a 'Professor of Economics' and referred to as such by Grasser in his answer below) had needed some time to unveil the trick. In his second example (not shown here) his main point is that despite the minister's contrary accounts in the recent budget-speech the financing of Federal teachers had in fact been reduced.

We could say that this opening of a storyline is rhetorically well constructed, not only because Van der Bellen succeeds in catching his opponent interactionally in the trap of revealing – evidently to all – his publicly known vanity while presenting an argument regarding his credibility. He also exemplifies the 'trickiness' of the ministers' 'creative accounting' on descriptions footing in the ministers' own representations (vdB: 'you will recognise these numbers ((shows the report)) these are your numbers, not mine'). But Grasser is a political professional, and his answer argumentatively and emotionally copes with the challenge of his opponent.

Transcript 5: ZiB-2-3-2005-Budget-speech

M: Please let's have the Minister of Finance answer to these
       accusations
G: Lets deal with (0.3) credibility, Mister Professor (.)
       uhhm (.) and, you said 'professor', I say, obviously *too*
       uhm *party* leader uhm Van der Bellen.
vdB: I do represent that too, [frankly speaking]
G: [Firstly/] (.) And for that you
       also sit here.
vdB: *Surely*
G: uhmm When I said 12 million *more* for federal teachers in
       my budget speech .hh then you obviously have overlooked
       that this occurs in the chapter of fin*a*ncial adjustment=
vdB: [Very true]
G: =[and in] financial adjustment it is part of an agreement
       with the federal regions to give 12 million *more* to the
       regions under the title of financial adjustment.
vdB: [(These are the ?)]
G: [Federal] teachers. I therefore record, it is (.)
       comp*le*tely (.) *right*. Objectively provable (.) *Fact*. .hhh
       Second: I don't think it is serious or credible when *you*
       say, and you did this yesterday already (.) on federal
       teachers we economize, you say and there's [less money]
vdB: [Cut]   not
       econom[ize, cut]
G: [Cut] Ok (.) But you don't mention, and I would
       expect this from a (.) serious personality who claims to
       be credible himself .hh you don't mention that in the
       realm of federal teachers we have at the same time twelve
       to thirteen-thousand pupils less …

Actually Van der Bellen was right, the budget for Federal teachers *was* cut by 30
million. I don't have the space here to prove that in technical detail, but the point
is, neither had Van der Bellen in the discussion itself: the moderator hadn't allowed
him to go much deeper into explanations on education expenses, as the topic of the
discussion was the budget as a whole, and the complexity of factual relations still
left leeway for 'creative accounting', so finally Grasser was able to establish his
interpretation in the discussion. The success of this is revealed through a detailed
analysis of Grasser's answer.

   Grasser takes up the numbers Van der Bellen had used in the second example
and accuses him of inaccuracy, thereby returning the accusation of lacking
credibility and seriousness. His answer touches the core of his opponents' attack
by firstly addressing the challenge to his identity. Grasser corrects the moderator's

introduction of Van der Bellen as university professor and adds that his opponent's role in the discussion was as opposition leader, i.e., guided by party interests, which Van der Bellen, scowling, ratifies (mind how this is similar to the way Van der Bellen had addressed the minister's popularity in the tabloids – as the 'ideal son-in-law' – before tilting this very picture). The insisting and condescending tone in which Grasser then addresses Van der Bellen, like speaking to a petulant pupil, and the irritated way Van der Bellen reacts, further deprives the latter of his professorial aura.

Grasser insists that his depiction of rising expenses for Federal teachers was '... right. Objectively provable. Fact', by shifting the focus of his statement to a technical subset of the budget, where this actually was true. This shift of focus is an example of 'ontological gerrymandering' (Potter 1996: 177), ironically used here to parry the accusation of misrepresentation. Grasser's second argument works similarly. Here, too, he veils his shift of focus by lengthily claiming that to consider the falling numbers of pupils would have been a requirement of objectivity which Van der Bellen had failed to observe.

Again, we see that identity ascriptions are crucial in tilting opponents' representations, and indeed this is a general pattern I have observed in numerous political panel discussions. Reframing interpretive frames works primarily through attacks on the opponents' identity, and additionally by engendering a shift of focus in the narrative account. It is a general function of framing and reframing (and not only by means of 'ontological gerrymandering' like here) that even a minor shift of aspects can tilt the whole assessment of relevancies, truth-values and moral evaluations of a case.

The central challenge of interactively establishing a frame on the level of political narrative is to create a network of mutually supporting, pseudo-logical references between single statements spread over the whole discussion. These networks can become interpretive frames to which all arguments are heard to be related, allowing for certain types of inferences and excluding others, making certain phenomena salient and letting others fade into the background.

How Grasser strategically selects certain 'facts' to support his overall argumentation, is one crucial step for preparing an argumentative 'storyline', another requirement is creating a certain 'wording'. To construct a consistent framing of political facts, problems and constellations politicians need to create a suitable 'wording' for casting these 'facts' into a pregnant categorisation. Creating a suitable 'wording' today is believed to be a basic skill of political actors and their communication advisors,[1] because a characterful categorization underlines the

---

1 '*Wording*' in German has become a technical term with a narrower sense than in English, also used by communication advisors who train Austrian politicians: to secure a homogene appearance in the press, party leaders, when discussing how to handle a certain affair or new situation, develop 'wordings' which they then give out to all party representatives who could be picked for media-interviews (fieldnotes Meyn 20 July 2007, Wagner 10 September 2007, Besenböck 29 October 2007).

ontological quality of representations: through 'wording' which highlights certain aspects – and backgrounds others – a strategically selected meaning is transferred into an 'innocent' descriptive term where the implicit valuation and argumentation appears as inner logic of matters themselves.

In Transcript 3 Pilz depicted the presumed involvement of socialist politicians in the construction-scandal as 'the year-long looking-away of politicians', *nominalising* as an intentional behaviour what later turned out to be just his own presumption. In the confrontation with Van der Bellen Grasser speaks of a 'governmental focus on education' – which is nothing more than 'symbolic politics' (Edelman 1990) to demonstrate his concern in spite of his budgetary cuts on schools and universities. Another one of his slogans, 'zero deficit' became almost a 'business card' for Grasser's politics. In the discussion analysed here he used the popular slogan to create the impression of a 'sinking financial debt' (another strategic 'wording'...), although when confronted with actual numbers the 'zero deficit' turned out to be only a political goal he tried to invoke. So, a clever 'wording' and a suitable interactive positioning of introduced representational elements are both important to the effort of constructing one's interpretive frame.

What in fact is crucial for constructing the core of an interpretive frame on the narrative level is creating the impression of a coherent 'story line', which builds on the pseudo-logical relations between these representational elements, as well as their relation to the adversarial frame presented by the other discussant. If we try to condense the narrative elements of the adversarial frames in the debate on the budget speech for 2006 in a combined figure, it would look somewhat like in Figure 4.2.

In summing up the narrative lines in this panel discussion there are some noticeable differences in what the two discussants present as their contradictory interpretive frames of education expenses and the budgetary situation. Not only does finance-minister Grasser's representation touch on more aspects to support his interpretation, there are also richer paralogical argumentative references between the elements of his narrative representation than in Van der Bellen's storyline.

The argument over Van der Bellen's main criticism that the current budget of Federal teachers was cut, clearly goes to Grasser. Grasser brings in sinking pupil numbers on Federal schools and alleged higher expenses for high schools to 'win' this important first argument, suggesting a rise in educational expenses relative to pupil numbers. He also starts to press his opponent that as a university professor Van der Bellen would need to admit the regularity of this calculation, thereby reinforcing his identity-ascription (party leader vs. professor) and embedding his education-expenses-argument in an appeal to Van der Bellen to stop 'polemics' and seek common solutions. Grasser asserts that expenses for education would be rising since the start of the conservative government, which finally stands unchallenged, although Van der Bellen had criticised budgetary cuts on education from the very beginning.

Grasser also settles another critical argument for himself, where Van der Bellen derogates his statement 'The financial debt is sinking?', which urges Grasser to admit 'In relation to the GNP, of course, when you look in here/' and he goes on to assert that relative numbers were 'more objective'. Van der Bellen adds that an annual rise of €6 billion could not be regarded as 'sinking financial debt', but this – originally striking – objection is finally 'parried' by Grasser who emphatically expresses optimism that Austria nonetheless is going towards 'zero-deficit', and cites several international newspapers which he says had congratulated him for a 'better performance than Germany'. In fact it needs some enthymemic thinking to see how this argument paralogically relates to Van der Bellen's critique of the raising national debt: it works only on one aspect, namely not on the fact itself, but on the (implicit) accusation, Grasser would try to euphemise the budgetary situation, where citing the 'compliments' from *Financial Times* and *Neue Zürcher* provides the supposition that euphemisms would not be necessary, because 'international authorities' depicted the situation of the Austrian budget as good. Van der Bellen in turn fails to doubt this construction.

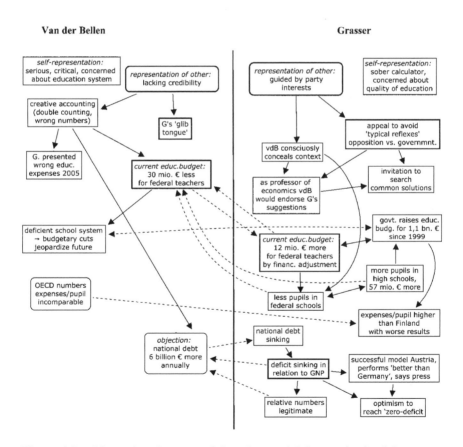

Figure 4.2   Narrative elements of the adversarial frames in the debate

Breaking down arguments into different aspects is the job of media-communication-advisors when preparing politicians to create handy formulas for every aspect in countering arguments they can expect from their opponents.[2] Grasser's 'richer' paralogical references between his statements appear as such a superior '*aspectisation*'. On another panel debate Gotsbachner (2008) shows how 'argumentative dominance' is manufactured by building a narrative 'storyline' on networks of paralogical references, touching on more and stronger aspects of a political problem than the opponent. On the level of political narrative we need an analysis of argumentation patterns – who introduces what propositions, how are they treated by the opponent, and what is finally left as unchallenged – to reconstruct the competing storylines which make up for the different framings and how they relate to each other (van Eemeren et al 1993).

Whilst analysing the 'rhetorical force' or even dominance of argumentative patterns is a complicated question to be treated with diligence, we can see that Grasser wins considerably more speaking time than Van der Bellen and opens more challenges his opponent cannot answer. Though of course this attests dominance only on the level of activity.

Observing developments in this panel discussion we can say that although Van der Bellen had built his narrative frame of the budget-situation on his critique of the ministers' 'creative accounting' from the beginning, he shows himself unable to reveal the ministers' practices when being interactionally confronted with them. That is to say that Van der Bellen fails to assert the cuts in educational expenses on the very case he had introduced, when Grasser does what Van der Bellen had predicted he would do repeatedly.

Still, if we consider which interpretive frame succeeds in paralogically 'overruling' the arguments of the opposite framing, the picture is ambivalent. Grasser 'wins' the argument over the question, if the budget on education is rising or cut, but Van der Bellen, although finally unable to counter the presentation of a rise of educational expenses, had somewhat pre-empted this by pointing to Grasser's 'creative accounting' and 'glib tongue'. In the end however it depends on which interpretive frame is regarded to be more credible,[3] if and how the true addressees of these adverse framings, the television audiences, ratify the contradictory accounts, or how they make sense of them. To analyse these framing effects of political panel discussions it would need an equally subtle and extensive reception research across socio-culturally and politically different groups of television consumers.[4] What we can analyse in panel discussions themselves is only what political actors do and how they do it.

---

2   Fieldnotes Meyn 20 July 2007, Wagner 10 September 2007.

3   Schön and Rein (1994 p. 30) about the very logic of 'frame conflicts': 'Evidence that one party regards as devastating to a second party's argument, the second may dismiss as irrelevant or innocuous'.

4   In our 'Frame Project' (September 2008 to March 2011), funded by the Austrian Science Foundation P20814-G03, we will explore the alignment of frames in audience

Social Knowledge and Dominant Frames

To achieve a kind of 'frame resonance' (Snow et al. 1986) the main task for political actors on the third level is to build their framings on socio-culturally established frames, values and ideologies which their narrative accounts of a political situation claim to be legitimate instantiations of. In the strict sense the narrative storylines of political discussants, although carrying some characteristics of 'frames' already, are not yet proper 'interpretive frames', i.e., semantic structures of 'social knowledge'. Nevertheless this is what the rhetorical efforts of political actors are all about, trying to disseminate their framings to the wider public so that they are taken on as appropriate, close-to-experience definitions of social reality.

Analysing what kinds of established frames and values political actors draw on in their narrative accounts is not difficult. Researchers, considering the unstated assumptions in the enthymemic construction of paralogical arguments, can analyse what discussants treat as social knowledge or value, if or how others challenge or ratify these instantiations, or how discussants compete about who is the legitimate representative of a certain stance (e.g. Grasser and Van der Bellen concurring in their concern about education – who 'stands' for a 'better' education system).

Many types of 'social knowledge' are socially bound and what certain social or political groups regard as close-to-experience 'knowledge', for others is pure ideology. While seeking 'frame resonance' a basic problem for political actors is that their addressees are highly heterogeneous in terms of political orientation and socio-cultural background. That political statements are subject to different reinterpretations by various audiences with different experiences and interpretive repertoires is due to the recognisability of certain ways of speaking as bound to a specific 'Weltanschauung' and perspective, the problem at the core of how understanding via interpretive frames works. In panel discussions we can often observe rhetorical tactics which suggest that political actors orient to these heterogeneous understandings. Although culturally available interpretive frames are saturated with patterns of values, belief and perception, this does not prevent them from being highly adoptable or appropriable. In fact, while trying to construct a credible narration of current political events on the narrative level, political actors often use *heteroglot rhetoric* drawing on popular topics of their opponents and thereby trying to make their own specific framings plausible even for those parts of the public, who are not (yet) part of their electorate. For example where a Green politician uses the nationalistically loaded term 'Heimat' (homeland), or a right populist invokes women's emancipation. Whilst on the face of it seemingly disjunctive with the political frame of the speaker, the first was in a discussion of minority rights while defending the right to a 'Heimat'-feeling even for ethnic minorities, and the second part of an argument discrediting immigrants with respect to Muslim women's headscarves. Only in considering the complete frame the rhetorical character of such heteroglossia becomes accessible, comparing

---

reactions. See <http://www.univie.ac.at/frame-project>.

how certain politically 'recognizable' arguments are used to pre-empt expected critique during the construction of an interpretive frame of a different political orientation.[5]

An example less transparent in its rhetorical endeavour is one we have already discussed in the construction-scandal-debate when Pilz, regaining the floor after Mayr's eruptive accusations, uses his first turn to express his concern about employment. His appropriation on the level of who-stands-for-what-kind-of-issues and who is regarded as competent and politically equipped to talk about them, is part of Pilz' bigger strategy. The provocation for Mayr, who again interrupts Pilz loudly (see Transcript 2), lies in the heteroglot 'appropriation' of the social-democrat's 'own' theme, through which Pilz starts to block his opponents' interpretation.

Later in the panel discussion Pilz turns Mayr's argument against Mayr himself. Pilz knows the argument from socialist politicians' previous newspaper-comments – that he would endanger working-places by 'unfounded accusations'– and he reasonably could expect that Mayr would use it also in the debate. He explains: 'That is the usual development in such scandals. In the beginning the responsible politicians say: that's all not true, lie, defamation – we have heard this already'. Referring to Mayr's own words Pilz starts to explain, how his opponents' argumentation usually develops, going on to explain that in the next step, 'when the facts, the evidence, the testimonies are on the table' social-democrats usually conceded there were some 'black sheep', until, as Pilz explains, during investigation '… all sheep turn out to be black. And the next step is: Ok, we knew it, but it was all for securing employment. We now approach this last rescue argumentation'.

In reframing his opponents' arguments, beginning with those heard some minutes before, then going on with suppositions about alleged 'facts' and 'evidence' (which Pilz actually failed to supply) and ending with a prediction of the arguments which will follow, Pilz constructs a double-bind-dilemma for Mayr, who then is unable to escape it (see the beginning of Transcript 3). Mayr, finally, undermines his own argument by involuntarily ratifying Pilz' prediction while introducing 'employment' as an important element of his own interpretive frame.

The strength of Pilz' tactics for constructing his interpretive frame around his opponents' recurring argumentation lies not only in interactively catching Mayr in a double-bind. Its plausibility is also created through connecting the 'directly perceptible' with established 'social knowledge': most audiences could easily recognise the recurring social-democrat argumentation – that different political nuisances need to be accepted in order to prevent unemployment.

To 'reframe' the political behaviour and strategy of the opponent in line with one's own explanatory patterns is an increasingly common rhetorical strategy of

---

5   Preliminary observations of TV receptions show that audiences still are vulnerable to such tactics, taking over interpretive elements of parties they do not sympathise with, or starting to use their inferentially loaded wordings while describing what is going on. See also Gotsbachner (2003).

political actors in TV debates, because revealing his or her 'ideology' and political motivations can 'tilt' the assessment and perception of the antagonist's whole framing. If successful, it can have the effect that this opponent – by following his argumentative routines – increasingly exposes himself to the interpretations bestowed upon him and involuntarily and unconsciously can be heard to support an interpretive frame contradicting his own (see Gotsbachner 2003, 2008).

If and how certain framings actually become accepted by different groups of recipients of course depends on many factors. In specific cases like the debate on the construction-scandal, one can show how the interpretive frame of Pilz was taken over by different opinion leaders and newspapers: Pilz' *bonmot* became a crystallisation point for explanations which started to take the charges of corruption serious, building their evidence on presumptions about the political situation during socialist majority. Journalists started to gather, select and arrange new information according to the storyline of Pilz' framing (Gotsbachner 2008), which is a strong indicator for how this storyline was taken on as an interpretive frame to comprehend social and political reality.

Summary

Enlightening details of how politicians try to establish their interpretations of political issues against concurring representations needs to analyse the interplay of a broad range of interactive and semantic elements. Indeed, Figure 4.1 has shown that even a gesture can be an important move eminently influencing the development and settlement of a whole panel discussion. How these different elements develop their 'force' is revealed through analysing the assertion of 'interpretive frames': a 'framing paradigm cautions researchers not to take fugitive components of messages and ask, how they *might* be interpreted' (Entman 1993: 56), but helps to reconstruct fundamental processes of actual understanding and constitution of meaning.

The approach sketched in this chapter tries to integrate different strands of rhetorical endeavours in political panel discussions around their contribution to establishing an 'interpretive frame' on the levels of interaction, political narrative and social knowledge. Successful rhetorical operation on each of these interdependent three levels depends on at least satisfactorily treatment of the others. The level of activity structure is basic to the negotiation of the interactional order: the local distribution of talking rights, the negotiation of participant roles and identities, and the definition of thematical foci of the discussion. To make their own political themes relevant, actors need to translate them into challenges for their opponents, like controversial assertions, accusations, calls for legitimation, or more subtly, for concession and cooperation, etc. They do so by manifold enforcing activities which expand their range of self-determination and which also carry implications for their identities. On the pragmatic level interpretive frames mainly are established as the lively enactment of representations, which are introduced by inference-rich talking activities preferably on certain points of a discussion, either introductory statements, or 'points of increased attention' created by critical challenges of an opponent. Actors essentially need to assert a certain grade of control over the local distribution of talking rights on the interactional level in order to enable them to coherently develop their descriptions on the second, narrative level.

On the level of a political 'narrative', required in establishing a certain 'storyline' of what is happening, actors in televised discussions need to occupy certain cornerstones of the pending debate: definitions of the current social/political problem and the distribution of roles, which assert who is responsible for what, and who is competent and equipped to do something about it. I have named this level political 'narrative', although the thematical representations I consider under this level are mostly only partially realised in the conventional narrative form. However they accomplish their rhetorical effect only as paradigmatic, prototypical 'narrations', as a 'plot' or 'storyline' interpreting a current political constellation or state-of-affairs. The narrative level is central in a way that an established 'storyline' can set the terms of relevance for all arguments and activities in the whole discussion, namely also for those of an opponent: it can tilt perceptions and determine what answer, what measurement etc., is relevant for what kind of pending problem. I have argued that the prudent selection, categorisation and 'wording' of certain aspects of reality is basic to creating a coherent narrative and political representation, establishing or hiding certain responsibilities, or setting relevant certain 'causal' connections and 'truth values'. However, eventually this is dependent on the ability of political actors to create a network of 'paralogical references' in their enthymemic arguments spread over the discussion. Creating such a network enables them to establish their interpretive frames at this level.

A main route for 'reframing' an opponent's argument or tilting a whole frame is to address and reframe their self-representations through adverse ascriptions of an identity. I have shown how these ascriptions can become relevant on all three levels, the activity level redistributing talking rights, on the narrative level determining the validity of positions, and on the third, socio-cultural level for renegotiating who-stands-for-what-issues. Basic to all reframing-devices is that they can tilt the whole interpretation of a certain case by considerably minor changes or refocusing of aspects which become eminently meaningful.

The positioning of interpretive frames on the third, socio-cultural level builds on the actor's awareness that appeals to 'common knowledge' are crucial to validity claims of narrative political accounts. However at the same time these intrinsic appeals to 'common knowledge' for most audiences are recognisable signs indicating the 'ideological position' of political discourses, which these audiences may not necessarily share. To influence the who-stands-for-what-kind-of-issues-dimension over a certain period, political actors in televised panel discussions need to enact their command over certain themes on the activity and narrative levels of their performance. An observable effect is that they often appropriate socio-politically allocated themes – keywords, social definitions and values – of opposite camps to blur the recognisability of their own ideological position and to address audiences, which are not (yet) convinced of their views.

Analysing the assertion of interpretive frames in televised political discussions needs a combination of methodological approaches adequate for each of these three different levels: a sequential analysis which expands the conversation-analytic premise – that answers indicate interpretations of preceding utterances – into realms of strategic interaction, tracing how discussants take up certain aspects of their opponent's enforcing moves; secondly, an analysis of argumentation-patterns sketching the paralogical references between single arguments, working out how the two 'storylines' relate to each other and how their fabrications of 'consistency' work. And lastly it requires an ideographic analysis to reconstruct how a certain discussion contributes to the redrawing of thematical/ideological boundaries, which may lead to a sociologically significant analysis of how certain interpretive frames become treated as 'social knowledge' by certain groups of interpreters and thereby influence the social career of political representations.

References

Bakhtin, M.M. 1998. Discourse in the novel, in *Literary Theory: An Anthology* edited by J. Rivkin and M. Ryan. Oxford: Blackwell, 674-685.

Bateson, G. 1972. *Steps into an Ecology of Mind: Collected Essays*. London: Intertext Books.

Bergmann, J.R. 1994. Ethnomethodologische Konversationsanalyse, in *Handbuch der Dialoganalyse* edited by G. Fritz and F. Hundsnurscher. Tübingen: Niemeyer, 3-16.

Cicourel, A.V. 1975. *Sprache in der sozialen Interaktion*. München: List.

Clayman, S.E. 1992. Footing in the achievement of neutrality: the case of news-interview discourse, in *Talk at Work* edited by P. Drew and J. Heritage. Cambridge: Cambridge University Press, 163-198.

Donati, P.R. 1992. Political Discourse Analysis, in *Studying Collective Action* edited by M. Diari and R. Eyerman. London: Sage, 136-167.

Entman, R.M. 1993. Framing: Toward clarification of a fractured paradigm. *Journal of Communication*, 43 (4), 51-58.

Fillmore, C.J. 1982. Frame semantics. Linguistics in the morning calm. Selected papers from SICOL 1981. *Linguistic Society of Korea*. Seoul: Hanshin, 111-137.

Gamson, W.A. 1992. *Talking Politics*. Cambridge: Cambridge University Press.

Gotsbachner, E. 1999. Identitätspolitik. Ausländerbilder als symbolische Ressource in Schlichtungsverhandlungen, in *Mediationsverfahren* edited by C. Pelikan. Baden Baden: Nomos, 189-240.

Gotsbachner, E. 2001. Xenophobic normality: The discriminatory impact of habitualized discourse dynamics. *Discourse and Society*, 12 (6), 729-759.

Gotsbachner, E. 2003. Normalisierungsstrategien in der Rhetorik der FPÖ. Die politische Alchemie, Kritik in Unterstützung zu verwandeln. (Normalisation stratiegies in the political rhetoric of the Austrian Freedom Party. The political alchemy of turning criticism into support). *Österreichische Zeitschrift für Politikwissenschaft*, 32 (4), 457-483.

Gotsbachner, E. 2008. Durchsetzung von Deutungsrahmen in politischen Fernsehdiskussionen. *Gesprächsanalyse*, Online-Zeitschrift zur verbalen Interaktion 9, 269-299; <http://www.gespraechsforschung-ozs.de/heft2008/ ga-gotsbachner.pdf>.

Gotsbachner, E. forthcoming. 'Ausgrenzung' oder: Hegemonialstrategien der FPÖ. Die politische Alchemie, Kritik in Unterstützung zu verwandeln, in *Multikulti light. Tagungsband der 8. Jahrestagung der Arbeitsgruppe 'Sprache in der Politik'* edited by F. Liedtke and C. Papen.

Holly, W., Kühn, P. et al. 1986. *Politische Fernsehdiskussionen. Zur medialen Inszenierung von Propaganda als Diskussion*. Tübingen: Niemeyer.

Iyengar, S. 1991. *Is Anyone Responsible? How Television Frames Political Issues*. Chicago, IL: Chicago University Press.

Kallmeyer, W. 1988. Konversationsanalytische beschreibung, in *Sociolinguistics* edited by U. Ammon, N. Dittmar and K. Mattheier. Berlin: de Gruyter. II, 1095-1108.

Kallmeyer, W. and Schmitt, R. 1996. Forcieren oder: die verschärfte Gangart. Zur Analyse von Kooperationsformen im Gespräch, in *Gesprächsrhetorik. Rhetorische Verfahren im Gesprächsprozeß* edited by W. Kallmeyer. Tübingen: Narr, 19-118.

Kallmeyer, W. and Schütze, F. 1977. Zur Konstitution von Kommunikationsschemata der Sachverhaltsdarstellung, in *Gesprächsanalysen* edited by D. Wegner. Hamburg: Buske, 159-274.

Müller, K. 1984. *Rahmenanalyse des Dialogs. Aspekte des Sprachverstehens in Alltagssituationen*. Tübingen: Narr.

Potter, J. 1996. *Representing Reality. Discourse, Rhetoric and Social Construction*. London: Sage.

Sacks, H. 1992. *Lectures on Conversation*. Cambridge: Cambridge University Press.

Schenkein, J. 1978. Identity negotiations in conversation, in *Studies in the Organization of Social Interaction* edited by J. Schenkein. New York, NY: Academic Press, 57-78.

Scheufele, D.A. 1999. Framing as a theory of media effects. *Journal of Communication*, 49 (1), 103-122.

Schön, D.A. and Rein, M. 1994. *Frame Reflection. Toward the Resolution of Intractable Policy Controversies*. New York, NY: Basic Books.

Snow, D.A., Rochford, B.E. et al. 1986. Frame alignment processes, micromobilization, and movement participation. *American Sociological Review*, 51, 464-481.

Tannen, D. and Wallat, C. 1993. Interactive frames and knowledge schemas in interaction: Examples from a medical examination/interview, in *Framing in Discourse* edited by D. Tannen. New York, NY: Oxford University Press, 57-76.

Tiittula, L. 2001. Formen der Gesprächssteuerung. in *Text- und Gesprächslinguistik* edited by K. Brinker, G. Antos, W. Heinemann and S.F. Sager. Berlin: de Gruyter. 2: 1361-1374.

Wetherell, M. 1998. Positioning and interpretative repertoires: conversation analysis and post-structuralism in dialogue. *Discourse and Society*, 9 (3), 387-412.

Chapter 5

Staging Public Discussion: Mobilizing Political Community in Closing Discussion Programmes

Hanna Rautajoki

Introduction

Socio-political television discussions represent a long-established programme format on the Finnish media. These familiar broadcasting formats may be considered intriguing or drop-dead boring, a valuable perspective opener or biased charade but, despite individual predilections, any competent member of the culture has some sense of them. In this chapter, I explore the details of the interaction through which the cultural recognizability of the programme format is accomplished *in situ*. I will focus on the closings of the discussions, asking how the relevant participant identities and the oriented-to task at hand are achieved in action. The analysis of interactional practices around closings opens up a perspective on broader democratic and nationalistic processes articulated through various strategies of address and ascriptions which are oriented to the audience, or 'us', as a political community. The theoretical framework of the study is ethnomethodological, and analytic tools are provided by conversation analysis and membership categorization analysis. My data consists of three live multi-party discussion programmes on 9/11.

The Public Sphere as a Members' Phenomenon

The concept of the public sphere derives from Jürgen Habermas's (1989) theoretization where he conceptualizes the ideal public sphere as the realm of social life in which the free exchange of information and views on questions of common concern can take place and public opinion formed. The rationally and critically generated public opinion is then taken to shape the policies of the state and the development of society as a whole. Since in modern society citizens can only be co-present in relatively small numbers, the mass media, dominantly television, has become the chief institution of the public sphere (Dahlgren 1995: 7-8). For Habermas, this institutional intervention has meant degradation, manifest through fragmentation, entertainmentization and vested interests. Be this as it may, mass mediation has not abolished the public sphere. Institutionalized encounters still create forums for practices which are relevant to viable political life (ibid: 9). In these processes the media is increasingly channelling the formation of public opinion (Housley and Fitzgerald 2007, and this volume). Yet, the public sphere is not just a place for information and opinion exchange but also a major societal mechanism for the production and circulation of the culture which frames and gives meaning to our identities (Dahglren 1995: 23). 'Us-ness' gets created in the fine-grained mechanisms of political discussion.

According to the ethnomethodological approach culture appears in action (cf Hester and Eglin 1997). Ethnomethodology highlights members' own situated orientations and sense-making practices and the collaborative maintenance of intersubjective understandings (Garfinkel 1967, Heritage 1984). Within the media environment, the aim of ethnomethodological inquiry is to describe the structures, practices and devices determining how a media text is produced and made recognizable (Jalbert 1999). Broadcast talk is a pervasive feature of everyday contemporary society although it has been studied relatively little (see, e.g. Scannell 1991, Livingstone and Lunt 1994, Hutchby 2006, Tolson 2006). One of the most distinctive features of broadcast talk in general is its 'double organization' (Scannell 1991) whereby talk is a communicative interaction between present participants but at the same time it is designed to directly address non-present overhearing audiences (see also Heritage 1985). Media talk attempts to engage the audience in a quasi-interactive relationship; for example, television talks to us in ways that invite our response, and in that process the individual audience member takes on a group identity (Tolson 2006: 15).

In mediated interaction the distanced and scattered constellation of participants allows creating extra-situational we-relations (cf Knorr Cetina and Bruegger 2002). The concept of participation framework (Goffman 1981) has been elaborated to investigate the positioning of the producers or receivers of talk in interaction (Goodwin 1987, Goodwin and Goodwin 1990). Participant roles are seen as mutual relations between participants, who are characterized as having specific discursive and social identities (Goodwin 1987: 119-120). The participant structure of television discussions is triangular. There are journalists and discussants present in the studio but talk is mainly targeted to a third party, the audience. Coordination of all these interrelated positions produces the organization of relevant identities. One device that the members use to manage mutual relations is the use of we-rhetoric. It can be deployed for inclusion and exclusion in categorizations, or as an invitation to self selection. The television audience is rarely categorized directly but it is constantly offered loci for identification through the ways the co-present speakers organize their talk (cf Housley and Fitzgerald 2007: 198). To get into the production of a public sphere in action, I will next investigate the machinery of political identity formation in the case of current affairs discussion programmes.

Methodological Toolkit

I will apply two methodological toolkits which are further elaborations of ethnomethodological considerations, both developed by Harvey Sacks, membership categorization analysis (MCA) (Sacks 1972a, 1972b) and conversation analysis (CA) (Sacks et al. 1974). Both see interaction as highly organized in the structures by which participants co-ordinate social activities in talk. CA provides tools for analysing the sequential organization of interaction, while MCA is targeted to explicate members' categorization work. Although emerging divisions and tensions between sub-methods have been evident since Sacks's death, there has been a move towards reconnecting the essential elements of both category and sequence in recent years (Watson 1997, Silverman 1998, Housley and Fitzgerald 2002a, Schegloff 2007). From this perspective, categorizing members and ascribing predicates to them, and making sequential moves in interaction are two sides of the same coin (Silverman 1998). Identities are developed reflexively in conjunction with the sequential flow of interaction (Fitzgerald and Housley 2002).

Media talk has also been of specific focus within CA under the institutional talk programme (Drew and Heritage 1992, Arminen 2005) which examines how institutional tasks, identities and inferences are accomplished in and through institutional practices (Arminen 2005: 27). Prior research on interaction in current affairs programs highlights the strategies of managing journalistic neutralism, and thus the institutional constraints of the conversation (Clayman 1992, Greatbatch 1992, Clayman and Heritage 2002). Whilst this approach has proved fruitful in highlighting the fine grained interactional work of interviews little is said about the wider socio-political context or address of the interaction. That is to say, although the methods of production are always local, the actions accomplished and identities evoked may, and often do, exceed the immediate interactional context. This perspective is facilitated by a reconsidered model of MCA, which provides access to the actualization of broader social relevancies (Housley and Fitzgerald 2002a). The wider social structure and processes can also be located, observed and described within situated action (ibid.: 60). Access to these is provided by looking closer at the moral organization of interaction, the normative and norm-in-action character of categorizations (ibid.: 65).

I approach democratic life and its public sphere as an interactional accomplishment that is located within discursive spaces, moments and sedimentations (cf Housley and Fitzgerald 2007: 189). In closing television discussions this domain of inquiry comes down to the aspects of question design, task completion and category-related rights and responsibilities. The initiation of the closing is sequentially organized in institutionally typical question-answer formats (Drew and Heritage 1992: 48). Asking and answering actualize the omni-relevant institutional categories of host and guest (Sacks 1995), but what's more interesting in relation to political identity formation, is the particular task that the question sets for the discussants to complete. The execution of the task is impregnated with various normative expectations, which invokes additional categories mapped on to the studio guest category (Hester and Fitzgerald 1999: 184). Particular rights and responsibilities are manifested in the formulation of the question as well as in the sequential unfolding of the talk. Just any answer won't do, but the journalists carefully manage a sufficient set of second pair parts to the question, to get to the underlying institutional goal. As certain categories can be used to implicate certain category-bound activities (Sacks 1972b), then also, certain activities serve as an implication of certain categories, thus can be used to make activity-bound identifications. The activated categories in television discussions are mutually related. I consider the triangular interrelations and expectations in my data a duplicatively organized unit (see Sacks 1972b: 220-221), in this case built around democratic political activity.

Data in its Finnish Context

My data consists of three Finnish discussion programmes on the terrorist attacks in the USA on 11 September 2001, all broadcast within a few weeks of these events. All were produced by YLE, the Finnish public service broadcasting company. Finnish television has always been a combination of commercial and public service operators. It is obvious though, that until recent decades, the televisual domain has been dominated by YLE. Thus, Finland has a strong tradition of public service broadcasting, which according to its ideology is expected to secure equal access to its content, support democratic process and political equality, create and develop domestic culture, offer programming for minority groups and further enlightenment and education (Hujanen 2002: 20). I will scrutinize what this ideology looks like in its micro-characteristics and how it is realized in the situated machinery of interaction.

All the discussions in the sample are live and conducted by two journalists, male and female. The number of discussants varies from 5 to 23, and they are not divided along political party-lines or binary opinions, as in election discussions or in bi-polarized debates. On the contrary, the discussants (experts, politicians and ordinary people) are gathered together for a crisis situation and for airing out as many reasoned opinions on it as possible. Programmes share the same topics and the same socio-political conditions, referring to the phase in the news story in which the USA had been attacked and had declared war on terrorism, but there had not yet been any retaliation on its part. A counter-strike at Afghanistan was on everybody's lips, but it had not materialized yet. Due to its acuteness, the potential counter-strike is an omnipresent topic (Housley and Fitzgerald 2007: 197) in all three discussions. As demonstrated in the analysis, it is also the topic around which the closings are thematically organized. The potential counter-strike functions as a topic-opinion device: the ultimate underlying question which the discussants are supposed to give their opinion to (Fitzgerald and Housley 2002: 592).

Despite similarities between programmes, the compositions of the discussions differ markedly from each other, as do their perspectives and strategies in covering the topic. My initial interest in this data arose from the opportunity to compare various combinations of situated public spheres. The news event under investigation was large enough to be covered in all possible current affairs programming items and to arouse discussion which continued for weeks. It provides a productive case of public discussion which all journalistic institutions had to contribute to. The only challenge for the journalists was to find distinctive ways of organizing the coverage. A controversial news story is a bonus for discussion programmes, as well as for their comparative analysis, but it is also one that limits the generalizability of the research results. While the findings of the study are not generalizable *per se*, explicating the patterns used in these programmes aims to offer analytic insight and procedural frameworks for further studies. I will now set my analytic gaze to the end of the programmes, focusing on the ways the discussions are brought to their closure, in order to demonstrate perceptively the participant roles and goals of the discussion. I have translated the discussions into English. The programmes are presented in chronological order.

Stimulating and Wrapping up a Running Political Debate

The closing procedures in the three quite different discussions on 9/11 resemble each other considerably where the following pattern recurs. At the initiation of the closing the political weight of the discussion is first stimulated by applying strategies of temporal orientation, as well as activating the task-relevant identities by all-inclusive question formulation. Whilst at the end the local discussion is wrapped up and tied into broader ones by drawing one view to the fore, and consequently, elevating it above all the others.

Case 1 – Our Morals, Your Politics

> PROGRAMME: TERVO AND PÄIVÄRINTA / 'TO WAR AGAINST TERRORISM?' 17 September 2001
>
> *Journalists: Kari Tervo (J1) and Susanne Päivärinta (J2)
> *Discussants: Peter Rappold (PRA, teacher in English and EDP, American), Nely Keinänen (NKE, lecturer in English, American), Eugene Holman (lecturer in English, American), Jeremy Gould (anthropologist, American) and Hamed Normand (HNO, human rights activist, Afghan)

The first of the discussions was broadcast six days after the attacks. The programme is called Tervo and Päivärinta, the names of the two journalists conducting the discussion. The guests on the programme consist of four Americans and one Afghan, all currently living in Finland and speaking good to fair Finnish. The four

Americans are introduced one by one from the beginning and talk first with each other, and the Afghan joins them in the middle of discussion. The tone is very critical of the actions and intentions of America and its leaders.

The following two extracts display the initiation of closing and the final closure of the discussion. I will first take a closer look at the question design and then the way this theme is brought to an end in the final words of the programme. Closing is prepared for by putting a future-oriented all-inclusive question to all the discussants. The extract starts from the journalist commenting on earlier discussion on the sense of USA's counter-strikes.

Data Extract 1.1

```
1J2:    --- a country where there is (.) a lot of poverty
2       and hunger as you said, .h a country which is almost put
3       into the ↑ground, (.) there is- practically nothing left
4  ►    to bomb,=.h but a ↑question #e# to all of you (.) ↑what
5  ►    (0.2) from now on (0.2) should we think and do
6       .hh so that (.) terrorism won't increase >so that ↑racism won't
7              ((points at Hamed while referring to racism))
8       increase<, .hh[h it] feels that ↑racism might also increase
9J1:                  [mm. ]
10      here  quick[ly and anger-]
11HNO?           [ hhhhh       ]
12        (.)
13J2: on [anger's accou]nt-
14HNO:  [ I am        ] for example a foreigner? (0.7) <but>
15      I don't think that I am an Afghan or
16      a Finn or ↑something, (0.2) .h when people (.) die
17      (.) in Africa (0.3) I feel the same, (0.3) in America the same,
18      (.) in Asia the same, ---
```

The emphasis of the all-inclusive question (4-5) is on thoughts, attitudes and future actions. It is seemingly distanced from the prior comment on the counter strikes by 'but', which marks a topic shift and works to neutralize the ground for the question. The question involves a potential threat in the future course of current events, and it is presented in open and sincere form. Everybody is expected to give their opinion. Hatred and racism are self-evidently taken as bad, which implies a shared moral community. The pronoun 'we' (5) is used inclusively here, referring to us humans involved in this experiential turmoil. Interestingly, the formulation of the question presupposes general allocation of competence. Every discussant is taken to be competent to undertake the challenge to resolve the potential problem – or at least to give their opinion on it.

Hamed starts the responses in overlap with the journalist (14). He produces an anti-nationalistic and emotive account of his own universal position in relation to racism and nationalism (14-18). After this, the others give their opinions in turn. The responses vary quite a lot, from personal attitudes to religious principles and criticism of the means intended to solve the situation. Positive prescriptions are also offered, as below, where Nely suggests organizing intercultural meeting places. She then gets rushed by the host because of lack of time. The subsequent final turn is from Jeremy, an anthropologist, who turns the moral viewpoint towards 'the hosts' themselves. I wish to pay attention to the way in which this turn is formulated, and then taken up by the journalists to provide the closure.

Data Extract 1.2

```
       ----- ((54 lines omitted))
73 NKE: -- it is ↑very ↑important that #e# this is ↑very- #e#   (.)
74        easy to talk about being a ↓world citizen but- .hhh
75        the important thing is that we organize ourselves .h
76        ↑meeting places, (.) where we can really (.)
77        <↑meet> .h other people and talk with them .h more
78        extensively, .h[hh       ]
79 ▶ J1:               [ sorry  ] Nely we're  [ru]nning out of time,
80 NKE:                                        [m.]
81   J1: Jeremy,
82 JGO: mt' .h
83 NKE: ↑I[ see. ]
84 JGO:  [<well>] (.) I'd say (0.3) two things to what from now on,
85        (.) the one is that in the long run (we) reduce poverty
86        in the world (.) then (.) then these
87 ▶     problems .hhh <erm> (.) will vanish but .h >if I may< .hh
88 ▶     give these (.) hosts of ours (.) some advice then I'd say e-
89        after .h this .h once #eeh# this fear and (.) and (.)
90        and confusion .h settles then >let's hope that<
91        Europeans .hh would consider (0.3) a bit more carefully
92        whether (.) whether th- (.) to what extent they want to be
93        on the ride with the Americans, .h on this (.) this (.) #e#
94        military expedition, .h against an unknown faceless enemy
95 ▶     and .h rather (.) the Europ- the Europeans
96 ▶     and Finns would act #eer# in favour of international
97        understanding and (.) cultural- (.) inter- .hh cultural (.)
98        understanding.=
99   J1: =>well now, that's (.) a good thing to [end with, we'll see]
100  J2:                                         [.thhhhhhh          ]
101 ▶ J1: >which< ride we are on, isn't that right Susa,
102  J2: hh that one must do,=Tony Blair <has> strongly expressed his
103       ((seems to be talking to Jeremy; not in any case to the
104       viewers ))
```

```
105        view that they (.) still support (.) the United States, #m#
106 ►      we hold our [ bre]ath and continue following the situation.=
107        ?:         [ (m).]
108        J2 =>thank you to all and (.)   [tha]n- (.) thank you #m#
109        ?:                              [m, ]
110        to those who sent >text< message. ((turns to the camera))
111        (.)
112        .h good (.) restful night.
113        (10s) ((a video insert on a shocked woman in a scarf))
114        *A PALESTINIAN AFTER ATTACKS IN ISRAEL*
115              ((text on the screen))
116        "How do I feel? How do American women feel now. It's the same
117        feeling. How do they feel now. Terrorist there, here.
118        Terrorism, everywhere."
119        ((signature tune))
```

By invoking the temporal contingencies of the air-time allocated to the debate as a reason, the host stops Nely from speaking further so that 'everyone is to have their say before the time is up' (79). However, and presumably unintentionally, this interruption also compromises the argumentative weigh of her comment. This impression is somewhat reinforced by allowing the next respondent to reserve himself a rather long turn (84) and to complete it without interruption. Jeremy first makes a short practical suggestion to reduce conflict in the world and then moves on to the second point of his response. This is marked as exceptional by asking permission to make the advisory remark and by presenting it in propositional form (87-88). At this stage it remains unclear what the speaker is referring to by the term 'hosts' but later on in the turn he explains it as the Europeans and the Finns (95-96). The moral prescription is generalized as a shared wish by 'let's hope' (90), which again marks particular values as self-evident and implies a shared moral community. However, the advice is directed 'outside', being offered to a population which the speaker excludes himself from. Morality seems to be a shared domain but political agency lies elsewhere, with the Finns and Europeans. The national division can be seen as a display of the public sphere at hand (Housley and Fitzgerald 2002b: 58). By locating the discussion in Finnish publicity, the speaker marks the Finns as the primary recipient of the discussion (cf Hester 2002: 36).

The categorical device of nationality is applied interestingly in the argument as the speaker warns against his own nation (93). This may imply resistance to the nationalistic cleavages which are quite heavily deployed in the programme. It may also serve as an account of his personal responsibility in opposition to the foreign policy of his own country. The speaker addresses Finns directly (97) which, together with the declared intention of giving advice, orientates them as an overhearing participant category in the discussion. The Finns (at least those who decide upon joining a war) are taken to be somewhere within earshot behind the camera lens. However, the journalist receives this prescription personally, as addressed to himself and his colleague 'Susa' (100-102). The journalists identify themselves either as literally 'the hosts' or as the metonymic targets of the prescription (we Finns) and confirms the moral stance by giving an account of updated alertness in this matter. In either case, the account is given from an institutional perspective. Reference to those in power and following the situation with a critical eye (106) produces a responsible 'journalistic us', a watch-dog who remains at a distance but completely informed of the events. The turn displays skilful management of both socially and institutionally proper journalistic morality. To sharpen the political edge of the discussion, it also works to stress the incompleteness of the situation.

The closing of this discussion demonstrates an upgrading of the omni-relevant institutional roles: the host asking questions, the others answering them. But most importantly, there are other member categories related to these discursive identities, which are manifested by orienting to and realizing activities relevant to the task at hand. I identify these categories as those of citizen and public servant. The citizen category is activated and made recognizable by ascribing the participants universalized competence and obligation to give non-expert societal opinions. The category of a public servant is mobilized within the institution of public service broadcasting by an additional account of undertaking critical surveillance of those in power. The moral agency is pointedly attributed to the journalists themselves. Emphasizing the commitment to serve the public is done under the categorization of the recipient being the Finns. This implicitly marks the boundaries of the public and reserves the journalists an important position on the side of it.

The firm acknowledgement of and provision of support for the moral condemnation in the last response manages to produce a hierarchy between the closing opinions of the discussants. The negative critical perspective on American actions and intentions remains as emphatic inference in the whole programme, and as such, it is granted more influence on the public opinion formation than the other views in the discussion. Finally, the thank yous and best wishes at the end (108-112) underline the rule over territory by the hosts, stress the guests' voluntary and non-routine visit to the studio, and establish a para-social bonding and enduring relationship with the audience. Paradoxically, immediately after condemning the Americans, the video insert again brings up cross-national universal humanity and individual experiences. The 'we' addressed is morally universal but follows national lines politically.

Case Two – Communal Accountability

PROGRAMME: A-TALK / 'WAR AGAINST TERRORISM' 19 September 2001

*Journalists: Riikka Uosukainen (J1) and Seppo Toivonen (J2)

*Discussants: Martti Koskenniemi (MK, professor of public international law), Erkki Tuomioja (ET, foreign minister), Heikki Palva (HP, emeritus professor of Arabic), Paavo Selin (PS, chief of security, security police) and Mika Kerttunen (MJ, major, national defence university)

The second discussion was broadcast eight days after the terrorist attacks. Like the previous one, *A-Talk* is a weekly current affairs discussion programme. It too has five guests, but the guest list is quite different. There is an expert in international law, the foreign minister, an expert in Arabic culture, a major from national defence university and a chief of security police. All the guests are sitting in the studio from the beginning. The particular emphasis in this programme is on expert accountability and information delivery.

The following data samples have been extracted from the formulation of the last question and the closing words, showing the initiation of the close and the end of the programme. The last question to the panel is derived from audience questions in which worries about possible threats of the intended means to handle the situation are raised. The question formulation stumbles a bit. It starts from insinuating irrationality and a contradiction between the means and ends, but ends up asking a closed question about the possibility of the conflict escalating into a world war in the future.

Data Extract 2.1

```
1   J2:>but that< (.) when the si- when the situation won't reso- (.)
2      solve (.) ehh be resolved if bin laden is caught <and> and=and
3      >a CYCLE of revenge< (0.4) >FEAR of the cycle< is clearly quite
4  ▶   widespread among our (.)↑viewers at least, .hh and there are (.)
5      several questions on whether this can expand (0.2)
6      into a larger war,=can this turn into a world war. (.)
7      hhhh (.) e- what kind of (.) ehhh eer (.) w- (.)
8      what kin[d of-]
9  ▶ J1:      [let's] answer tha- #e# let's [ take] a round on that.
10  J2:                                     [yeah,]
11       (.)
12  J1: what- whats- >let's start from<, (0.5) the foreign minister.=
13  ET: =no.
14       (0.4)
15  ET: .hhhh <and> (.) of course when one says this (.) it has to be
16      in a sense a self-fulfilling (0.2) eer (.) se- prophecy ---
```

The contrastive 'but that' (1) marks the topic as unfinished business, as a question that is still unanswered and lacks a proper second pair part, thus pushing the discussants to respond and express their view on this matter. Indirectly the concern is again the USA's counter-strikes against Afghanistan, the omnipresent topic of the programmes. The contradiction in the preface of the question (1-2) throws a rational and moral challenge to the respondents, which awakes the expert accountability based on knowledge and authority. As in the previous programme, the issue is about speculating on future events and possible courses of action. The audience is pointedly used as a third person referent, which secures journalistic neutrality and puts even more pressure on answering. Viewers are depicted as afraid and in need of information and clarification, and the group of experts is obliged to provide them. Although the audience is allowed a mediated voice, it is excluded from opinion formation. The initial question formulation implies an opinion, but it is flattened down to an inquiry in the end (6). With the categorization 'our viewers' the journalist implements an institutionalized journalistic 'we', who represent the audience and looks after its interests, pressuring the experts to deliver answers to its viewers' questions.

The round question format (where each expert answers in turn) (9) is used as a strategy to stress the importance of the topic and to insist on universalized expert accountability, commonly on an issue that carries potential discrepancy or contradiction. Again, everybody is involved in the preparation for closing which means upgrading the omni-relevant 'respondent' identity with membership in an 'expert' collection. It is noteworthy that the turn order is changed from the physical round of respondents, privileging the foreign minister to start the round. His response is an instant denial of the possibility of war (13) and continues with an elaboration in which he states that things are not entirely out of control. After the minister, the question goes on to the legal expert, Arabic expert and the major, ending with the chief of security. Some of the respondents only reply to the threat of a world war, but others take a more critical stance on the intended counter-strikes implied in the question preface. The following extract starts from the end of the last response in the round by the security police, after which the turn is handed yet again over to the foreign minister who gets the last word.

Data Extract 2.2

```
    ------- (( 78 lines omitted ))
95  PS: -- at the moment we know that .hh terrorist organizations (.)
96      have used gas. (.) poison gas. (.) and poison gas is
97      indeed .hh very dangerous (.) in the hands of terrorists.
98      (.)
99 ▶J1: =>Tuomioja  [once more.
100 ET:       [.hhhh
101     (0.5)
102 ET:#eer# it's also worth considering the fact that (.) hhhh (.)
103 ▶     >most < countries in the world are not (.) in the same way
104 ▶     .hh organized (0.2) democratic (.) transparent
105 ▶     societies a- hh constitutional states .hhh as in Europe.
```

```
106        .hhh and this then means that (.) these- when
107        talking about these chains< then ↓if in some end there
108        is .hhh an extremist terrorist .hhh #ee# group,
109        .hh in the same society there may then be
110         in the (.) m- continuum all (.) all the way to the government
111        .hhh eer-connections which are never quite clear as to
112        where the official organization (.)sort of begins and
113        .h where be- eer- (.) m- be- (.) >begins< (.) .thh begins #eer#
114        (.) an underground terrorist organization >.hhh< but ↑this
115        (.) >should I say this ↑shock< (.) effect that this (.)
116        strike has had (.) m- it must (.) now be taken
117        advantage of in a sense so that ↑these chains
118 ▶     are also cut. (.) >.h< if all the leaders of the world .hhh
119        have=↑and <I believe quite genuinely >, (0.4) like condemned
120        this and blanched at this .h (then) from that it must ↑follow
121 ▶     then that=that in all the own (.) conflicts as well or
122        in potential .h possible .hhh conflicts
123        you disengage from violence and (.) >commit to<
124        peace processes and >cut< the connections .h and isolate
125        (.) those who still use violence.
126 ▶     ((moderators lean backward at the table))
127        ((signature tune))
```

The chief of security ends the round by elaborating the threat even further and aligning with the potential risks of the violent counter-action. However, the turn is allocated back to the foreign minister. 'Once more', marks the turn as additional, adding up to and continuing the round response already given (99). This additional post-sequence may have to do with the status and hierarchy of the speaker, since it allows him to have an additional opportunity to put his view, which indeed turns out to be the final word of the whole programme. Granting one of the discussants the locus of conclusion assigns him substantial definitional power over the news event (cf Drew 1992).

The response creates a contrastive categorization between us, the 'civilized European societies', and them, the 'numerous other corrupted countries' (103-105). This division between 'us' and 'them' locates the threat elsewhere and serves to diminishes it. It serves to reassure people and invites the audience to identify with our kind of good system (see also Sloboda this volume). Another categorization, 'the leaders of the world' (118) defines the actor in charge. The moral agency lies with the leaders and the moral prescription is addressed to them. By providing an account on the proper way of handling any potential 'own conflicts' (121-125) the speaker identifies himself as one of the leaders, invites the audience to identify with his moral evaluation and indirectly provides his view on the omnipresent topic. The audience is subjected to the power of formal authority, but it also represents the source of legitimation for power. While in the previous discussion prescriptions are given by ordinary people, from bottom-up, the perspective in the example above is from top-down. The minister's account activates a relational pair of a democratic leader and the people. It is consistent with the way in which expert category (us-in-charge and us-knowing) is mobilized by manifestations of public accountability throughout the discussion.

Repressing institutional intervention at the end of discussion (126) seems exceptional. It may be due to the ultimate running out of airtime but it may also indicate a proper fulfilment of conventionalized programme ending, an accented public moralization on the current topic. In any case, it serves to accomplish appropriateness by maintaining the impression of journalistic neutrality. By declining thank yous or overall summaries, the journalists put the emphasis of the programme on information delivery by experts under public accountability. The topic-opinion question is presented for the experts to analyse but the formation of an opinion is seemingly left up to the audience to decide – if only it is slightly guided by letting the minister draw the conclusion. The only goodbye to the viewers is a programme logo which appears on the screen while the minister is speaking. It says 'the discussion will continue' and has an internet address attached to it. This small symbolic gesture works to build identity for the programme and its viewers, and it further accentuates the impression that the local discussion has been a part of some greater unfinished business.

The extract shows how us–them division can be deployed to foster communal expert agency. The accountable expert formulates a societal system and a domain of governance which unifies certain group of people. He proposes identification for the audience as a better-equipped privileged community which should be led by restraining from violence in handling any conflicts of their own. The same device is used a bit differently in the next extract where the conclusive us-them division is made by the journalists. They first execute a vote among discussants and then ascribe agency to everybody within the privileged community in peace and isolation which must now rise up to the occasion by getting involved in the rest of the world and acting against a circle of revenge.

Case Three – Universalized Responsibility

PROGRAMME: AJANKOHTAINEN KAKKONEN / 'WAR BETWEEN WORLDS' 2 October 2001
*Journalists: Helena Itkonen (J1) and Jan Andersson (J2)
*Discussants: Khodor Chehab (KCH, imam, Islamic Society of Finland), Pertti Mäki-Hakola (PMÄ, member of parliament), Nely Keinänen (NKE, lecturer) Hamed Normand (HNO, human rights activist), Leena Kaartinen (LKA, doctor), Jyrki Käkönen (JKÄ, professor of international relations), Olli Kivinen (OLK, columnist), Teija Tiilikainen (TTI, head of research), Matti Myllykoski (MMY, docent in theology), Sylvia Akar (SAK, Islam researcher), Raija-Leena Punamäki (RPU, professor of psychology), Mustafa Kara (MKA, chair of Tampere Islamic Society), Jaakko Laakso (JLA, member of parliament), Pertti Multanen

(PMU, developing countries researcher), Otso Kivekäs (OKI, activist), Erika Weckström (EWE, activist), Ulla Karvonen (UKA, activist), Mikko Kuustonen (MKU, musician, UN goodwill ambassador), Heikki Hult (HHU, colonel), Liisa Eränen (LER, fears researcher), Juha Pihkala (JPI, bishop), Maija-Leena Pajari (MPA, missionary).

The third programme is a special broadcast called a theme evening, which is organized three or four times a year, produced by the makers of a weekly current affairs magazine programme, Ajankohtainen Kakkonen (Current Channel Two). The theme of the evening, 'War between Worlds', refers to the potential conflict between Muslims and Christians in the war against terrorism. This discussion differs from the two previous ones in its size and longer duration. It was broadcast three weeks after the attacks, but in terms of the news story, the conditions have remained the same. The USA's retaliation is still undetermined. The group of studio guests is bigger and broader than in the other programmes with twenty-three guests altogether. Four of them join in one by one as interviewees at the beginning of each sub-theme. There is huge variation in the roles and status and opinions of the participants, and indeed the general approach to issues is confrontational.

The following extract takes place right before the closing interview and the concluding words from the journalists. It is a 'hand vote' (show of hands) on justifying the USA's possible retaliation against Afghanistan. Since not showing one's hand is considered a stance, there's no possibility to abstain from the vote. Everybody is obliged to take a stance on the matter. However before getting to the vote the initial formulation of the question is mildly criticized, which then escalates into outright objection, leading to the journalist trying to reformulate the question. The transgression of the institutional order implies tensions embedded in the task. Institutional order is regained by negotiating additional specifications for the question but persisting with the topic and pushing the discussants to comply with it.

Data Extract 3.1

```
1   J1: .thh ↑and (.) now dear view- (.) dear (.) discussants
2 ▶     it's time for (.) A2's ((programme's name)) traditional hand
3       vote,.hhh and this time (.) the question is that
4       (.) .mhhh if (0.2) the united states (.) mounts (.) a strike?
5       (.) in afganistan, .hhhh then (.)
6       ↑is this (.) #e# >military< (.) strike (.)
7       <justified>. (.) .hh those who think that it is
8       ↑justified (.) please raise your hand.
9       (1.2)
10 ((some raise their hands at once, including HHU and OLK, but then
       start to criticise the question))
```

```
11 ▶ HHU: the question is a bit wr[ong.
12   JLA:                          [wrongly      [put.
13   OLK:                          [very wrong  [question
14   MMY? [it is (.)
15   OLK: [im- impossible question to answer,]
16   MMY? [badly (.) not (.)                    ]not po[ssible to-  ]
17 ▶ J1:                                              [↑well (.)↑if ] I
18       [ask  that-  (.) that (.) i- ] is it (.) is it
19   OLK: [>impossible question to answer<.]
20        right- (.) does: the u- united state have the right (.)
21        >the united states<have the right (.) is it
22        justified to mount a military counterstrike.=
23   JLA?=.thh[h the question is ( )-   ]
24   OLK:     [the united states has a ↑cle]ar right to <strike> (0.2)
25        against those terrorists pres- after presenting the ↑evidence
26        that they are the ones ↑behind this,=most >clearly< has the
27        right .h to strike (.) >specifically against those< [who-
28   J1:                                                      [↑with
29   J1: this specification, [those who (.) think so (.) they   ]
30 ▶ J2:                     [based on this han- (.) hands up.  ]
31 ▶ J1: raise their hands up.
```

Several sensitivity markers appear in the formulation of the question. Discussants are addressed with the warm token 'hyvät' (closest to 'dear' in English) (1), which creates a solid and cohesive atmosphere for the vote, and presumably serves to smooth the upcoming contrast. The temporal reference 'it's time' in the question preface (2) also obscures the speaker's intentionality and her own involvement in 'causing trouble'. The question seems to come to them in a self-determined and temporally unavoidable fashion. Again, the question employs a journalistic 'we'. The programme has a history of public hand votes as part of its tradition through which the question invites the audience to identify with the tradition. The question posits a propositional future scenario for the discussants to evaluate (4-7). Again, all discussants are involved in this moral challenge.

In this programme the topic opinion task in the final all-inclusive question is most extreme. A clear-cut split is a risky business in morally sensitive questions, since it implies a division into right- and wrong-minded people (7-8), especially when there is a limited chance to offer reason for one's stance. The fierce escalation of criticism (11-15) from a cautious remark to extreme case formulations supports this impression. There are problems in reformulating the question (17-22) and, after two self-repairs, the journalist practically ends up repeating the original question, albeit now in generalized and abstract form. Sticking stubbornly to the topic and its moral challenge displays a task which must be accomplished in order to get the structure of the programme work. In the end it emerges that this vote is needed to glean a publicly-produced opinion from the discussion. The discussants remain resistant and start negotiating the premises of the question in return for their compliance in voting (24-27). While putting strong pressure on for taking an action on the vote (30-31), the journalists have to accept the additional qualifications to get the job done (28-31).

The transgression in voting insinuates the power potential invested in journalistic inferences where the journalists are not only conducting public opinion formation but also allocating potential moral identities. The extracts shows that members can demonstrate their orientation to the task relevant duties through complying to take a stance but also by appearing reasoned and responsible in challenging that task on some moral or technical grounds. A public discussant can be held accountable for both. The transgression also demonstrates that the discussants take the task given to them very seriously. The hand vote is not oriented to like a light-minded game in a TV programme, but as a well-considered stance-taking in an open political decision. Seriousness displays voters understanding of being a part-taking citizen within a broader political process. After getting the vote co-ordinated, the journalists count the hands and state the majority result (that surprisingly few people support the retaliatory strikes). One voter from each side is then asked to state the reasons for their vote. The hand vote episode is followed by an interview sequence, in which a missionary is asked to describe and give tips on the peaceful co-existence of two religions and cultures. The final closure below takes the form of an explicit conclusion, addressed directly to the camera.

Data Extract 3.2

```
      ------ (( 105 lines omitted ))
136   J1: .hhhhh (0.2) <↑when> (.) (they say) that the world has got
137 ►     smaller maybe >this< is what it means, .mthh we >can no
138       longer <<close> our eyes (.) to the rest of the world, .hh
139       the world is (.) right here (0.2) >today<.
140       (0.2)
141 ► J2: .thh we are >all< (.) responsible for the kind of
142       (.) world we (.) >up<hold, (.) all the
143 ►     >evil< acts need <not> recur in ten
144 ►     generations.
145       (0.3)
146   J1: .thh <and> now dear discussants thanks (.) to you?
147       (.) .th thanks (.) to the viewers, .thh <and> (.)
148       have a peaceful evening, (.) in spite of everything.=
149   J2: =sleep tight.
150                      ((signature tune))
```

The concluding sequence is separated and marked as an action of its own. It draws persuasively on a common saying (136) and an inference (137) which is supposedly drawn from the preceding discussion. The demonstrative 'this' compresses the lesson learned although with the third party referent not specified provides the journalist with the authorization to make a statement. The statement is structured around an us–them division (138-139). The category 'we' here refers to nationality, us Finns, and the opposition is the rest of the world. The journalist acts as the didactic voice of gradually achieved enlightenment. The conflict at the outset of discussion has turned into consensus by the end. Since moral prescription is addressed to everybody (141), including the audience at home, viewers are involved in the group of morally accountable political actors. Strong audience inclusion at the end markedly intensifies us-ness within the triangular participant structure. The implicit moral prescription encourages breaking the cycle of evil acts (143-144). Interestingly, this creates a moral hierarchy between the voters in terms of responsible and irresponsible suggestions. One of the opinions is marked as better. Furthermore, the conclusion is put out as locally and democratically produced public opinion to the omnipresent question.

Before departing, thanking the visitors and the viewers (146-148) is used to manifest control over studio territory, but it also explicates nicely the contribution of all those who are needed to accomplish the intended activity (us programme makers, the discussants and the audience). Furthermore, the good night wishes (148-149) establish a caring para-social relationship with the audience (Horton and Wohl 1956). The phrase 'in spite of everything' sends the message that 'we are in this together' and suggests a shared identity for all the participants as belonging to the same time and place and experiential landscape, as members of the same moral and political community.

Again, the categorizations and memberships deployed and acted out in this closing are multilayered. There are duties that relate to being a guest in a discussion, being an accountable moral actor and being a part of a particular type of political system. Thus, whilst the underlying morality is broader than that of politics as participants have access to moral evaluations universally, the framework for acting and making moves is national. All three of the programmes conclude with this abstract nationalism. The political community is equated with the national community. Correspondingly, the addressed overhearing recipients of the discussions are categorized as citizens of a nation. Beside suggesting an identity for the viewers and sustaining a commonsense order of politics, this grouping indicates the characteristics of the public arena. Instead of specified target group niches, television discussions are played out on a stage of overarching national publicity. This 'holistic audience scaling', targeting the whole nation, is one way of accomplishing the identity and the task of a programme, aiming at the ideals of accessible public service broadcasting.

Summary

The analysis has shown that to grasp the closing procedure in television discussions and the identities that it evokes one needs to consider members' categorizations and sequential actions as a combination. There is an upgrading of omni-relevant roles in all three programmes as discussions start to approach their end. This is realized through the format of all-inclusive questions. The journalists present a question and push on with answering it and every single discussant gives an answer or takes a stance on it. Besides discursive duties, however, there are other roles and orientations involved in these questions, which suggest broader social responsibilities. Firstly, the action at hand is not just any discussion. It is a serious, important and urgent one on a current issue. The political nature of discussion is achieved by topicalizing a shared concern which will require some political action and decision in the near future. This is already motivated at the beginning of the discussions. In the closings, a political community is remobilized by sketching a potential threat in the proceeding situation. Interestingly, this communal identity building is emphasized not by reporting the current situation but by speculating about the future. The approaching threat raises the need for some kind of response or reaction. In the all-inclusive question sequences the journalists obligate discussants to occupy a topic-opinion position in relation to the omnipresent burning question on counter attacks and the discussant take up the task in their responses. This procedure demonstrates an attempt to execute a process of public opinion formation *in situ*. Instead of just offering citizens scattered raw material for opinion building, television discussions aim at displaying and accomplishing the idea of a public sphere in the structures of its local practices.

The strategy of handling the threatening situation locally displays understanding of the form and mechanisms of political activity, whereby the democratic system is oriented to by staging a scene of public discussion. Public discussion is not just a location category, being in public, but an oriented-to institution of its own. It is activated by stressing the openness and incompleteness of the current situation (sketching future scenarios), together with encouraging or obliging the discussants to take a stance (all-inclusive questions). The principles applied in the closing question sequence resonate with broader democratic ideals. Eliciting different opinions on the matter, equity in voicing them, putting perspectives in dialogue or in parallel, voting on the issue and declaring a majority result, are indicators of these ideals. In the framework of public discussion, stance-taking becomes relevant only at the stage where discussion still has the potential to influence the related political actions and decisions. Just as in news broadcasting an unfinished story determines the newsworthiness of the event (Thornborrow and Fitzgerald 2004: 351), in broadcast public discussion the incompleteness of the situation maximizes the sense of societal participation. The local activity of stance-taking is taken to be distributed into global ones by its instant connection to related processes elsewhere (cf Latour 2005: 204). Incompleteness creates a sense of being part of something bigger and it invites audiences to identify with the political community that is now trying to solve the dilemmas aroused by the crisis.

One central strategy in building 'us'-ness is the use of moral rhetoric and references to shared values. However, membership in a moral community is not equated with the political one. While morals cross nationalities, politics is situated in a national domain. A nation state is depicted as the agent and the location of political activity (cf Billig 1995: 177). In the end, the national domain is where morals have to be applied and where the democratic procedure resides. Thus, the locus of identification offered for the audience is nationalistic as well as moral and political. In the triangle of participant positions, the identity of the audience is related to the positions adopted by journalists and discussants. An understanding of the ongoing democratic process is displayed by activating the categories of citizen, expert-authority and public servant in the closings. I perceive these actor positions and their related obligations as interconnected elements of the same unit, namely a democratic political system, which are mobilized by activity-bound identifications. A citizen is to give a non-expert opinion or to take stance on the topic, an expert-authority is to provide public accounts to the people, and a public servant is to elicit those opinions, put pressure on answering, uphold public accountability, observe those in power, inform and educate the people across the nation and facilitate the formation of public opinion. The groupings of these incumbents vary across the programmes, but they all share an orientation towards an institutionally intermediated spread of political information and opinions for the wider public in the form of discussion. The triangle in which journalists are included as an institutionalized us, also serves to strengthen media's status as integral part of a functioning democracy.

Finally, activities are not quite as ideal and pure as they might appear. There are implicit unofficial power practices going on in the closings. Being media products to consume, with a limited amount of time and fierce competition over the audience, raises expectations of coherence and completeness for the programmes. The tricky questions at the opening of the programme, designed to tempt viewers, wire up expectations of achieving a solution or at least clarification in the course of the discussion. Conclusions at the end are laden with additional force in relation to these expectations. The concluding position affords precious control over putting facts together (Drew 1992: 510). It is the last description of events which sticks in the viewers' mind. As it happens, the journalists manage to raise one view above the others at the end of all three programmes. This is done by privileged turn allocation or by complimenting and commenting on a particular remark or by making a moral judgement on the contrary opinions. In television discussions allocating turns means allocating political agency. Paradoxically, creating a hierarchy of relevance between responses serves to facilitate broader public discussion, in terms of sending out a more condensed opinion, while it simultaneously erodes the ideals of open, equal and impartial discussion at the local level. For television discussions, supporting democracy remains the cake to pursue – but it is left up to programme makers to strike a balance between having it and eating it too.

References

Arminen, I. 2005. *Institutional Interaction: Studies of Talk at Work*. Aldershot: Ashgate.

Billig, M. 1995. *Banal Nationalism*. London: Sage.

Clayman, S. 1992. Footing in the achievement of neutrality, in *Talk at Work,* edited by P. Drew and J. Heritage. Cambridge: Cambridge University Press, 163-198.

Clayman, S. and Heritage, J. 2002. *The News Interview: Journalists and Public Figures on the Air*. Cambridge: Cambridge University Press.

Drew, P. 1992. Contested evidence in courtroom cross-examination, in *Talk at Work*, edited by P. Drew and J. Heritage. Cambridge: Cambridge University Press, 470-520.

Drew, P. and Heritage, J. 1992. Analyzing talk at work: an introduction, in *Talk at Work*, edited by P. Drew and J. Heritage. Cambridge: Cambridge University Press, 3-65.

Dahlgren, P. 1995. *Television and the Public Sphere: Citizenship, Democracy and the Media*. London: Sage.

Fitzgerald, R. and Housley, W. 2002. Identity, categorisation and sequential organisation. *Discourse and Society*, 13 (5), 579-602.

Garfinkel, H. 1967. *Studies in Ethnomethodology*. Englewood Cliffs, NJ: Prentice-Hall.

Goffman, E. 1981. *Forms of Talk*. Philadelphia, PA: University of Pennsylvania Press.

Goodwin, C. 1987. Forgetfulness as interactive resource. *Social Psychology Quarterly*, 50 (2), 115-131.

Goodwin, C. and Goodwin, M.H. 1990. Context, activity and participation, in *The Contextualization of Language*, edited by P. Auer and A. di Luzo. Amsterdam: John Benjamins, 77-99.

Greatbatch, D. 1992. On the management of disagreement between news interviewees, in *Talk at Work*, edited by P. Drew and J. Heritage. Cambridge: Cambridge University Press, 268-301.

Habermas, J. 1989. *The Structural Transformation of the Public Sphere*. Oxford: Polity Press.

Heritage, J. 1984. *Garfinkel and Ethnomethodology*. Cambridge: Polity Press.

Heritage, J. 1985. Analyzing news interviews, in *Handbook of Discourse Analysis*, vol. 3, edited by T. van Dijk. London: Academic Press, 95-119.

Hester, S. 2002. Bringing it all back home, in *Language, Interaction and National Identity*, edited by S. Hester and W. Housley. Aldershot: Ashgate, 16-37.

Hester, S. and Eglin, P. (eds) 1997. *Culture in Action*. Washington, DC: International Institute for Ethnomethodology and Conversation Analysis.

Hester, S. and Fitzgerald, R. 1999. Category, predicate and contrast, in *Media Studies*, edited by P.L. Jalbert. Lanham, MD: University Press of America, 171-193.

Horton, D. and Wohl, R. 1956. Mass communication as para-social interaction: observations of intimacy at a distance. *Psychiatry*, 19 (3), 215-229.

Housley, W. and Fitzgerald, R. 2002a. A reconsidered model of membership categorisation analysis. *Qualitative Research*, 2 (1), 59-84.

Housley, W. and Fitzgerald, R. 2002b. National identity, category and debate, in *Language, Interaction and National Identity*, edited by S. Hester and W. Housley. Aldershot: Ashgate, 38-59.

Housley, W. and Fitzgerald, R. 2007. Categorisation, interaction, policy and debate. *Critical Discourse Studies*, 4 (2), 187-206.

Hujanen, T. 2002. *The Power of the Schedule: Programme Management in the Transformation of Finnish Public Service Television*. Tampere: Tampere University Press.

Hutchby, I. 2006. *Media Talk. Conversation Analysis and the Study of Broadcasting*. New York, NY: Open University Press.

Jalbert, P.L. (ed.) 1999. *Media Studies*. Lanham, MD: University Press of America.

Knorr Cetina, K. and Bruegger, U. 2002. Global microstructures: the virtual societies of financial markets. *The American Journal of Sociology*, 107 (4), 905-950.

Latour, B. 2005. *Reassembling the Social*. Oxford: Oxford University Press.

Livingstone, S. and Lunt, P. 1994. *Talk on Television*. London: Routledge.

Sacks, H. 1972a. An initial investigation of the usability of conversational materials for doing sociology, in *Studies in Social Interaction*, edited by D.N. Sudnow. New York: Free Press, 31-74.

Sacks, H. 1972b. On the analyzability of stories by children, in *Directions in Sociolinguistics*, edited by J. Gumperz and D. Hymes. New York, NY: Holt, Rinehart and Winston, 325-345.

Sacks, H., Schegloff, E.A. and Jefferson, G. 1974. A simplest systematics for the organization of turn-taking for conversation. *Language*, 50, 696-735.

Scannell, P. 1991. Introduction, in *Broadcast Talk*, edited by P. Scannell. London: Sage, 1-13.

Sacks, H. 1995. *Lectures on Conversation*, volumes I and II. (ed. G. Jefferson). Oxford: Blackwell.

Schegloff, E.A. 2007. A tutorial on membership categorization. *Journal of Pragmatics*, 39, 462-482.

Silverman, D. 1998. *Harvey Sacks: Social Science and Conversation Analysis*. Cambridge: Polity Press.

Thornborrow, J. and Fitzgerald, R. 2004. Storying the event. *Communication Review*, 7 (4), 345-352.

Tolson, A. 2006. *Media Talk. Spoken Discourse on TV and Radio*. Edinburgh: Edinburgh University Press.

Watson, R. 1997. Some general reflections on 'categorization' and 'sequence' in the analysis of conversation, in *Culture in Action*, edited by S. Hester and P. Eglin. Lanham, MD: University Press of America, 49-75.

Chapter 6
'Doing Public Policy'
in the Political News Interview

Johanna Rendle-Short

Introduction

Announcing policy information to the public is an important part of the political process. Within the Australian context, such policy announcements are frequently made through the news media, including printed media, television and radio broadcasts, or political news interviews. Although talkback radio presents a legitimate forum for the discussion of national public affairs and provides a way to break policy initiatives to the wider voting public (Ward 2002), this chapter will show how a very different forum, the political news interview, can also be a site for constructing, shaping and reflecting on political policy for, and on behalf of, the overhearing listening audience.

The Interactive Nature of the Political News Interview

One of the distinctive features of media talk, whether it be television and radio broadcasts, political news interviews, or talkback radio, is the interactive nature of the medium. Such interactivity is, however, not limited to the two (or more) speakers who are directly taking part in the interaction; it includes the silent, yet listening, audience. Different approaches to media analysis emphasise the interactive nature of media talk to a greater or lesser extent, depending upon the medium being analysed (e.g. television, radio, news interviews, talkback radio), the analytic framework being utilised (e.g. conversation analysis, membership categorisation analysis, discourse analysis, critical discourse analysis), and the researchers' own methodological assumptions and background (e.g. media studies, linguistics, sociology). Although it is not the aim of this chapter to tease apart these very diverse frameworks and methodological assumptions,[1] it is useful

---

1 One of the difficulties in even attempting to tease apart the different frameworks and methodologies is that in this area of communication research there tends to be a high degree of overlap, with many researchers analysing the data within a variety of frameworks and methodologies.

to situate the notion of interactivity within the particular analytic contexts from which they emerge.

Tolson (2006), for example, from a media studies perspective, emphasises the fact that the audience is an active listener, directly involved in the interactive media event. Drawing on a variety of methodologies, including conversation analysis, he demonstrates how political news interviews are designed for an overhearing audience through the way in which journalists frame and follow up their questions and through the way in which politicians provide answers to these questions. Tolson argues that because politicians' answers tend to be quite long, certainly more than minimal responses, it is clear that they are not designed for the immediate co-participant, the interviewer, but for the invisible unseen audience 'out there' (p. 11). He shows how this unseen audience exerts pressure on the interviewees to 'come across' well and to perform. As a result, interacting with the invisible silent audience requires a listener-friendly approach, full of what Tolson calls 'liveliness' and spontaneity.

Even if the interview is not actually happening in real time, interviewers can adopt a rhetoric of liveliness in a variety of ways (Ellis 2000). For example, they can demonstrate liveliness through direct forms of address or through the use of expressions such as 'now', 'today', 'here' and 'we'. By emphasising the context-dependent nature of their talk they are able to give the illusion that they are talking at the same moment of time as the audience hears them. Thus, in broadcast communication, the absent audience can be spoken to as if it were co-present and in lively ways as if the interaction were spontaneous and interactive (Tolson 2006).

Through the use of relaxed and spontaneous modes of address participants can create a pseudo-intimacy that on the one hand encourages and includes the absent, non-present audience, whereas on the other hand, through its non-responsive silence, it remains distant. As Scannell (1991) argues, today's audience do not want to be spoken to as part of a crowd, but as individuals; they expect 'to be spoken to in a familiar, friendly and informal manner, as if they were equals on the same footing as the speaker' (p. 3). Thus, although the broadcast output is articulated in the public domain as public discourse, it is received 'within the sphere of privacy, as an optional leisure resource' (p. 3). Such a shift reflects both the 'conversationalisation of public discourse' (Fairclough 1994) and the 'immediacy of distance' (Moores 2000), whereby participants are brought together in live time with the immediacy of co-presence being captured in circumstances of absence.

This notion of the audience being thought of as a community, of sorts, has also been discussed by Kane (1998) who states that talkback radio 'provides the opportunity for personal thinking, outrage and validation by persons whose views would not be of great interest or relevance to more established and traditional forms of media' (p. 159). As such, the audience become part of an 'imagined community' (p. 159) who have a sense that they are heard because they know themselves to be valued in a certain way. Fitzgerald and Housley (2007) similarly show how talkback radio can engender an imagined community that is treated, at times, by the host and others as a political public.

The dialogic nature of media interaction, through 'dialogical networks', has been taken up by Leudar and Nekvapil (2004) who show how non co-participants demonstrate their orientation to the 'network' though their use of language within the public sphere. Just as Austin (1962) argued for the performativity of all speech acts, so too, Leudar and Nekvapil (2004) argue that the media (for example, newspapers or radio) do not simply describe happenings, rather they play a performative role, as demonstrated through the sequential structure of texts and interactions. It is through such sequential structures, similar to conversational adjacency pairs, that networks are created and cohesion maintained.

Taking a linguistic discourse analytic approach, Montgomery (2007) addresses the issue of interactivity when making a distinction between accountability interviews (typically the political news interview) and other types of interviews, such as the experiential interview, the expert interview and the affiliated interview. He argues that one of the distinguishing features of accountability interviews is that the audience is invited to identify with the interviewer (generally the journalist) as their spokesperson (p. 159), rather than with the interviewee (generally the politician). Characteristic of this accountability interview is that the interviewer asks questions on behalf of the audience, whereas the interviewee is presented as estranged and evasive and not readily willing to present a clear and truthful account of the matters under discussion.

Much of the research on media talk has relied on earlier conversation analytic research on the political news interview. Using conversation analysis, Heritage (1985), emphasises the interactive nature of the news interview by showing how political news interviews are more than just a series of questions and answers between the interviewer (IR) and interviewee (IE). Interviewers, often journalists, demonstrate that although they are listening and responding to the politician's talk, they are not, in fact, the intended audience. They do this by refraining from producing response tokens or verbal acknowledgements, such as 'yeah', 'mm mhm', 'mhm' which might indicate that they are the intended recipient of the talk; they refrain from producing news receipts, such as 'oh' or 'really', which might indicate an acceptance or project acceptance of the factual status of the IE's response; they avoid assessments which overtly affiliate or disaffiliate with the stated proposition; and they avoid commenting on, editorialising, or presenting their own opinions concerning public issues (Heritage 1985, Clayman and Heritage 2002). In other words, in order to demonstrate their objectivity and balanced perspective towards issues of public interest and concern, they limit themselves to only asking questions (Heritage 1985, Clayman and Heritage 2002). If they do make an assertion, they attribute it to a third party; and if they do need to provide background information necessary for the question, they design their turn to ensure that the background information, normally in the form of a declarative statement, is heard as 'belonging to' the question.

More recently, Hutchby (2006), also within a conversation analytic framework, has analysed media and broadcast talk more generally. He also focuses on the interactive nature of broadcast talk, although arguing that to refer to the audience as the 'overhearing' audience gives a false impression that they are in some ways illicitly overhearing the talk, rather than being the intended recipients of the talk. He therefore argues that the audience of broadcast talk should be referred to as 'distributed recipients' in order to capture the sense in which 'the audience is addressed, albeit often indirectly, and situated as a ratified (though non co-present) hearer rather than an eavesdropper' (p. 14).

However, a different way to examine how the audience, often the 'public', is incorporated into media talk is through linguistic interactional analysis. In particular, through analysis of person reference terms, it is possible to examine the way in which journalists and politicians use and modify person reference terms within their talk. Although linguistic analysis of person reference terms frequently focuses on textual coherence, emphasising the way in which participants use anaphora or pro-terms to track a particular referent (e.g. Akmajian et al. 2001), the focus of this chapter is to interactionally examine how person reference terms are used within the political news interview. Through examination of terms such as 'the Australian public', 'the tax payers', 'the listeners', 'those earning under five thousand dollars', this chapter explores how politicians and journalists variously use person reference terms to describe and display their understanding of policy and how it relates to, or affects, particular audience members. Through the design of their talk, participants can choose to present their ideas and policies in certain ways and for certain people. By examining the interactional environments, and under what circumstances the public are specifically named as third parties to the interaction, this chapter demonstrates how both journalist and politician involve 'the public' within the process of 'doing policy formation'.

Data and Methodology

The data under analysis comprises 16 political news interviews collected in 2004 during the lead up to the Australian federal election. As Faine (2005) comments, this was an especially interesting time as politicians made a particular point of being available for radio and television news interviews during this pre-election period. As a result, politicians participated in a large number of radio and television news interviews in the nine months preceding the date of the federal election, held on 9 October 2004.

In this current data set, taken from a larger corpus of 287 radio and television interviews, data is sourced from both the Australian Broadcasting Commission and commercial programs. The 16 political news interviews selected for analysis focus on interviews between the leaders of the two major political parties (John Howard as the leader of the Liberal Party of Australia and Mark Latham as the leader of the Australian Labor Party) and six senior journalists (Tony Jones,

John Laws, Catherine McGrath, Laurie Oaks, Kerry O'Brien), with each journalist interviewing each politician within the same very short time period. The interviews ranged from short 3-4 minute grabs to more detailed interviews, lasting more than an hour. The interviews were transcribed using conversation analysis (CA) transcription conventions.

Taking a linguistic perspective, the methodological framework for the current analysis will use principles from conversation analysis (CA), with emphasis on the analysis of language as social action, focusing on what it is that the talk is actually *doing* as participants interact in everyday institutional settings. In particular, through the methodological framework of conversation analysis, the following analysis will examine how person reference forms within the political news interview are utilised to involve the overhearing audience within the policy formation process.

Analysis

Making the overhearing audience relevant

Although the political news interview is a two-party interaction between journalist (IR) and politician (IE), it is clear that the interview is being performed for, and on behalf of, the overhearing audience. Australian politicians are increasingly aware of the overhearing audience and frequently encourage audience participation in order to open up opportunities for talking to the public and to create a forum for the exchange of ideas. The following extract shows the way in which one politician demonstrates his understanding of such a forum for public debate.

Extract 1 (IR is John Laws and IE is John Howard [30 August 2004])

```
1. IR: okay, Prime minister.
2.     you're in for a busy time aren't you?
3. IE: I am and I'm looking forward to it.
4.     I have great stamina,
5.     and I have a great commitment.
6.     I want to go on in the job, John.
7. →   I love working for the Australian people.
8.     it's a tremendous privilege to have this job.
9.     I care about it very much.
10. →  I never tire of interacting
11. →  with the Australian people.
12.    I like talking to them and listening to them.
```

Extract 1 shows how the then Prime Minister of Australia, John Howard, directly involves the Australian people within the political process, through the way in which he demonstrates his understanding of the three-way interaction between politician, journalist and the audience, 'the Australian people', and the role played by the public within the democratic process.

Such references to the overhearing audience are not limited to introductory statements at the beginning of a political news interview, as in Extract 1. In the data under consideration, there are frequent references to the listening radio and television audience.

1. And all of **your listeners** in small business will remember the … interest rates.
2. But for **voters around Australia** who are listening to you …
3. But Tony, what I'm asking the **Australian people** to do, and what I'm asking **your viewers** to do, is to look at the here and now.
4. Well can I just say that **people who are walking past their television sets** now have heard you say that.
5. Why should **people watch this** and say well you mean it this time.
6. I'm sure **your viewers** understand Labor's tax policy.
7. And I don't think there'd be **a listener to this program** who wouldn't acknowledge that we have done an excellent job.
8. And I can assure **your viewers** of this, that what I will say will not be driven by a preference deal.

The above examples show how journalists and politicians refer directly to the audience. By so doing, they remind participants that the interview is not simply occurring for the politician and journalist, but that even though the audience may not have a voice, they have an opinion concerning the variety of policy issues under discussion (they listen, remember, hear, understand, acknowledge).

The above examples also show how, when doing such referring, journalists and politicians categorise the overhearing audience in different ways, as listeners, viewers, voters, Australian people. Such categories work to both draw out similarities and create differences. For example, in (3) above, where the speaker initially says 'what I'm asking the Australian people to do' and then adds 'what I'm asking your viewers to do', the question immediately arises as to what is the difference between 'the Australian people' and 'your viewers'? Why are two categories invoked in this instance? One possibility is that such descriptions are maximally inclusive in that they include both those who are the Australian public (whether they happen to be viewing at the time or not) and those who may not identify as part of the Australian public, but are viewers. By so doing, the politician ensures that all members of the imagined community 'out there' feels part of the discussion rather than just being observers to the discussion.

Additionally, however, the above examples demonstrate that it is not just being any viewer or listener that is relevant, but it is being a listener or viewer of a particular program ('*your* listeners', '*your* viewers', 'a listener to *this program*', 'voters who are listening to *you*', 'people watch this and say well *you* mean it this time'). Such direct linking of listeners or viewers to a particular program and to program participants (interviewers and interviewees) works to increase the intimacy between speaker and overhearing audience. It is not just any listener that is being referred to, but listeners who choose to listen to this particular program and as such 'belong' to this group or community of people. Such a group or community is in direct contrast to people who might just happen to hear the interview because, for example, they are 'walking past their television sets now' as in (4) above.

However, given the frequent reference to viewers or listeners in utterances (such as in 1-8), the question also arises as to why speakers may choose *not* to mention viewers or listeners as in Extract 1. By choosing to refer to the broad category of 'Australian people' (lines 7 and 10-11) rather than specifically mentioning viewers or listeners who at that particular time may be watching or listening to the news interview, Howard is able to claim not only that he is enjoying interacting with the Australian people within this particular political news interaction, but also that he 'loves' and 'never tires' of interacting with the Australian people more broadly.

Thus it is clear that politicians have choices as to whether to refer to the overhearing audience or not. However, if they do refer to the audience, they also have choices as to how such person references emerge in the talk. Do they only provide one description of members of the audience? Which description should that be? Is it a description that ensures that everyone is included, or one that strengthens the intimacy between the speaker and audience? Deciding upon the appropriate reference term, and thus the appropriate descriptor or category, will depend on what it is that the politician is trying to do within a particular interaction. However, as the following analysis will show, choosing a particular person reference term is also directly related to the sequential environment in which the category choice occurs and to the way in which politicians make public policy directly relevant to the listening audience.

Issues of accountability

References to the public, or sub-sets of the public, frequently occur within contentious adversarial environments. Journalists use person reference terms as a technique for legitimising unsourced assertions or contentious questions. Politicians use person reference terms as a technique for justifying a particular response or as a way of preventing further questioning on a particular topic. By so doing, both journalists and politicians are demonstrating their orientation to the notion of accountability. This is particularly relevant for journalists who have to balance opposing requirements for neutralism or objectivity, on the one hand, with the need to be adversarial and to ensure that politicians adequately answer difficult questions, on the other hand (Clayman and Heritage 2002).

Extract 2 occurs within a contentious adversarial context in which the journalist (IR) calls on the listening audience, 'the voters around Australia', to legitimise her suggestion that the politician may have given voters the wrong impression concerning divisions within the Labor Party.

Extract 2 (IR is Catherine McGrath and IE is Mark Latham [14 February 2004])

```
1.  IE:    we're looking at the options
2.         and getting ready for what we hope
3.         will be a very good
4.         and progressive Labor ↑[tax policy.
5.  IR: →                     [but- (.)  but
6.      →  for voters around Australia who a:re eh (.)
7.      →  listening (.) to you:
8.         th:inking >that you're promoting
9.         an image of a very united party<
10.        there are very serious divisions about this.
11.        do- do you accept that,
12.        and it could create problems for you.
```

Extract 2 shows the journalist orienting to the overhearing audience as a reminder that this interaction is primarily for the listening audience. By so doing, she also uses the audience, 'voters around Australia who are listening', as justification for pursuing a response. Such justifications are sometimes called 'devils advocate' challenges (Clayman and Heritage 2002) with journalists specifically referring to a third party in order to maintain their neutralistic stance. Extract 2 also demonstrates the sort of contentious environment in which such an orientation to the overhearing audience is most likely to occur, with the journalist commencing her turn with the disjunctive, 'but', in overlap with the end of the politician's turn. It is in such contentious adversarial environments that the tension between neutrality, accountability and the journalist's need to challenge the politician is most evident.

Calling on the public to provide additional support

Politicians and journalists can also directly involve the audience in their presentation of public policy. In the following example which again occurs within a contentious adversarial context, the politician calls on the Australian public to demonstrate their understanding of the policy under discussion.

Extract 3 (IR is Laurie Oaks and IE is Mark Latham [19 September 2004])

```
1.   IE:   well >Laurie< I've answered your question.
2.         I've answered your ques[tion¿
3.   IR:                          [oka:y, °wull-°
4.   IE:   I've shown you THE CABINET DOCUMENTS¿
```

```
5.              I'VE SHOWN YOU THE GOVERNMENT'S WEBSITE,
6.              I'VE TRIED TO EXPLAIN TO YOU THE NATURE
7.              OF THE FAMILY DEBT CRISIS¿
8.    →         MATE IF YOU DON'T GET IT¿
9.    →         if you don't get it, I can assure you: (.)
10.   →         one point four million Australian families ↑do:¿
11.             (.)
12.             coz they'[ve got the nightma:re=
13.   IR:                [okay,
14.   IE:       =of having to deal with Centrelink
15.             >to deal with this problem<¿
16.   →         if journalists don't get it, well ba:d luck;=>THE
17.   →         AUSTRALIAN PEOPLE DO:,
18.             AND LABOR'S GOING TO SOLVE
19.             THE ↑PROBLEM FOR THEM<.
20.             LA[BOR IS GONNA SO:LVE THE PROBLEM FOR ] THEM,=
21.   IR:         [°well° what I get- what I get is that]
22.   IE:=       AND >I TELL YOU WHAT<;
23.             THEY'RE A MI:LE AHEAD UNDER our policy.
```

Extract 3 shows the politician invoking the audience, 'the Australian people', in order to provide support for his statement concerning family payment policy. Although the politician has 'answered the question' (lines 1 and 2), shown the journalist 'the cabinet documents' (line 4), 'the government's website' (line 5) and explained the 'nature of the family debt crisis' (line 6 and 7), it is clear that the journalist still does not understand the policy, as demonstrated by line 21. The politician even tells the journalist that if he doesn't get it 'one point four million Australian families ↑do:¿' (line 10) because they have the nightmare of living with this situation.

In this adversarial environment, the politician is calling on the listening audience to provide additional support for his family payment policy. Initially the complaint that the journalist doesn't 'get it' is specifically directed towards the journalist, as evidenced through the address term 'mate' and the second person 'you' (lines 8 and 9). This is in contrast to 'one point four million Australian families' who do 'get it' (line 10). However, the politician then goes on to broaden his complaint from this particular journalist who doesn't 'get it' to *all* journalists who may not understand his policy and also broadens his third party reference from 'Australian families' to 'the Australian people' (line 17). By generalising his argument to include the wider community (and repeating this statement for emphasis) he is able to make his policy relevant to a larger group of people, present the audience as being able to understand his policy initiatives even though journalists may not understand them, and to justify his policy in the light of public understanding of the difficulties of dealing with 'Centerlink' (the Social Security Department in Australia).

So this extract demonstrates how the politician is simultaneously doing a number of things. On the one hand, he aligns himself with the Australian people, those who are currently suffering under the current policies. By so doing he shores up his policy initiative by claiming that the Australian public understand it even if the journalist doesn't. Although 'journalists' can also identify as members of the category of 'Australian people', the politician focuses on the differences in order to create a clear distinction between Australian people who understand (because of their experience with the problem), and journalists who don't understand (because of their role as cynical questioners of all policy initiatives). The politician strengthens the alignment with the Australian people by reminding them of his Labor party affiliation, a party that is known for its working class roots and so is in touch with struggling families. It is in this capacity that 'Labor is going to solve the problem for them' (lines 18 and 19).

However, although the politician is creating this strong alignment with the Australian people, at the expense of journalists, he is still maintaining his alignment with this particular journalist, Laurie Oaks. First, though his use of the address term 'mate' (line 8), he emphasises the closeness of their relationship in that they are both members of the same group that can call each other 'mate', a term that is not generally used in radio interviews.[2] The use of 'mate' in this context mitigates the challenge that follows. Second, although he initially complains that the interviewer doesn't get it, he maintains his alignment with the individual journalist by generalising the complaint to all journalists. As a result, the 'problem' belongs to all journalists, rather than to this particular person.

Making policy relevant to particular categories of people

Policies can be made directly relevant to the public through the way in which different groups or categories of people are referred to, and thus incorporated into, policy discussions. Through the use of non-recognitional terms (Schegloff 2007) to refer to non-present third parties, listeners to political news interviews can be caught up within an 'imagined community' (Fitzgerald and Housley 2007) of those who identify their own personal experience through a common social experience. By hearing references to third parties 'as-for-me' (Fitzgerald and Housley 2007), listeners can be directly involved in policy making discussions.

---

2   Using 'mate' in this position is a highly marked form. First, because when politicians use a pre-positioned address term (normally a first name in the Australian context) it demonstrates their orientation to the contentious nature of the talk that has overstepped the boundaries of what counts as acceptable, neutralistic news interview practice (Rendle-Short 2007b). Second, because using the address term 'mate' in a political news interview (regardless of the sequential environment) is extremely rare. (Of the 1435 address terms used by politicians in this 2004 data set, 'mate' is only used once.) For further discussion of 'mate' in the Australian context, see Rendle-Short (2009).

The following example shows a journalist and politician incorporating particular groups of people into their discussion of a new tax initiative.

Extract 4 (IR is Kerry O'Brien and IE is Mark Latham [7 October 2004])

```
1.    IR:   and ↑yet you didn't cover
2.          everybody under fifty-two thousand,
3.          there were some that you missed as we:ll.
4.    IE:   °°no that's not right°°
5.    IR:   we:ll in your annual tablet- ugh (.) ta:ble,
6.    →     the: (.) low single-income earners with kids
7.    →     the sole parents with kids, there are blocks
8.    →     of people who uh who actually (0.3)
9.          lo:se money once the Government's six
10.         hundred dollars ↑is taken out of the °equation°.
11.   IE:   but everyone under fifty-two thousand gets a ↑tax
12.   →     cut. the working tax bonus¿ ↓uh superannuates,
13.   →     ↓uhm ↓uhm self-funded u:h retirees,
14.   →     ↓uh taxpayers, uh they're all receiving? a tax
15.         cut uh under the Australian Labor Party ↑pla:n.
```

Extract 4 shows both the journalist and politician expressing different perspectives as to who 'everybody under fifty-two thousand' refers to (line 2). The journalist initially provides a three-part list of those who might lose money as a result of the policy, including, 'low single-income earners with kids', 'sole parents with kids', and other 'blocks of people'. In contrast, the politician presents a different three-part list of those who are going to benefit from the tax cut (redefined as a 'working tax bonus') including, 'superannuates', 'self-funded retirees' and 'taxpayers'. Although both lists are meant to be inclusive of 'everyone under fifty-two thousand', they set up a contrast between those losing or benefiting from the tax policy and between those with children and older tax payers. By setting up an alternative list of those who benefit from the tax policy, the politician avoids addressing the issue raised by the journalist that low income earners with children will be worse off overall, although difficulty connected with setting up his alternative list is evident, as demonstrated by the multiple 'uhs' and 'uhms' (7 in total) preceding key words (lines 12-15).

Choosing which groups to refer to and how such third party references should be categorised is crucially important in generating public policy discussion. Although the politician does not directly refute the journalist's categorisation of people 'under fifty-two thousand', through re-naming the tax cut as a 'working tax bonus' and through listing alternative categorisations of those 'under fifty-two thousand', the politician is able to demonstrate his disagreement with the journalist. Thus, through alternative reference forms that emerge in the moment-by-moment talk, the politician is able to defend and sell his policy to the listening audience while avoiding any direct reference to the fact that not all groups will benefit from the new tax initiative.

Sometimes speakers themselves repair their reference to a particular group or groups to ensure that they are presenting their policy in a more inclusive format.

Extract 5 (IR is Laurie Oaks and IE is John Howard [3 October 2004])

```
1. IE:    it will leave the budget in very healthy surplus,
2.        and once agai:n, it's performance Laurie.
3.        ↑we (.) have delivered (.) budget surpluses.
4.        it's one thing to have delivered those surpluses,
5.        and to make targeted commitments, including tax
6.    →   cuts for small business, and for working mothers.
7.    →   and (0.2) >fathers for that matter.<
8.        it's one thing to deliver those surpluses
9.        and to make those commitments.
10.       another thing, the Labor Party is >doing<, is
11.       ((talk continues))
```

Extract 5 shows the politician modifying his list of tax cut recipients. The expression 'targeted commitments' (line 5) foreshadows the idea that there are specific groups of people who are beneficiaries of the surplus. The politician lists the categories who have been given a tax cut – 'small business' and 'working mothers' (line 6). He then goes on to add 'and fathers for that matter' to complete the three part list. By repairing the list to include 'fathers', he does a number of things. On the surface, by including the category of 'fathers' he is demonstrating that they should not be excluded from the list. The different nature of this group is made clear through the marked talk, including, the 0.2 second pause just prior to saying 'fathers', the way in which this descriptor is presented with faster talk as an aside, the emphasis given to the word 'fathers' (in contrast to 'mothers'), and the addition of 'for that matter' which makes the category of 'fathers' in some way special. However, by adding 'fathers' as an afterthought, the politician is demonstrating his own normative assumptions around child care and who is most likely to be the primary carer of children.

Thus, speakers have choices as to how they formulate lists and in what order they include various groups within a list. Through the way in which the list is created and subsequently modified, the politician in the above example shows his own assumptions about particular groups (in this case working mothers) while at the same time giving the impression that his public policy formulation is inclusive and directly relevant to the listening audience.

Choices of group categorisation

Because people belong to multiple categories, speakers have choices as to how to refer to particular groups of people. But such choices are not neutral; rather they are 'inference-rich', often used to accomplish particular tasks (Sacks 1992).

The following example shows how person reference terms can accentuate particular descriptors, thus highlighting who exactly is being invoked within a particular policy initiative.

Extract 6 (IR is Kerry O'Brien and IE is John Howard [7 October 2004])

```
1.  IR: well speaking of integrity (.) Mr Howa:rd,
2.      a month ago:, >a little over< a month ago:,
3.      ah you said, (0.6) a that you wanted.
4.      ah to see an e:nd, to logging in
5.      old-growth forests. but at the same ti:me,
6.      >ah< you would a:h you would not ↓a:h be a party
7.   →to:: (.) >putting hard working Australians or
8.   →their communities< [on the scrap  heap.]
9.  IE:                  [°°mhm°° °mhm° °mhm°]
10. IR: so: with three go- da:ys to go to the
11.     election, (0.3) where is your policy on
12.     old-growth forests for Tasmania.
13. IE: I'll be making a statement uh about that issue,
14.     not tonight¿ .hh >But I'll be making a statement
15.     about that< issu:e before the campaign ↑°ends°.
16. IR: three days to go: Mr Howard, what ↓a:h (.) what
17.     respect are you showing, (0.4) to
18.  → Tasman°ians°, those people >you don't want to put<
19.  → on the scrap heap, (0.3) by sitting until
20.     the last minute on your policy on old-growth
21.     forests. when you reflected that view
22.     >more than a month ago<, that you wanted
23.     [to   see   an   e]nd to old-growth logging.
24. IE: [well the >view I-<]
25. IE: well the view I reflected wa:s °that I-° I
26.     I thought most Australians wanted to see an
27.     end .HH to old-growth >logging<=myself included,
28.     .hh >but I didn't want to< see it at ↓uh (.) the
29.  → expense of the livelihoods and the hopes and
30.  → aspirations of small isolated timber communities
31.     in Tas>mania<, I will be making a detailed
32.     statement on that, but I'm not going to make it
33.     tonight. ((talk continues))
```

Extract 6 shows the same group of people being described in multiple ways. Whereas the journalist calls them 'hard working Australians or their communities' (lines 7 and 8) and 'Tasmanians who you would not want to put on the scrap heap' (lines 18 and 19), the politician invokes quite different descriptors, such as 'small isolated timber communities' who have livelihoods, hopes and aspirations (lines 29 and 30). By the end of the interview, the politician refers to them as 'the people of Tasmania' and 'ordinary Australians living in Tasmania' (not shown on the transcript). In other words, by the end of the discussion, this group is no longer seen as disadvantaged (on the scrap heap) but just like other ordinary Australians.

Through the emerging characterisations of these groups of people we are able to see how journalist and politician express their different attitudes and perceptions. Although this extract occurs within the context of an adversarial environment, as evidenced by the way in which the journalist frames his questions in pursuing a response from the politician, including his marked use of address term 'Mr Howard' (Rendle-Short 2007a), there is no overt challenge as to how the groups should be described or categorised.[3] As a result, the journalist categorises them as 'hard working' and possibly on the 'scrap heap' while the politician emphasises that fact that they are just like other 'ordinary Australians' with 'hopes and aspirations'. Such embedded corrections (Jefferson 1987) permit journalist and politician to avoid overt disagreement of previous descriptors as they create and develop public policy on air, in real-time.

The following example, again within an adversarial context, similarly shows politicians and journalists making choices as to how to refer to groups of people in order to jointly construct the idea of what counts as 'good policy'.

Extract 7 (IR is Tony Jones and IE is Mark Latham [5 October 2004])

```
1.  IE:    ↓°uh° TEN percᴇɴᴛ (.) of our hospital beds
2.         no::w ↓°uh° in the public system,
3.     →   are taken up by frail aged people, who, if the
4.         hosp- nursing home beds were available,
5.         could be transferred >out<, freeing up¿
6.         significant resources in public hospitals.
7.         s[o:   Goᴏᴅ ] ᴘᴏʟɪᴄʏ Goᴏᴅ=
8.  IR:     [but- y- y- ]
9.  IE:    =ᴘᴏʟɪᴄʏ [makes it's (o:wn efficiency gains). ]
10. IR:           [>but you don't- but  you don't< but]
11. IR:    just to confirm you don't have any projections
```

```
12.        →   as to what'll happen when .hh these hu:ge
13.        →   numbers of- of elderly people come on li:ne,
14.            and are eligible for this policy.
15. IE:        well Tony the projection would be:
16.            that if the population doubles, ↓uh most likely
17.            the waiting lists will double. >now< what a
18.        →   calamity if senior Australians have to
19.            wait two years instead of one year to get
20.            eye, knee and hip operations. we're doing this,
21.            not only about the policy that looks
22.        →   after our seniors, but significant efficiency
23.            gains in the health system.
```

In line 3, the politician refers to a particular group of people as 'frail aged people' who are taking up hospital beds. In response, the journalist refers to a larger group, 'these huge numbers of elderly people' who will 'come on line' (lines 12 and 13). This larger group presumably refers to the large number of 'baby boomers' who are becoming increasingly old and who will soon fill up hospitals and nursing care facilities. The politician then invokes the category of 'senior Australians' (line 18), again with the idea that such people may 'have to wait two years instead of one year to get eye, knee and hip operations' (lines 19-20). Finally this group becomes 'our seniors' (line 22), who will need to be 'looked after'.

Such shifts demonstrate some of the available choices for describing and categorising groups of people. As in earlier examples, such categorisations occur within the context of an adversarial environment. In lines 8 and 10, the journalist commences his talk in overlap with the disjunction 'but' before the politician has finished his turn construction unit (TCU). The politician orients to the contentious nature of the talk by prefacing his response with 'well Tony', thus retrospectively constructing the prior turn as being a personal attack that has overstepped the boundary of what counts as acceptable, neutralistic, news interview practice (Rendle-Short 2007b).

However the categories themselves are not marked as being contentious, with no hesitation markers, no emphasis, no discussion or challenge as to why a particular category was chosen. Rather the categories emerge, without any overt marking to show that one category is more applicable than another and without any discussion as to how this particular group 'should' be referred to. Following the journalist's categorisation (line 13), the politician changes 'frail aged people' to the more neutral 'senior Australians' (line 18). The latter term emphasises the status inherent in being 'senior Australians', even though they may have medical (eye, knee, hip) problems, in contrast to the more friendly and familiar 'our seniors' (line 22), even though they too will require care and attention.

Thus, different person reference terms within the context of an adversarial environment in which differing views are being presented demonstrates how politician and journalist are jointly constructing the idea of what counts as 'good policy' (lines 7 and 9). As a result they are jointly creating a picture of who is being referred to and the nature of the attributes such a group might have. Thus one outcome of the way in which the different choices are presented is that by the end of the sequence, those who will be affected by the policy, can be characterised as 'elderly' or 'senior Australians' who have the attributes of frailness, age, being in large numbers, being Australian, needing eye, hip and knee replacements, belonging to us, and needing our care.

Through such characterisation shifts journalists and politicians are able to present their perspective, often with moral overtones, as to how such groups (in this case the elderly) are perceived within a community of talk. It demonstrates how policy relating to an efficient health system is played out at a micro, personal level, rather than in a more formal, 'reasoned' manner (Housley and Fitzgerald 2007). But these micro-level discussions do not occur in private. The talk is designed for the overhearing audience, thus ensuring that they are an integral part of the policy framing process, part of the imagined community of seniors or carers of seniors who are directly affected by policy outcomes.

In contrast, the following example shows how the idea of 'angry loggers' put forward by the IR is not challenged or modified and so remains a non-contested category.

Extract 8 (IR is Kerry O'Brien and IE is Mark Latham [7 October 2004])

```
1.      IE:    that's what election campaigns are about.
2.             (0.3) choices. about the big issues of the future,
3.             how do we save the environment, .hh and pass
4.             on these wonderful natural assets ↓°uh° for
5.             the next generation of young ↑°Australians°.
6.      IR:→  but those loggers are your rank-and-file.
7.             and you went down there a few months ago and told
8.             them they wouldn't lose their jobs. do you really
9.          →  think, that all those angry loggers no:w¿
10.            (0.3) are in a frame of mi:nd, to sit down
11.            quietly and absorb the eight hundred million
12.            package that you say will guarantee them
13.            jobs (.) >into the future<. (.) because they
14.            still believe you've sold them ↑out
15.            .h if you'd released that policy even a week ago
16.            or ↑two weeks ago:, wouldn't they have had
17.            >a little< more ti:me to calm down a bit,
18.            look at your policy properly¿
19.      IE:   we:ll, they can look at our eight hundred million
20.            dollars versus Mr Howard's ↓suh fifty¿
21.      IR:   >but right now they don't want to.<
22.          →  [they're too ↑angry.]
```

```
23.   IE:   [well    °well°      ] well well Kerry
24.         the reality is when- I: uh saw the Gunns
25.         ↓u:hm >uh< veneer plant in Tasmania,
26.         I saw old technology¿
```

Although once again this discussion occurs within the context of an adversarial environment as the journalist challenges the politician as to why his 'eight hundred million package' was not delivered in time, the shift of categorisation from 'those loggers' (line 6) to 'all those angry loggers' (line 9) is unchallenged. All subsequent references to this group by the politician are with third person pronouns, 'they' or 'them' (lines 12, 13, 14, 16, 19, 21, 22). As a result, within this contentious environment where the journalist could be charged with not maintaining a neutralistic stance (as demonstrated by the disjunctive 'but' (line 6), the adversarial complex question (lines 6-18), and the politician's use of an address term in line 23), the politician does not provide an alternative account as to whether the loggers are angry, nor does he provide any justification as to how his approach could have ameliorated their strong reaction to his policy. Thus, because the opportunity for providing an alternative account was foregone, the politician also forewent the opportunity to justify and defend his 'eight hundred million package' within the public sphere of the political news interview.

Concluding Remarks

As the above examples demonstrate, the audience is an integral part of the political news interview, with references to the public, or sub-sets of the public, often occurring within contentious, adversarial environments. References to the audience may be used by journalists as a technique for legitimising unsourced questions or assertions; they may be used by politicians as a technique for justifying a particular response or as a way of preventing further questioning on a particular topic. By so doing, both journalists and politicians demonstrate their orientation to the notion of accountability. For journalists, accountability is intricately tied with the need to balance opposing requirements for neutralism or objectivity with the need to ensure that politicians adequately answer difficult questions.

For politicians, the notion of accountability relates to the democratic principles of ensuring that because they have been elected by the public, politicians have a responsibility to represent, and therefore be answerable to, the public. One way to demonstrate this accountability is through the way in which politicians involve the public, the overhearing audience, in their talk, as they respond to journalists' questions and challenges, and as they both gather public opinion, while simultaneously generating, modifying and justifying public policy associated with issues of health, education, taxes, terrorism and the like. Thus the political news interview is not simply a forum for politicians to break policy initiatives to the wider voting public. Rather, the news interview is increasingly being used as a space in which journalists and politicians are able to question, challenge, defend, generate and sell public policy. Therefore this chapter has not been principally interested in how the media plays a role in mediating between politicians and the public, with emphasis on how to translate politician's ideas to the ordinary everyday people. Rather the emphasis in this chapter has been on how politicians, journalists and the audience collaborate to ensure that key macro events such as public policy emerge through the micro detail of interaction. Because of the way in which the audience is incorporated into the talk, they are included in the policy formulation process, with policy being created, modified and constructed in real-time, produced through moment-by-moment interaction for the overhearing audience.

Choosing a particular descriptor or characterisation is not a neutral action. In addition, as Scannell (1991) notes, the important thing to focus on is '*how* things are said, why and for what possible effects' (p. 11 italics in original). By focusing on what and how something is said it is possible to demonstrate how journalists and politicians *do* public policy through the political news interview. Through the different ways in which participants categorise key players within policy discussions, politicians both create and modify policy for the listening public, while at the same time respond to journalists' challenges concerning the detail of the policy information. Simultaneously, the audience is invited to be part of an imagined community that hears the various categorisations as-relevant-for-me. As pointed out by Fitzgerald and Housley (2007), the audience need to be able to identify their personal experiences as *common* social experiences, to recognise that 'I feel included because others are similar to me'. Thus, through the various categorisations, their voices can be heard and made relevant, even though they are silent within the participation framework of the political news interview. As such the audience is mobilised and directly involved within the policy formation process as politicians and journalists present, propose, create and formulate public policy.

Any talk, including political news interviews, is designed for an audience (Bell 1984). As Howard told Jon Faine, Melbourne radio journalist, in 2004, 'I don't come in to talk to the presenter but I come in to talk to your audience' (Faine 2005: 177). One way to involve the audience is through the generation and modification of person reference terms by the parties to the interaction. By so doing, it becomes possible for overhearers of the news interview to obtain a better understanding of how policy is being conceived of, and created by, the key players in policy formation. Such a process becomes 'democracy-in-action' with the audience directly involved in the democratic dialogue through the creation of public policy. As Faine (2005: 188) said of the Australian situation, talk radio 'has become an integral part of the democratic debate and the political culture of the nation'.

Therefore, the political news interview is not just a series of questions and answers where journalists try to undermine, debate, or challenge politicians; nor is it just a forum for politicians to break policy initiatives to the wider voting public. Rather, as journalists question and challenge, and as politicians defend and sell, the political news interview becomes a site for the constructing, shaping and reflecting on political policy for, and on behalf of, the overhearing audience.

References

Akmajian, A., Demers, R.A., Farmer, A.K. and Harnish, R.M. 2001. *Linguistics: An Introduction to Language and Communication.* Cambridge, MA: MIT Press.

Austin, J. 1962. *How to do Things with Words.* Oxford: Oxford University Press.

Bell, A. 1984. Language style as audience design. *Language in Society*, 13, 145-204.

Clayman, S. and Heritage, J. 2002. *The News Interview.* Cambridge: Cambridge University Press.

Ellis, J. 2000. *Seeing Things: Television in the Age of Uncertainty.* London: I.B. Tauris.

Faine, J. 2005. Talk radio and democracy, in *Do Not Disturb: Is the Media Failing Australia?*, edited by R. Manne, Melbourne: Black Inc, 169-188.

Fairclough, N. 1994. Conversationalization of public discourse and the authority of the consumer, in *The Authority of the Consumer*, edited by R. Keat, N. Whiteley, and N. Abercrombie, London: Routledge, 253-268.

Fitzgerald, R. and Housley, W. 2007. Talkback, community and the public sphere. *Media International incorporating Culture and Policy*, 122, 150-163.

Heritage, J. 1985. Analyzing news interviews: Aspects of the production of talk for an 'overhearing' audience, in *Handbook of Discourse Analysis, Vol. 3, Discourse and Dialogue*, edited by T. van Dijk, London: Academic Press, 95-119.

Housley, W. and Fitzgerald, R. 2007. Categorization, interaction, policy and debate. *Critical Discourse Studies*, 4 (2), 187-206.

Hutchby, I. 2006. *Media Talk: Conversation Analysis and the Study of Broadcasting.* Maidenhead: Open University Press.

Jefferson, G. 1987. On exposed and embedded correction in conversation, in *Talk and Social Organisation*, edited by G. Button and J.R.E. Lee, Clevedon: Multilingual Matters, 86-100.

Kane, T. 1998. Public argument, civil society and what talk radio teaches about rhetoric. *Argumentation and Advocacy*, Winter, 34 (3), 154-161.

Lerner, G. 2004 (ed.). *Conversation Analysis: Studies from the First Generation.* Amsterdam and Philadelphia: John Benjamins.

Leudar, I. and Nekvapi, J. 2004. Media dialogic networks and political argumentation. *Journal of Language and Politics*, 3 (2), 247-266.

Montgomery, M. 2007. *The Discourse of Broadcast News: A Linguistic Approach.* London and New York: Routledge.

Moores, S. 2000. *Media and Everyday Life in Modern Society.* Edinburgh: Edinburgh University Press.

Rendle-Short, J. 2007a. Catherine, you're wasting your time: Address terms within the Australian political interview. *Journal of Pragmatics*, 39, 1503-1525.

Rendle-Short, J. 2007b. Neutralism and adversarial challenges in the political news interview. *Discourse and Communication*, 1 (4), 387-406.

Rendle-Short, J. 2009. The address term 'mate' in Australian English: Is it still a masculine term? *Australian Journal of Linguistics*, 29 (2), 245-268.

Sacks, H. 1992. Lectures on conversation. Oxford: Blackwell.

Scannell, P. 1991. Introduction, in *The Relevance of Talk, in Broadcast Talk,* edited by P. Scannell, London: Sage Publications Ltd, 1-13.

Schegloff, E.A. 2007. A tutorial on membership categorization. *Journal of Pragmatics*, 39, 462-282.

Tolson, A. 2006. *Media Talk: Spoken Discourse on TV and Radio.* Edinburgh: Edinburgh University Press.

Ward, I. 2002. Talkback radio, political communication and Australian politics. *Australian Journal of Communication*, 29 (1), 21-38.

Chapter 7

Press Scrums: Some Preliminary Observations

Patrick Watson and Christian Greiffenhagen

Introduction

In this chapter we want to contribute to the study of the day-to-day practices of media operatives, focusing on a specific form of news gathering: the press scrum – quick, informal, unscripted encounters, in which reporters question, e.g., politicians about their views on particular topics.[1]

While in contemporary journalism reporters are increasingly bound to their desks and rely on information that is sent to them in the form of wire copies, official statements, or press releases (cf, Davies 2008), at other times materials have to be actively collected. Press scrums – a method of news data collection involving journalists from different media outlets physically bunched together so that they are all within hearing/recording distance of the person they want to talk to – are a common method for obtaining materials to compliment news stories. Such scrums are familiar scenes in places where reporters can hope to find people of interest: outside parliaments or public offices (law courts in particular), in front of the homes of people currently in the public eye, or following sporting events, to name a few.

Our case study focuses on the work of reporters covering the Ontario Legislative Assembly (OLA) in Toronto, Canada. Since the assembly is a reliable source of political news, local news outlets have reporters present throughout the legislature's working day. At various times, particularly when politicians were known to be leaving the assembly to return to their offices, reporters would 'scrum' around them in the corridor and question them about recent events for subsequent newspaper reports or radio/television broadcasts.

Press scrums are akin to other forms of interactions between reporters and politicians, such as news interviews (e.g., Greatbatch 1988, Clayman and Heritage, 2002a) or press conferences (Schegloff 1987, Clayman and Heritage 2000b). Like news interviews, they largely follow a question-answer format. However, whilst

---

1   The term 'scrum' (or 'scrummage') originates in rugby, where it designates 'an ordered formation in which the two sets of forwards pack themselves together with their heads down and endeavour by pushing to work their opponents off the ball and break away with it or heel it out' (Oxford English Dictionary).

the news interview is meant to be 'a finished product in its own right' (Clayman and Heritage 2002a, 1), a press scrum is not broadcasted or published as a whole. It is meant to produce materials that can be reformulated into (part of) a news story or that can be quoted or replayed, providing 'sound bites' or 'pictures' which are valued formal elements of news reports.

Our analysis of press scrums is based on a two-month period of fieldwork, in which we were able to capture ten scrums. The study is thus in the tradition of ethnographies of news production and news gathering, but particularly influenced by more recent studies of news and media discourse, which examine audio- or video- recordings of media products in great detail in order to make visible the taken-for-granted practices of journalists (cf, Greiffenhagen 2009).

There is a long tradition of ethnographies which have tried to open up the 'black box' of news production and gathering. While early studies were particularly concerned with issues of 'gatekeeping' (e.g., White 1950), i.e., with questions of how and why certain stories are selected over others, in the late 1970s a number of ethnographers tried to reveal the processes through which the news are 'assembled', 'made', or 'manufactured' (e.g., Tuchman 1978, Schlesinger 1978, Golding and Elliott 1979, Fishman 1980). These studies sought to demonstrate the social construction of the news, i.e., they argued that news, rather than being a simple mirror of reality, is at best only a selective version of it (with news stories being shaped as much by media values as by the 'facts' being reported). Whether through the examination of media output or through observations of decision making in news rooms, the dominant concern was to show that the news report represented no more than one possible – and from the analyst's view, tendentious – rendering of the news materials.

These kinds of studies were soon rivalled by approaches drawing on the rapidly expanding interest in analyses of discourse, which originated in and drew from a variety of different disciplinary sources. In many cases, these studies sought to combine an interest in discourse with the increasingly prominent idea of the social sciences as essentially 'critical' disciplines. The rediscovered Frankfurt School and the increasing influence of Michel Foucault very powerfully propelled this critical direction. In Britain, Stuart Hall (1980, 1982) and the Glasgow University Media Group (1976, 1980) were particularly influential in demonstrating that the (linguistic) forms of representation adopted in news media were not neutral in the way that news agencies projected themselves to be. Rather news reports embodied a 'hidden agenda' of communication, that of giving the dominant ideology an apparently congenial form. As the Glasgow University Media Group (1976: 1) put it: 'the news is not a neutral product; [...] it is a sequence of socially manufactured messages, which carry many of the culturally dominant assumptions of our society'. The claim was not necessarily that journalists were personally biased, or deliberately deceitful, but dominant assumptions were embedded in and reproduced by news presentations. More recent approaches, such as critical linguistics (Fowler 1991) and critical discourse analysis (Fairclough 1995, Fairclough and Wodak 1997, van

Dijk 1988) have aimed to demonstrate more specifically how linguistic factors contribute to, and are constitutive of, ideological representations of reality.

Alongside these 'critical' approaches to media discourse, other approaches to discourse, which could be labelled 'descriptive-explicative', have evolved. Researchers working in this tradition work with the same kind of data as their 'critical' colleagues, but put different questions to these data. Rather than asking, for example, whether language represents reality (successfully, objectively), the question becomes what work the language is put to by participants. There are a variety of theoretical origins of such 'explicative-descriptive' studies, for example sociolinguistics (cf, Bell 1991). However, our own study is most directly influenced by ethnomethodology and conversation analysis.

Ethnomethodology (Garfinkel 1967) has as its aim to make visible the taken-for-granted practical methods that people use to accomplish various practices. Conversation analysis and membership category analysis (Sacks 1992, Sacks et al. 1974) have focussed on the methodic practices that are employed by members when engaged in various forms of social interaction. These approaches have been used to analyse a variety of media products: newspaper headlines (Lee 1984), newspaper stories (Schenkein 1979, Eglin and Hester 2003, Barthélémy 2003), letters-to-the-editor (Fitzgerald and Housley 2006), talk shows (Hutchby 1996, Hester and Fitzgerald 1999, Housley 2002), or news interviews (Heritage 1985, Greatbatch 1988, Clayman and Heritage 2002a).

In an important exchange (Schegloff 1997, 1999 a and b, Billig 1999 a and b), Schegloff has tried to clarify the difference between 'critical' and 'descriptive-explicative' approaches by arguing that the former employs the standard of the *researcher* to analyse materials, whilst the latter aims to ground the analysis in the standards and values exhibited by *participants* (see also Anderson and Sharrock 1979). Thus while critical approaches employ an external standard to reveal factors that are 'hidden' or 'invisible' to participants, descriptive-explicative studies aim to exhibit the factors that participants *themselves* are attuned to. In the former, it is typically the researcher who decides whether a particular news product is 'neutral' or 'objective'. In contrast, researchers working within ethnomethodological approaches try to exhibit how participants themselves deal with issues of neutrality or objectivity (e.g., Clayman and Heritage 2002a).

There have been very few studies that have tried to combine the focus of the ethnographic studies on the *processes* of news assembly with the fine-grained, real-time analysis that is typical of studies of media discourse. That is to say, most previous conversation analytic or ethnomethodological studies have analysed media *products*. Three notable exceptions are Heath and Nicholls's (1997) video-based examination of the production of news stories in an international news agency, Clayman and Reisner's (1998) study of how 'front page' stories are selected using audio-recordings of editorial conferences, and Broth's (2006, 2009) investigations of the camera work during a live TV production based on video recordings of the control room. Following these, we have tried to base our own study on audio recordings of press scrums to exhibit the real-time creation of media materials. The aim has thus not been to demonstrate any hidden motives or ideologies on the part of journalists or politicians, but rather to show, with concrete examples, how it is that through the interaction between journalists and politicians they accomplish 'the news'.

The Scene

Our analysis of press scrums is based on a two-month period of fieldwork in 2004 following press-, radio- and television-reporters covering the Ontario Legislative Assembly (OLA). The fieldwork encompassed the time prior to and during the government's budget announcement.

Reporters at the OLA were based in a lounge which sat between the government press office and the legislative chamber from which they were able to move to the press gallery in the debating chamber. Certain reporters (particularly those working for newspapers or the wire service) would spend time watching the debates, while others (predominantly television reporters) would show up in mid-afternoon, in time for the politician's departure from the debating chamber. Reporters received information through two official channels: the government press office, which would release a package each morning, and the party press offices, which would release their own news as well as comment on the government release.[2] This, for the most part, informed the agenda of each of the press scrums. Reporters representing the wire services and newspapers would often be leafing through the press releases, watching a 24-hour news channel on the lounge television or wandering between the office, the lobby (where scrums were conducted) and the legislative chamber. In the mid afternoon, after the regular debating session in the legislative chamber had ended, the lobby of the OLA would become more active. Members of the press would assemble near the doors through which ministers and other politicians (e.g., critics or shadow ministers) would leave the floor to return to their offices. As soon as the relevant politician was spotted, reporters would 'scrum' around her or him in order to ask a series of questions. In general, these scrums were brief (roughly one to ten minutes) and fluid affairs (reporters could come and go as they saw fit). The smallest scrum observed involved two reporters while in the largest about twenty reporters and camera operators were present. In the larger scrums, reporters would stand in uncomfortable proximity to each other, often pressing against each other, using their fellow reporters to prop up their microphones and recorders. Some scrums were setup in advance, e.g., when reporters were informed by ministerial aides of the impending arrival

---

2   There were any number of non-official channels, such as 'leaks', comments from outside authorities, stories relating to but not emanating from the OLA itself, etc. These could become topics in the scrums, but generally questions came from the government's agenda of the day (see Jaworski et al. [2004] for how leaks are presented, and contested, in radio news broadcasts).

of ministers in the lobby. In other scrums, crews and equipment transferred very quickly from one politician's location to the next, once the appropriate comment had been recorded. Following the scrums, politicians would return to their offices to conduct the rest of the day's business whilst reporters from television would head to edit suites and radio and print reporters would file their reports at offices off site.

An initial sense of press scrums can be gained from Transcript 1, which reproduces one scrum in its entirety.

Transcript 1, Minister of Finance with 6 reporters (in entirety, Data Set 1)

```
1      (2.0)
2  I1:twenty five thousand jo:bs lost in:n (.) close to a month
3      (0.3)
4  M: well we had uh::h fifty one thousand three hundred jobs
5     created since we've been (1.0) the government uh:h thet goes
6     back to October (0.5) and the ↑economy is growing at a rate
7     of about uh four point eight per cent annualized ◦hh from the
8     third quarter of last year so wuh (.) ↑the economy is doing
9     uh ◦hh ↓reasonably well and a one month's::uh (.) numbers do
10    not add up to a trend= so this is happened in the past it
11    happened (0.5) two thousand and one (0.5) there was a thirty
12    one thousand job loss figure (1.0) tween January and February
13    that time (0.5) uh (.) it happened again uh let's see uh in
14    two thousand and three? in April two thousand and three
15    there were twenty two thousand jobs lost ◦hh so uh ↑these
16    are not trending numbers= i-it's un one uh months (.) numbers
17    (0.5)
18 I2:have you tracked to see where they are?
19    (1.2)
20 M: uh it's uh yin uh (.) variety of (0.5) uh (0.5) uh (0.5)
21    industries (.) it's in uh (0.5) business services uh building
22    (1.0) uh but generally in services
23    (1.0)
24 I2:does that give you any (1.5) cause (0.5) for the creating of
25    a strategy (.) turn that sector around=
26 M:                              =well ah I repeat uh
27    one month does not make a trend so we have to look at this as
28    uh as as a one month indicator oh what's [going on   ]
29 I3:                                          [so if it's] a
30    second month like this then we're starting a Bob Rae debt
31    spiral again is thet [the problem?]
32 M:                      [↑oh (.) my ] (.) my heh that's its
33    heh far from it ↓uh even two months we (.) we are looking at
```

```
34    uh °hh projected growth for this year of about three per cent
35    for the economy and about three point five per cent for next
36    year so we have uh °hh an economy that's recovering from (.)
37    last year where we had a real dip in the numbers and uh (.)
38    we expect uh positive growth this year and next
39    (0.5)
40 I2: on a lighter note a guy from Ottawa a guy from Toronto
41    square off today=
42                 ((reporters relax, three leave the scrum))
43                 =you're in the black suit with the red strips (2.0)
44    aren't you a leaf f[an]
45 M:                    [no] this is grey red stripes uh there's
46    a lot of blue out there as you can see (0.5) blue on this
47    [tie and this shirt]
48 I2: [   you    can    ]   rationalize anything [can't    you ]
49 M:                                             [heh heh heh heh]
50 I2: ((puts down microphone and walks away))
51 I4: you::uh you uh rootin[for the leafs?]
52 M:                      [this  is  for ] Toronto
53    Toronto's going to win tonight
54    ((remaining parties walk away))
```

On the way back from the assembly to his office, the Minister of Finance is stopped by several reporters who question him about a report of declining employment figures over the previous quarter. What is at first perhaps surprising is the relative shortness of the scrum, lasting only one minute ten seconds. Also of note is the abrupt way in which the scrum begins: there are no greetings, introductory remarks, or lead-ins. Instead, upon the arrival of the minister, reporters gather around him and one reporter initiates the exchange through a question-like statement (line 2). Neither is the scrum brought to a formal close, but rather comes to completion with the politician's remark on Toronto's hockey team (lines 52-53), after which reporters simply walk away (line 54; although some reporters had already left before, see line 42).

The scrum is organised as a two-party turn-taking system between reporters and politicians, which mostly follows a question-answer format typical of news interviews (cf, Clayman and Heritage 2002a), but also features challenge–comment pairs. For example, the reporter's first utterance in line 2, although not formulated as a question, is treated by the minister as one (and thus seems to be heard by him as containing an implicit 'Would you comment on that ...?'). However, in contrast to news interviews, reporters' questions do not contain prefaces designed for an 'overhearing audience' (Heritage 1985, Clayman and Heritage 2002a: 120-126) and presume significant shared knowledge on both sides. For example, the initial question (line 2) presupposes knowledge of a recent news story (the job losses in the month prior) and is based on the assumption that the minister is an appropriate person to ask for comment on that story (since it was not a formal topic of discussion on the floor of the legislature that morning).

No discernible order as to who of the reporters gets to ask a question is apparent, but this lack of predetermined sequence of questioners does not imply that scrums are chaotic. Instead, different reporters ask questions around the same topic. For example, I2's question in line 18 can be heard as a follow-up to I1's question in line 2. Reporters do not seem to compete for the right to ask questions, but rather collaborate with each other, although it is generally accepted and expected that television reporters would ask the first question. The general idea, as reporters described it, is to ask the type of questions that would unnerve the politician; other reporters would often allow a single reporter to use whatever necessary time in the scrum if they were succeeding at doing so.

Looking at the scrum in its entirety, it becomes clear that this is a routine affair. The absence of any setup, the relative brevity and abruptness of questions and the limited amount of time spent conducting the scrum all point to the fact that these exchanges occur frequently and are part of the mundane business of both politicians and reporters.

Openings

Activities have beginnings or openings, which frequently are marked in a variety of ways (cf, Turner 1972: 369, Sacks 1992: 105). Some activities are verbally marked, for example, teachers' 'good morning' or 'come on settle down' in classrooms (Payne 1976, Greiffenhagen 2008) or the announcement 'Be upstanding in court...' in courtrooms (Atkinson and Drew 1979: 87-91). Press scrums typically start with a reporter's first question. In other words, there are no greetings, preambles or requests to whether reporters could ask a question. Instead, almost all scrums begin as the one in Transcript 1: with one reporter asking a question.

Of course, both parties, reporters and the politician, have to work to be in a position where one reporter can ask a question. Thus there are elaborate 'pre-beginnings', in which both parties 'get into position'. Reporters gather in the lobby outside the debating chambers about half an hour before they expect the ministers or other politicians of interest to leave the floor.[3]

Sometimes reporters are already in a state of readiness, waiting for the politician to exit, in which case the politician walks to the designated position facing the reporters. At other times, politicians stand in the lobby waiting for the reporters to assemble around them. Reporters would wait for those politicians who

---

3   Ministers would leave through the session, after they concluded their business on the floor, but the session could be expected to continue after they had left. It was typically only one or two politicians (minister and opposition member) who would leave around the same time.

were most likely to be the potential source of newsworthy material. In this setting, reporters always gathered around the exit of the government party and would only subsequently walk up to opposition members who had left the chamber.

A politician walking up to the reporters signals that the scrum is about to begin. It is at this point that the reporters – and the researcher – would start their recorders. Most recordings gathered from the site therefore start with a silence before the first turn (as in line 1 in Transcript 1). This silence represents the phase in which participants are 'almost ready', but are not yet starting the verbal exchange.

Reporters not only check whether the politician is ready to be asked a question, but also whether fellow reporters are ready (e.g., have positioned themselves appropriately and turned on their equipment). At times, this is explicitly addressed. For example, in the following transcript, one reporter (I1) is talking to another reporter (I3) who is having problems getting his recording device to start. A third reporter (I2) is waiting for I3, before producing the first question (line 3).

Transcript 2, Minister of Health and 5 reporters (lines 1-7 of 92 lines, Data Set 4)

```
1  I1:it's the other side (.) ok (.) hghm
2     (2.0)
3  I2:ready (.) ok so you have said that you will do a
4     judicial review= you've asked a:uh judge to come in and do a
5     judicial review but °hh a-ya (.) the family doesn't believe
6     you went furthenough= they want a stop to all audits= why
7     can't you do [that]
8  M:            [right] ↑oh I understand that [...]
```

In another instance (Transcript 3), the minister walks up to the assembled press scrum. Upon his arrival, the television reporter (I1) is informed by the camera operator that there is a small problem with the camera. Consequently, rather than asking the first question, the reporter asks the whole scrum to 'hold on' (line 2). The eventual start is so long forthcoming that the politician produces a rare greeting (line 6), which is answered by one of the reporters (line 8).

Transcript 3, Minister of Health and 15+ reporters (line 1-12 of 222 lines, Data Set 5)

```
1     (4.0)
2  I1: hold on
3  I2: ha::irahgh ((clearing throat))
4     (2.0)
5  I3: Neil MacQuinn ((into microphone, perhaps a check))
6  M:  how's everybody doing
```

```
7       (0.5)
8   I4: pretty good minister
9       (1.0)
10 I3: [so ]
11 I1: [min]ister let's just start with your reaction to t-today's
12     report [...]
```

Although in this instance all parties are in the right physical position for the questioning to begin in line 1, the problem with the television camera delays the expected first question. In other words, both reporters and politician monitor the group to see whether everybody is 'ready'. It is not the case that the scrum could not start without every reporter being ready, but reporters are willing to wait for their colleagues to adjust their devices before proceeding with the scrum.

As mentioned, the beginnings of scrums rarely include greetings, pleasantries, or requests, but reporters rather go straight to questioning, since all parties know what Schenkein (1971: 30-31) refers to as the 'reason' for the encounter, which includes expectations as to 'why' the encounter has been arranged, 'what' the projected conversation will be about and 'how' the participants will spend time in conversation with each other (30). While in Schenkein's case, a conversation between an insurance salesman and a customer, participants have to work at 'getting to' the reason for the encounter, in press scrums reporters go straight to questioning. There are good reasons for this, for instance the parties to a press scrum already know each other and know that due to their busy schedules, ministers are only available for a few minutes and will have to move on quickly. Pleasantries are therefore an unwanted intrusion into the scrum's time with the minister (see also Fitzgerald and Housley (2002) for how hosts during radio phone-ins may launch straight into a question).

Questions are also formulated in a very succinct and compact manner and based on a variety of presuppositions (which includes the issues that are currently relevant, why the interviewed person is in a position to comment on it and what aspects might be explored). In Transcript 1, for example, the reporter does not explain that the relevance of his question (line 2) is premised on the report released that morning (which pointed to rising unemployment figures) and the minister is not surprised by the question (since he presumably understands that with a report mentioning rising unemployment, reporters will ask what the government will do about it). Similarly, in the next transcript, the reporter's first question (lines 2-5) asks about the 'OPG / Hydro One deal', but does not mention that this question is prompted by the government's decision to make public the salaries of employees of the recently privatised electricity utility.

Transcript 4, Leader of Third Party with 5 reporters (lines 1-8 of 185 lines, Data Set 2)

```
1     (4.0)
2  I1: is (0.8) what:i- what is what is it do you think the
3      government uh stalled this or (0.3) what do you think
4      happened here and °hh does this finally lift- lift the veil
5      of secrecy on this whole O P G hydro one deal
6      (0.2)
7  O:  no it doesn't it doesn't ah lift the veil of secrecy because
8      there's still going to be situations...
```

The reporter's question (lines 2-5) is opaque without sufficient background information. There is no explication of what had just happened, why this was a relevant question to ask, or how the characterisation of the deal (in terms of secrecy) is a relevant one. However, the interviewee has no difficulty understanding what the question is asking, thereby displaying that the reporter's question is designed for the politician – rather than a potential news audience.

Sacks (1992: 564) remarked that conversationalists operate under the maxim of 'recipient design', i.e., that one should 'design your talk to another with an orientation to what you know they know'. The way reporters design their questions in press scrums is in relation to the knowledge of the people in the room (the politician and the other reporters). It is interesting to compare this with broadcast news interviews, where much talk is not designed as such, since it is not a conversation between interviewer and interviewee, but a conversation for the benefit of an 'overhearing audience'. Clayman and Heritage (2002a: 60) note that, for example, news interviews are characterised by very elaborate openings prior to the interviewer's first question. These openings typically consists of (1) headline (detailing the topic for discussion), (2) background (providing the information necessary to understand the questioning) and (3) lead-in (in which interviewees are introduced), where this opening 'is addressed explicitly to the audience rather than to the interviewee' (59). Furthermore, interviewees are frequently introduced in a way that identifies why they are relevant to the topic under the discussion, e.g., as 'participant', 'expert', or 'advocate' (pp. 68-72). Similarly, in talk shows 'guests are introduced as incumbents of membership categories which are recognisably relevant to the topic of the show' (Hester and Fitzgerald 1999: 177). The reason for such introductions is that the talk produced is predominantly designed for an 'overhearing audience', which frequently needs more background information than the actual parties in the room.

In contrast, the compactness of questions in press scrums and the absence of elaborate introductions demonstrate that the scrum is not meant to be a media product in itself, but part of the gathering of materials for eventual products. Questions in press scrums are thus not designed to be understood by the eventual audience specifically, but by the parties present in the scrum (e.g., the politician). These questions are meant to elicit materials which, if framed in the appropriate manner will be relevant to the audience. Clayman and Heritage (2002a) characterise the news interview 'as a "strictly business" encounter that has been planned in advance and is now being orchestrated on behalf of the media audience' (pp. 68). Press scrums are similarly 'business-like', but they are not directly arranged for an overhearing media audience.

Closings

Scrums can be brought to an end by either side, i.e., by politicians or reporters. In the case of the former, it is typically not the politician who explicitly imposes a limit or says that he or she has to go, but instead the aide accompanying the politician. One frequent practice is to indicate that the politician would only take a few more questions.

Transcript 5, Minister of Health and 10 reporters (lines 189-196 of 231, Data Set 7)

```
189 M:  [...] we'll uh always be seeking to do? to make sure that
190     ∘hh as many of thu::h precious dollars that we have are::uh
191     dedicated tuh:: tuh things that ∘hh Ontarians ↑need to stay
192     healthy and to ↓get healthier
193 MA:(.) [two more]
194 I4:    [ may I ] ask you how soon you hope to get thee fast
195     foods or the fatty foods out of school cafeterias= do you
196     hope to have it by the new school year o[r::r]::
```

In the above transcript, the minister produces a relatively long answer (lines 176-192). Once the minister has finished the answer, and after a short pause, the minister's aide makes a quick remark (simultaneously with one of the reporters asking the next question), indicating that the minister would take two more questions (line 193). Similarly in the next transcript:

Transcript 6, Minister of Health and 15+ reporters (lines 194-201 of 227, Data Set 3)

```
194 M:  [...] well here here's my you know
195     (.) at the end of the day uh::h you can uh you can decide
196     to make that uh to make that inference from my uh from what
197     I've said (.) what I've said to you (.) is uh completely uh
198     completely uh clear
199 MA: [two more questions thanks]
200 I4: [so back to these p threes] there'll be no new p threes
201     (0.8)
```

Dealing with the press is only one of a politician's daily tasks. Although politicians are obligated to talk to the press, this does not have to occur for extended periods of time. The aides' interjections ('two more', 'two more questions please') are a way of acknowledging that reporters would like to ask more questions, but reminding them that the minister has other things to do. Having the aides rather than the politician himself 'wind down' (Clayman and Heritage, 2002a: 76) the scrum, also provides them with a way to get ministers from difficult situations. The press secretary of the OLA indicated that as part of the media training for minister and their staff, aides would be instructed on how to monitor the minister's performance, and to spot trouble signs in the questions and responses. Although no evidence of this occurs in our data, reporters were aware that this could happen, and did not appreciate the fact that ministers could escape if the reporters were getting too close to a negative event.

If a scrum is ended by a reporter, this is not accomplished through any formal markers. There are typically no farewells or thank yous at the end of a scrum, but rather the scrum simply ends with the final answer of the politician. It is instructive to compare this with the closings of news interviews, which are also characterised through an absence of ritualised farewells, but which do involve the interviewers thanking the interviewees for their participation (Clayman and Heritage 2002a: 74). These thank yous allow the interviewer to close the interview in accordance with a predetermined and fixed time frame, sometimes even cutting into the interviewee's final answer. The rigidity of scheduling with live-to-air broadcasts is not an issue with the scrum, as the completed product only involves partial segments of the scrum's entirety and as a result no marker is required to signal to the interviewee that the time for speaking has concluded.

In the scrums observed, rather than using a verbal marker (such as 'thank you') to indicate that reporters want to end a scrum, reporters would instead indicate through bodily behaviour that the questions were exhausted for today. For example, some reporters would stop their equipment and move away while the other reporters continued questioning. In particular, television reporters would often leave after two or three minutes. Schegloff and Sacks (1973) remark on such 'non-verbal' means of closing:

> [...] there may be some conversation whose closing is accomplished solely by 'non-verbal means' (as when one of the parties has become involved in a side conversation, and his erstwhile co participant seeks to depart without interrupting) (p. 323, footnote 20).

The visible behaviour of reporters (stopping equipment, closing notepads, walking away) indicates to the politician that the interview is about to end and therefore no verbal markers are necessary.[4] For example, in Transcript 1, it is apparent to

---

4   See Laurier (2008) for an analysis of how conversationalists in cafes can use 'silent yet visible ways' (174) to indicate that an ending may be immanent (e.g., pushing a coffee cup away to indicate that one has finished drinking).

all parties that the minister's answer (lines 52-53) would end the scrum, which is exhibited by reporters turning off their equipment and starting to turn away. The following scrum is also not 'formally' closed, but comes to an end with the minister's affirmative answer:

Transcript 7, Minister of Health and 15+ reporters (lines 216-222 of 222, Data Set 5)

```
215 M:  [...] when uh:h it's appropraite for her to step outside
216     that role and to (.) and to make comment and:uh we're very
217     much aligned with the direction ∘hh thet's uh:h
218     suggested in the two repo[rts]
219 I6:                          [so ] we will see something in- an
220     in sixty da[ys ]
221 M:             [yes]
222     (4.0)
223     ((reporters leave; so does the minister))
```

In this example, the Minister of Health provides a long answer (lines 199-218) to a reporter's question. The reporter produces a quick follow-up confirmation-seeking statement, which is answered succinctly by the minister (line 220). Since no further question is forthcoming and reporters start to 'pack up', the minister walks away without any explicit verbal termination of the scrum.

Although verbal closings to scrums are infrequent, that a closing was forthcoming was occasionally foreshadowed in a change of topic or questioning. Reporters can indicate that a closing was forthcoming by asking a question that is hearably slightly 'off-topic', e.g., more humorous or away from the more serious news of the day. For example, in Transcript 1; one of the reporters initiates the final topic through the utterance 'On a lighter note [...]' (line 40), before launching into a question about the minister's allegiance to one of the provinces two hockey teams, who were playing each other at the time. Although the exchange continues for a few more lines, the reporter's initial question (line 40) indicates that a closing was immanent. Similarly:

Transcript 8, Opposition Finance Critic with 15+ reporters (lines 163-170 of 191, Data Set 8)

```
163 I5: on a lighter note here (.) what's it say when a guy from
164     Ottawa squares off with a guy from Toronto and the guy from
165     Ottawa's wearing a blue suit
166     (1.0)
167 O:  (∘huhuhuhuh) ∘hh I'll tell you Dalton McGuinty::uh:::h the
168     only good decision he's made uh ∘hh since he took power was
169     to be an unabashed supporter of thee Ottawa Senators [...]
```

Again, the preface 'on a lighter note' (line 163) indicates that the formal business of the day has been fulfilled, but since the politician did not yet seem desperate to move on, there was an opportunity for a humorous topic to be pursued, which would only be of interest to a few reporters. Some reporters took this as an occasion to conclude, and either relaxed their posture or exited the scrum altogether.

Routine Nature of Scrums

The popular image of press scrums is one of an aggressive, exciting encounter between the press and a person of interest. However, this picture is based on extraordinary scrums, where the scrum itself becomes a matter of public interest. This was not often the case at the OLA, where scrums were part of the mundane, routine work of news reporters. This routineness was institutionally built in: this was the place and time where and when scrums were supposed to happen. Politicians were not surprised by the fact that reporters were waiting for them.

Much of the time, the gathered materials were also mundane to reporters. Frequently what politicians had to say was not itself the main news materials, but provided story filling, giving government reactions, opposition responses, pictures, sound bites and the like. Big announcements by the government would be handled through press conferences, which were attended by the same press corps. On rare occasions politicians would meet with individual members of the press shortly after a scrum. What was actually said in a scrum was rarely extraordinary (not a 'scoop'), but typically ended up complementing other materials (gathered through press releases, and so on). Published or broadcast news stories are often a heterogeneous construction of different materials from different sources, and the scrum contributed accordingly.

Scrums are everyday occurrences. As remarked above, this means that reporters could get straight to business and that both parties could presume a 'history known in common', since it could be expected that most people will have been present at previous press scrums. For example, in the following transcript a minister introduces his answer as a repeat of an answer that he had given already yesterday.

Transcript 9, Minister of Health and 15+ reporters, (line 142-147 of 222, Data Set5)

```
142 I7:  how come the province doesn't have a pandemic flu plan in
143      place (.) thuh federal government does local government from
144      uh::h two different (.) local cities are working on them
145      so where's the province
146 M:   wull people are working uh-I think I said yesterday Mike
```

```
147      in answer to a question that I re:ally belie::ve that
148      °hh the pandamic flu pla- flu plan is about continuous
149      improvement [...]
```

The reporter asks about the pandemic flu plan of the Province (a topic which had become relevant due to the recent SARS crisis) and mentions that both the federal government and two municipal governments have begun developing such plans. The minister, rather than answering the question directly, alludes to statements made on the previous day (in relation to the release of a government report). Similarly, in the following transcript, the minister makes reference to previous scrums.

Transcript 10, Minister of Health and 10 reporters, line (132-145 of 231, Data Set 7)

```
132 I7:  whuh ↑why do ↓you want to
133      increase the number of uh::h working poor in Ontario by uh:h
134      allowing p trees uh::h (.) cause that's the message that's
135      coming from uh:h some union leaders and u[h:h  ] ↑the
136 M:                                            [whuah]
137 I7:  pharma[cist ]s=
138 M:         [fer::]
139 I7:             =association of Ontar[io ↓and so on]
140 M:                                   [well let's be] clear
141      about a few things firstly I haven't endorsed p threes end
142      you know that very well °hh cause you've had the
143      opportunity at least five or six times to be in these scrums
144      where I've clearly said that it's my ministeral
145      colleague David Kaplan who's involved in that process [...]
```

The reporter asks a relatively heavy-handed question, which includes the presumption that the government is deliberately aiming to decrease the wages of public health employees (which is typically assumed to be the result of privatisation). The minister is quick to distance himself from the implication by reminding reporters that he has not personally endorsed privatisation (line 141) and also that it is not even his decision to make. In other words, it is not his place to speak for the government on these matters.

In these exchanges, not only do ministers refer to previous encounters with the reporters, they also can use these encounters as a defensive manoeuvre in order to attenuate the question ('I've answered this already...'). Although it is common for reporters to ask a question repeatedly (either in the same scrum or on different occasions) in order to try to get new information or possibly catch the politicians contradicting themselves, politicians use this as a way of converting a particular question into one that has already been answered. This is then an economical manner in which politicians can say that although they are aware that reporters are hoping for a 'non-standard' answer, if they continue to ask questions along these lines, they will only get repeats of the 'standard' response.

Scrums as Collaboration

There is clearly some degree of competition between different media (e.g., television versus print) and different media outlets (e.g., *Toronto Star* and *Globe and Mail*). There is a need for exclusivity in certain cases. However, not all aspects of news gathering are competitive in nature. Many of the materials through which news is assembled are available to everyone (e.g., press releases, press conferences, or public reports). The primary objective at the OLA was to secure adequate amounts of materials and although it may be beneficial to have exclusive materials, this was generally not necessary. Since what is said in scrums is available to all those who were present, scrums are characterised by a high degree of collaboration among reporters. Everyone is within hearing distance of what is said and the fact that a particular reporter asks a question does not give her or him proprietorship over the answer. Consequently, it is generally accepted that reporters would benefit by working together.

This collaboration among reporters becomes visible in a variety of ways. When discussing openings we had already remarked that reporters typically wait for other reporters to be ready before proceeding. There is also collaboration between different kinds of media. Reporters oriented to a rule of 'television people go first' and allowed them to ask the first question. The reason for this is that television people only needed small amounts of footage to air alongside a more in-depth story, and that camera operators suffered under the load of their equipment. Since television cameras are most difficult to setup, allowing them to ask the first question also almost always ensured that everyone else was ready to begin.

Reporters in the press scrum did not resemble the aggressive, guarded and individualistic stereotype (e.g. Smith 1980). 'Getting materials' was more easily achieved when each reporter oriented to the team and treated the assembly as such. This is nicely demonstrated in Transcript 1, in which lines 2-39 all centre on one particular topic (job losses). Although reporter I1 introduces the topic with the scrum's first question (line 2), it is the second reporter I2 who produces a first (line 18) and a second (line 24-25) follow-up question, before yet another reporter, I3, asks the final follow-up question (lines 29-31). What this demonstrates is that reporters are working together to explore a topic, i.e., they collaboratively pursue a line of questioning.[5] This can also be seen in the following excerpt:

---

5   Schegloff (1987: 224) notes that reporters during press conferences, in which it was the politician who nominated the next reporter who could ask a question, had to decide whether to use their turn to follow up on the preceding question-answer exchange (of another reporter) or to ask their own (prepared) question.

Transcript 11, Minister of Health and 15+ reporters (lines 16-21 of 227, Data Set 3)

```
16 M:   I'm not planning for any more p thr[ees]
17 I2:                                     [what about the  uh]
18 I3:                                     [what about Markham]
19 I2:  yeah what about Markham Stouville?
20      (0.2)
21 M:   what about it?
22      (0.2)
23 I2:  is that going on?
```

In this instance, two reporters (I2 and I3) both start to ask the next questions (lines 17 and 18). However, there is no visible competition over whom the question belongs. Once I3 has formulated his question ('what about Markham'), I2 agrees that this is a relevant question to ask ('yeah what about Markham Stouville?').

Reporters also tend to refer to themselves as a collective. In informal interviews during the fieldwork, reporters would use 'we' rather than 'I' to describe their activities (e.g., 'we like to get up close'; 'we were upset when the premier stopped doing press scrums'). Also, in one scrum, the minister's answer (that he was not planning for any more public–private partnerships) is treated by one of the reporters as surprising to all reporters (line 54), rather than as only surprising to the reporter asking the question:

Transcript 12, Minister of Health and 15 plus reporters (lines 49-57 of 227, Data Set 3)

```
49  M:  [...] I'd never rule anything in and I'd never
50      rule anything out because ∘hhhh the minister of
51      public infrastructure renewal is conduting
52      the ∘hhh conducting the review and is gonna be
53      helpng to develop those optio[ns]
54 I6:                                [we]'re just a little
55      concerned beause you were TOUTing (.) private sector
56      involvement in health care in the= in the house there
57      (0.5) just SURPRISING (.) for a lot of us
```

In sum, there is a strong communal sense of reporters in scrums, with no proprietary rights over who elicits information. The differentiation between media outlets occurs after the materials had been generated in the scrum (when materials can be 'individualised' by saying, for example, 'The Minister of Health yesterday told the *Globe*', which doesn't mention that he also told other reporters).

Conclusion

As mentioned in the introduction, most studies of media discourse focus on media *products*, such as newspaper or radio/television broadcasts. Our study is an attempt to explain the discursive practices of the *processes* through which such products are assembled. This has so far primarily been studied through ethnographic investigations – with the exception of the studies we mentioned in our introduction.

A consequence of this shift from product to process is that it brings the journalist back into the analysis, since journalistic practices could perhaps be seen as the 'missing what' of recent studies of media discourse. What we would suggest is that by understanding the questions of how media products are collected, assembled and disseminated, the understanding of the fifth estate as an institution will become more sophisticated and accurate. It is not uncommon for media operatives to accuse academics of talking past the issues or misrepresenting their practices (e.g., Ericson et al. 1987) and by taking seriously the role of reporters, editors and other practitioners of media production, this weakness can be overcome.

Press scrums are one way through which journalists gather materials for their stories. Scrums resemble other forms of media interaction in their question–answer format, but nevertheless constitute a particular speech-exchange system in which we have several questioners and only one respondent. Reporters' questions are not of one kind, but include, for example, requests for further information, clarifications, as well as probes and challenges. This reflects the different aims and purposes that reporters pursue during a scrum. Perhaps predominantly they would try to gather materials for stories-already-in-process (as, e.g., prompted through a press release). However, they would also try to 'find', or even generate, stories in the scrum, through their questioning, putting politicians in positions where they might say newsworthy things.

One way in which our study could be usefully extended would be to 'follow stories around' (to adopt the subtitle of Latour 1987), i.e., to investigate the different ways in which the materials gathered in the scrum end up in newspaper articles or radio/television broadcasts (as direct quotes, paraphrases, and so on). As we stated above, we believe this would lead to a more complete picture of both the media's function and functionality within a broader society. The process of understanding the news in completed form is understandably complimented by a comprehension of how that form came about as a collaborative effort between news makers and news reporters.

References

Anderson, D.C. and Sharrock, W.W. 1979. Biasing the news: technical issues in 'media studies'. *Sociology*, 13 (3), 367-385.

Atkinson, J.M. and Drew, P. 1979. *Order in Court: The Organization of Verbal Interaction in Judicial Settings*. London: Macmillan.

Barthélémy, M. 2003. Temporal perspectives in the practical-textual handling of a European public problem. *Social Science Information*, 42 (3), 403-430.

Bell, A. 1991. *The Language of News Media*. Oxford: Blackwell.

Billig, M. 1999a. Whose terms? whose ordinariness? rhetoric and ideology in conversation analysis. *Discourse and Society*, 10 (4), 543-558.

Billig, M. 1999b. Conversation analysis and the claims of naivety. *Discourse and Society*, 10 (4), 572-576.

Broth, M. 2008. The 'listening shot' as a collaborative practice for categorizing studio participants in a live TV-production. *Ethnographic Studies*, 10, 69-88.

Broth, M. 2009. Seeing through screens, hearing through speakers: Managing distant studio space in television control room interaction. *Journal of Pragmatics*, 41 (1), 1998-2016.

Clayman, S. and Heritage, J. 2002a. *The News Interview: Journalists and Public Figures on the Air*. Cambridge: Cambridge University Press.

Clayman, S. and Heritage, J. 2000b. Questioning presidents: journalistic deference and adversarialness in the press conferences of Eisenhower and Reagan. *Journal of Communication*, 52 (4), 749-777.

Clayman, S. and Reisner, A. 1998. Gatekeeping in action: editorial conferences and assessments of newsworthiness. *American Sociological Review*, 63 (2), 178-199.

Davies, N. 2008. *Flat Earth News*. London: Chatto and Windus.

Eglin, P. and Hester, S. 2003. *The Montreal Massacre: A Story of Membership Categorization Analysis*. Waterloo, ON: Wilfrid Laurier University Press.

Ericson, R.V., Baranek, P.M. and Chan, J.B.L. 1987. *Visualizing Deviance: A Study of News Organisation*. Milton Keynes: Open University Press.

Fairclough, N. 1995. *Media Discourse*. Arnold: London.

Fairclough, N. and Wodak, R. 1997. Critical discourse analysis, in *Discourse as Social Interaction, Volume 2 of Discourse Studies: A Multidisciplinary Introduction*, edited by T.A. van Dijk. London: Sage, 258-284.

Fishman, M. 1980. *Manufacturing the News*. Austin: University of Texas Press.

Fitzgerald, R. and Housley, W. 2002. Identity, categorization and sequential organization: the sequential and categorial flow of identity in a radio phone-in. *Discourse and Society*, 13 (5), 579-602.

Fitzgerald, R. and Housley, W. 2006. Categorisation, accounts and motives: 'letters-to-the-editor' and devolution in Wales, in *Devolution and Identity* edited by J. Wilson and K. Stapleton. Aldershot: Ashgate, 111-126.

Fowler, R. 1991. *Language in the News: Discourse and Ideology in the Press*. London: Routledge.

Garfinkel, H. 1967. *Studies in Ethnomethodology*. Englewood Cliffs, NJ: Prentice-Hall.

Glasgow University Media Group. 1976. *Bad News*. London: Routledge and Kegan Paul.

Glasgow University Media Group. 1980. *More Bad News*. London: Routledge and Kegan Paul.

Golding, P. and Elliott, P. 1979. *Making the News*. London: Longman.

Greatbatch, D. 1988. A turn-taking system for British news interviews. *Language in Society*, 17 (3), 401-430.

Greiffenhagen, C. 2008. Unpacking tasks: the fusion of new technology with instructional work. *Computer Supported Cooperative Work (CSCW)*, 17 (1), 35-62.

Greiffenhagen, C. 2009. Analysing media discourse. Forthcoming in *Doing Social Science: Evidence and Methods in Empirical Research*, edited by F. Devine and S. Heath. Basingstoke: Palgrave, 167-188.

Hall, S. 1980. Encoding/decoding, in *Culture, Media Language: Working Papers in Cultural Studies, 1972-79*, edited by S. Hall et al. London: Hutchinson, 128-138.

Hall, S. 1982. The rediscovery of 'ideology': return of the repressed in media studies, in *Culture, Society, and the Media*, edited by M. Gurevitch et al. London: Routledge, 56-90.

Heath, C. and Nicholls, G. 1997. Animated texts: Selective renditions of news stories, in *Discourse, Tools, and Reasoning: Essays on Situated Cognition*, edited by L.B. Resnick et al. Berlin: Springer, 63-86.

Heritage, J. 1985. Analyzing news interviews: aspects of the production of talk for an overhearing audience, in *Discourse and Dialogue, Volume 3 of Handbook of Discourse Analysis*, edited by T.A. van Dijk. London: Academic Press, 95-117.

Hester, S. and Fitzgerald, R. 1999. Category, predicate and contrast: some organizational features in a radio talk show, in *Media Studies: Ethnomethodological Approaches*, edited by P.L. Jalbert. Washington, DC: University Press of America, 171-193.

Housley, W. 2002. Moral discrepancy and 'fudging the issue' in a radio news interview. *Sociology*, 36 (1), 5-21.

Hutchby, I. 1996. *Confrontation Talk: Arguments, Asymmetries, and Power on Talk Radio*. Mahwah, NJ: Lawrence Erlbaum Associates.

Jaworski, A., Fitzgerald, R. and Morris, D. 2004. Radio leaks: presenting and contesting leaks in radio news broadcasts. *Journalism*, 5 (2), 183-202.

Latour, B. 1987. *Science In Action: How to Follow Scientists and Engineers through Society*. Cambridge, MA: Harvard University Press.

Laurier, E. 2008. Drinking up endings: conversational resources of the cafe. *Language and Communication*, 28 (2), 165-181.

Lee, J.R.E. 1984. Innocent victims and evil-doers. *Women's Studies International Forum*, 7 (1), 69-73.

Payne, G.C.F. 1976. Making a lesson happen: an ethnomethodological analysis, in *The Process of Schooling: A Sociological Reader*, edited by M. Hammersley and P. Woods (eds). London: Routledge, 33-40.

Sacks, H. 1992. *Lectures on Conversation* (Edited by G. Jefferson). Oxford: Blackwell.

Sacks, H., Schegloff, E.A. and Jefferson, G. 1974. A simplest systematics for the organization of turn taking in conversation. *Language*, 50 (4), 696-735.

Schegloff, E.A. 1987. Between micro and macro: Contexts and other connections, in *The Micro-Macro Link*, edited by J.C. Alexander et al. Berkeley, CA: University of California Press, 207-234.

Schegloff, E.A. 1997. Whose text? Whose context? *Discourse and Society*, 8 (2), 165-187.

Schegloff, E.A. 1999a. 'Schegloff's texts' as 'Billig's data': a critical reply. *Discourse and Society*, 10 (4), 558-572.

Schegloff, E. A. 1999b. Naiveté vs. sophistication or discipline vs. self-indulgence: a rejoinder to Billig. *Discourse and Society*, 10 (4), 577-582.

Schegloff, E.A. and Sacks, H. 1973. Opening up closings. *Semiotica*, 38 (4), 289-327.

Schenkein, J. 1971. *Some Methodological and Substantive Issues in the Analysis of Conversational Interaction*. PhD thesis, University of California, Irvine.

Schenkein, J. 1979. The radio raiders story, in *Everyday Language: Studies in Ethnomethodology*, edited by G. Psathas. New York, NY: Irvington, 187-201.

Schlesinger, P. 1978. *Putting 'Reality' Together: BBC News*. London: Constable.

Smith, A. 1980. *Goodbye Gutenberg: The Newspaper Revolution of the 1980s*. New York, NY: Oxford University Press.

Tuchman, G. 1978. *Making News: A Study in the Construction of Reality*. New York: Free Press.

Turner, R. 1972. Some formal properties of therapy talk, in *Studies in Social Interaction*, edited by D. Sudnow. New York, NY: Free Press, 367-396.

van Dijk, T.A. 1988. *News as Discourse*. Hillsdale, NJ: Lawrence Erlbaum Associates.

White, D.M. 1950. The 'gate keeper': a case study in the selection of news. *Journalism Quarterly*, 27 (3), 383-390.

Chapter 8

Styling for Hegemony: The West as an Enemy (and the Ideal) in Belarusian Television News

Marián Sloboda

Introduction

The interest in media, policy and interaction in democratic societies may naturally draw analysts' attention to highly interactive broadcast formats such as the debate, the news interview or the panel discussion, in which the public participates. However, when dealing with non-democratic settings where such interactive formats are marginal, attention to other formats or types of media discourse is pertinent in order to understand political issues and the role of the media in them. Accordingly, the aim of this chapter is to examine how political contestation and dialogue take place in the news discourse of Belarusian national television. The chapter centres on stylistic methods – particularly on the situated use of contrast, moral categorization devices and editing – for the discursive production of political accountability and responsibility for national and international relations in a non-democratic society.

Belarus and Belarusian Television

Belarus, a post-Soviet country, is often dubbed 'the last dictatorship in Europe'. Whatever the adequacy of this description is (cf Ioffe 2008, Marples 2005), the fact remains that, during his 15-year-long government, the first, and still the last, president of this country has taken the executive, legislative, and judicial powers of the state under his control. The centralized state administration directly influences and controls many spheres of social life in Belarus; the media is not an exception. The President's Office itself publishes the country's largest newspaper; other large newspapers as well as the four TV channels that broadcast nationwide – BT, ONT, Lad, and STV – are state-owned and state-controlled. The same is true of the satellite channel Belarus-TV. In addition to these Belarusian channels, several Russian channels and Euronews also enjoy popularity in Belarus. Private Belarusian channels only broadcast locally and news reporting on them is societally marginal (cf IREX 2001-2008). In 2004-2005 when the data for this chapter were gathered, news broadcasting on the four national channels was dominated by short daily news bulletins and longer evening news, which, as a rule, did not include any live interviews or live reports.

Data and Methodology

The data corpus consists of video recordings of eighteen newscasts of three national channels: BT, ONT and Lad. They mostly include the daily evening news (BT *Panorama*, ONT *Nashi novosti*, Lad *Naviny*), but also weekly newsmagazines (BT *V tsentre vnimaniya* and ONT *Kontury*). The data was recorded in October 2004 and July-August 2005, when the geopolitical category 'the West' featured prominently in the news. This was in relation to two events: (1) the October 2004 elections and referendum on a constitutional amendment which would allow the president Aleksandr Lukashenko to run for a third term; and (2) the Belarusian–Polish diplomatic conflict of Summer 2005 over a Polish minority organization in Belarus. This data was analysed using Membership Categorization Analysis, as described in Chapter 1 of this volume. The main focus of this chapter is on contrastive and moral categorization, including both personal and non-personal categories.

Interviewees' Positions

News interviews, debates, talk shows and other interactive broadcast formats provide an opportunity for members of the public to participate in media discourse. Media programmes thus become sites of interaction between different positions (views, perspectives) on various aspects of societal life and the interactive formats, where public policy is debated, are therefore considered sites of 'democracy-in-action' (Housley and Fitzgerald 2007). However, even the format as interactive as the debate can, to the contrary, serve undemocratic purposes in some countries (Zhong 2002). At the same time, there seems to be a tacit presumption in interaction-focused studies of media discourse (e.g. Clayman and Heritage 2002, Housley and Fitzgerald 2003, 2007, Hutchby 2006) that different positions are voiced by different participants in the media, a presumption which may also be culture-specific. In this section, we will thus examine how interviewees' participation and positions are produced in the news of Belarusian national television.

Extract 1 presents a news item broadcast during the 2004 referendum and election campaign.

Extract 1 (BT Panorama 14 October 2004)

(Transcripts of all extracts with video stills can be found at http://www.sloboda. cz/marian/MPI).

Displayed baseline text:

'International observers fulfil their mission at the referendum and
     parliamentary elections'

Sound:

1 PRESENTER: a number of prominent politicians and public figures,
2 from various countries of the world, are coming to Belarus
3 as observers. in order to give their own assessment of the event,
4 they want to see with their own eyes, how a serious political
5 campaign is conducted in our republic.
6 NARRATOR: she has a number of world records on her account,
7 including the women's world record in spacewalk.
8 an aviator-cosmonaut, twice awarded the Hero of the Soviet Union
9 medal, Svetlana Savitskaya, arrived to Belarus as an international
10 observer. (.) as a deputy of the Russian State Duma, she is a
11 member of the observer group, of the Union of Belarus and Russia.
12 she knows well, what parliamentary election is about. she has
13 already experienced it. and Svetlana Savitskaya's experienced eye
14 discerns right away, specific features of the serious political
15 campaign, in Belarus.
16 'SAVITSKAYA': a pre- pre-term voting is taking place now, i:t,
17 by the way, it proceeds, pro- proceeds in very different ways
18 in many countries, uh, i:n some countries, almost by post, u:h,
19 well they try even on the Internet, (.) here, uh, the legislation,
20 hh ensured a transparent, transparent mechanism of pre-term voting,
21 there's no, you know, such psychological stress, no psychological
22 pressure, no hypnotising of the voters, by gaudy posters, well by
23 the war, mm, of posters, information materials. here, thank god,
24 everything proceeds peacefully, there is information here, I see
25 people are coming and understand perfectly well, and know, who they
26 are voting for. ↑and well you know, there will always be a
27 critique. whilst, a policy of national independence, (.) that is
28 while this policy will be carried out, and while policy will be
29 carried out not in the interest of a- a small circ- capitalist
30 circle, but exactly in the interest of a majority of the
31 population. (.) the:n, president will displease the West. of
32 course, it's not pleasing. because like hungry wolves, they are
33 standing on the borders, and are ready, to rush Belarus, as well as
34 the Ukraine, although the situation in economy is much worse, than
35 in Belarus, well you see what mess is happening now in the Ukraine
36 uh: uh: in the election campaign. (.) so, because the West has
37 plunged its hands right there, you see? (that's) a strategic qu-
38 ques- question. that's a strategy! a strategic approach- well to
39 seize positions in Uk-in the Ukraine, m:: to me, frankly speaking,
40 even ju:st, well, in a, (.) moral sense I can't but envy those who

```
41 live in peaceful Belarus. let's hope tha:t, this peaceful life, (.)
42 continues in Belarus. I'd like to hope in this very much.
43 (..)
44 REPORTER'S VOICE: thank you so much.
45 'SAVITSKAYA': well, I'll move to another district ((smiles)).
```

In this extract a number of personal and non-personal categories emerge and
are then reconfigured in four stages as the news item unfolds. The first stage or
part is the presenter's opening (lines 1-5) consisting of categories ('prominent
politicians', 'public figures', 'observers'), action ('are coming to Belarus')
and reason ('in order to give their own assessment of how a serious political
campaign is conducted') (cf Thornborrow and Fitzgerald 2004).

The second part of the news item (lines 6-15) is marked by a speaker change
from presenter to narrator as well as by a different structuring of the discourse;
the narrator 'thickens' the opening story, i.e. is produced as elaborating on it (cf
Thornborrow and Fitzgerald 2004). She starts describing a person who can be
heard as an incumbent of the previously introduced personal categories and who
is there to witness ('see with their own eyes') how elections and referendum are
done in Belarus. The subsequent shots and explicit categorization of 'Svetlana
Savitskaya' as an observer and prominent politician soon confirms this.
From the viewpoint of the news production it is important that the narrator's
categorization work introduces the interviewee as an expert on elections by
attributing relevant experience and knowledge to her (lines 12f.).

Positioned this way, in the third part of the news item (lines 16-26), the
interviewee introduces a contrast between Belarus ('here') and 'some [other]
countries' based on 'voting mechanisms'. This contrastive geopolitical device
Belarus–Other Countries is then elaborated on: in Belarus, the voting mechanism
is 'transparent', without 'psychological pressure', 'war of posters' etc., resulting
in everything proceeding 'peacefully' and voters being well informed. This is
compared to 'some [other] countries', where voting is opaque ('almost by post'
and 'even on the Internet', lines 18f.) and – by way of unstated contrast to
'here' (in Belarus) – 'other countries' are ascribed psychological pressure and
an information war during elections and referenda.

A resetting of the interviewee's intonation (line 26) marks the beginning of
the final, fourth, part of the news item. This part foregrounds other categories
predicated to the geopolitical category pair Belarus–Other Countries, namely,
'the president', who makes 'the policy of national independence ... in the
interest of a majority of the population' in Belarus, and 'the West' who 'like
hungry wolves' causes 'mess' 'in the interest of a small capitalist circle' in the
Ukraine (lines 27-39).

In this news item, the category pair Belarus–Other Countries became a
prominent categorization device around which other categories were organized.
Presented as a Contrastive Device, its members ('Belarus' and 'Other Countries')
were ascribed significantly different characteristics or actions pertaining to the

same object (e.g. to 'voting mechanisms'). As we will see below, Contrastive Devices are a most active type of categorization devices used in Belarusian TV news discourse in general.

Let us examine another news item from the same newscast. The presenter opens this news item by saying: 'Belarusians have to make their choice in favour of stability. This is the opinion of a majority of the inhabitants of Moldova'. A narrator then introduces, one-by-one, four interviewees *qua* 'inhabitants of Moldova'. Extract 2 shows one of them.

Extract 2 (BT Panorama 14 October 2004)

```
Shots of a city [see Figure 8.1]
1   NARRATOR: and one more comparison. the Belarusians live better
2   than the Moldovans! this is the opinion of an inhabitant of
3   Transnistrian Bender Alla Lopatyeva. she obtained a passport
4   of our country and on the seventeenth of October she will cast
5   her vote for Belarus. as for the country in which one can live
6   with dignity.

Baseline text: 'Alla Lopatyeva, chair of the Coordination
Council of the Belarusian Communities in Moldova' [See Figure
8.2]

7   'LOPATYEVA': one immediately feels order in the republic.
8   discipline. uh::uhm cleanliness. people can freely go out at night
9   and in the evening, (.) all companies work, goods are produced,
10  demand for which exists not only at uh::: the local market,
11  but also far abroad.
```

The narrator starts this part of the news story by introducing a contrast between the living conditions of Belarusians and of Moldovans (lines 1f.). The interviewee 'thickens' the presenter's and the narrator's statement of the reason for Belarusians to 'make a choice in favour of stability' (presenter) and to 'vote for Belarus' (narrator, line 5). For a western viewer, it might be surprising to see that it is 'stability' in the sense of 'what is already there' that is made so important for Belarusian voters here and not 'change' (of the present state), a category frequently employed as positive in western politics. This unstated contrast between 'stability' and 'change' relates to the dramatic socioeconomic changes in eastern Europe after the fall of the Soviet Union which have had negative consequences for the respective societies and have lead to the restoration of the Soviet style of government in Belarus. Belarusian TV news seems oriented to this context in contrasting Belarus with post-Soviet countries in transition, such as Moldova or the Ukraine, as countries lacking stability.

Figure 8.1   Shots of a city

**Figure 8.2   Alla Lopatyeva, chair of the Coordination Council of the
Belarusian Communities in Moldova**

Both the interviewees from Extracts 1 and 2 describe Belarus as Peaceful and
Stable, a country where people live well. All the other three interviewees
representing the 'opinion of a majority of the inhabitants of Moldova' in the latter
news item as well as eleven other interviewees in the rest of the whole newscast
were shown as sharing the same position. At the same time, the newscast did not
produce any interviewee who took a different position, that is, all interviewees
were shown to share the same views. This feature is not unique to this newscast
only, but is characteristic of the data as a whole. For example, the news item in
Extract 3 features the same categorizations and devices (especially the 'Peaceful
and Stable Belarus' device), even though it was broadcast almost a year later and
concerns a different event (the Belarusian–Polish conflict over the Polish minority
in Belarus). The two interviewees of this news item are shown as if taking turns
and responding to each other (cf also the orientation of their faces in Figures 8.3
and 8.4), yet they do not take opposing views as is common in the 'western' media,
but 'thicken' the presenter's story on Belarus as a country of interethnic peace,
concord and stability (lines 1-4).

Extract 3 (BT Panorama 30 July 2005)

```
1 PRESENTER: Belarus has been, a common hospitable home
2 for many nationalities. as well as a country, which as no other
3 has the full right, to proud itself of interethnic peace and
4 concord. .hhh and they realize, but do not accept, the attempts
5 from outside to destabilize, to play a political game in Belarus. ...
```

Baseline text: 'Khizri Asadulayev, chairman of the International
Civil Association of Dagestanis "Hearth"' [see Figure 8.3]

```
27 'ASADULAYEV': concerning the state policy, and the people's
28 attitude in general, (.) uh well there's no reason to wish anything
29 better. I'd say like that. and that's indeed so. without exaggeration.
```

Baseline text: 'Oleg Kozlovskiy, the head of the civil
association "Belarusian Gypsy Diaspora"' [See Figure 8.4]

```
30 'KOZLOVSKIY': everything fine, thank God. I'd wish, that
31 it continues like this. .hh just flourishing of our Belarus.
32 and especially-, not especially of our nationality, but of all
33 the nationalities who live peacefully here, and in stability. .hh we
34 do not want revolutions either, you see. we the Gypsy nationality
35 are (for the) stability in general. we live in those countries,
36 where there's stability and well-being. (.) that's all we want.
37 we don't want wars, no revolutions. ...
```

What is interesting in the extracts above is that although mutually opposing
positions do not appear between speakers, they do appear *within* speakers'
utterances. For example, in Extract 3, the presenter produces the interviewees'
positions not as opposing each other, but as opposing 'the attempts from outside to
play a political game in Belarus', by stating that the interviewees 'do not accept'
these attempts (lines 4f.).

Styling Opposing Positions through Category Work[1]

In order to explore further how Belarusian TV news produces opposing positions
within utterances, we will examine a news item in which they are more pronounced
(Extract 4).

---

1   'Style' is understood here broadly as the integrative principle of selection,
modification and organization of means of expression (Chloupek and Nekvapil 1993).

Figure 8.3   Khizri Asadulayev, chairman of the International Civil Association of Dagestanis 'Hearth'

Figure 8.4   Oleg Kozlovskiy, the head of the civil association 'Belarusian Gypsy Diaspora'

Extract 4 (BT Panorama 26 July 2005)

DISPLAYED BASELINE TEXT:
'Poland continues to complicate bilateral relations with Belarus'
SOUND:
1 PRESENTER: Poland, continues to complicate, bilateral relations
2 with Belarus. having proposed, to a Belarusian diplomat, to leave,
3 the territory of Poland, .hh the Polish side forced Belarus, to
4 take reciprocal measures. .hh in conformity with the principles,
5 of international politics, a counsellor of the Polish embassy in
6 Minsk, Andrzej Olborski, is expelled from our country in return.
7 .hh this is already a third case that Warsaw, provoking a
8 diplomatic conflict, with our country, a:nd in spite of declaring
9 good intentions, .hh tries to infringe the interests, of
10 Belarusian citizens. .hh namely, speculations about, ethnic Poles
11 living in Belarus, .hh including the members, of the Belarusian
12 Union of Poles. have become frequent recently. we, have learnt
13 about incidents, when Warsaw threatened them, with a denial of

14 visa, for the entry into the Polish territory, in return for
15 their refusal to participate in political intrigues. .h and this
16 furthermore, I remind, concerns people, who have <u>Polish</u> roots.
17 .hh Belarus has always stood up for a:nd, is further going to, (.)
18 stand up for, the rights, of its, citizens, a:nd our country,
19 evidently, can respond, to similar visa pressure on the Belarusian
20 Poles, adequately. .hh (.) continuation of this topic, in the
21 programme Postskriptum, immediately after, .hh the news
22 programme, Panorama.

The news item in Extract 4 shows opposing positions being taken by 'Poland' (or 'Warsaw') and by 'Belarus' (or 'our country'). From the point of view of category work, oppositionality can be understood as a special case of contrast where two categories are produced doing disjunctive/alternative characterizations of, or actions to, the same object. In Extract 4, Poland is shown as carrying out activities aimed against 'Belarusian citizens' (lines 7-10, 12-15), whereas Belarus as carrying out activities in their support (lines 17-20). However, the news producer goes further than to the mere production of opposing positions. An important move takes place when members of the 'Belarusian Union of Poles' are categorized as both 'Belarusian citizens' and 'ethnic Poles'/'people who have Polish roots' (lines 9f. and 15f.). As 'Warsaw' (Poland) is also heard as belonging to the latter, the result of this categorization work is that Poland does not attack only Belarusian citizens, but, at the same time, their own people.

'Government Attacking its Own People' – a moral categorization device

'Government Attacking Its Own People' is an important moral categorization device Belarusian TV news either uses, or refrains from using. The latter strategy can be illustrated by the ONT news broadcast two days later. In this newscast, the press secretary of the Belarusian embassy in Poland states that the Union of Poles in Belarus, *qua* ethnic minority organization, should occupy itself with 'the issues of culture, education, language support and its own traditions, but when the issue acquires and is linked to a political dimension, then, of course, unpleasant moments for both bilateral relations and the organization itself arise' (ONT *Nashi novosti* 28 July 2005). Unlike on Belarusian television, details about these 'unpleasant moments' for the Union of Poles were broadcast on Euronews (Extract 5).

Extract 5 (Euronews News 29 July 2005)

1 NARRATOR: ... of Poland and Belarus, after the Belarusian police,
2 rushed the office of the non-governmental organization Union
3 of Poles in Grodno. Warsaw turned to the EU for help. the police
4 raid, reasons for which are unknown, resulted in the arrest of no

```
5  less than twenty activists of the Union of Poles. soon they were
6  released, but the police still controls the organization's office.
7  (..) they forced us to leave the building yesterday, policemen
8  tore my shirt. says a representative of the Union of Poles. (..)
9  yesterday they took from us our cars, continues another activist
10 of the organization, which represents the rights, of a four-
11 hundred-thousand minority in Belarus. (.) …
```

In contrast to the Euronews report above, Belarusian television did not mention the 'raid' by the Belarusian police on the Union of Poles. The non-inclusion of the Belarusian police raid in the Belarusian TV news is significant as it prevented the audience from hearing the raid as Belarus' attack on their own citizens, i.e. as the very same action that had been invoked earlier to condemn the Polish government and to contrast it to Belarus which 'has always stood up for the rights of its citizens' (Extract 4, lines 12-18). This categorization move enabled the whole responsibility for the conflict to be ascribed to the Polish side and to foster the omni-relevance of 'Peaceful and Stable Belarus'.

'Peaceful and Stable Belarus' as an omni-relevant device

'Omni-relevance' of a categorization device means that discourse participants demonstrably orient to it, although they are simultaneously using other categories or devices, and that they invoke it at various points of discourse sequence. Or as Sacks (1995) originally put it:

> An 'omni-relevant device' is one that is relevant to a setting via the fact that there are some activities that are known to get done in that setting, that have no special slot [in the conversational sequence], but when they are appropriate, they have priority. Where, further, it is the business of, say, some single person located via the 'omni-relevance device' to do that and the business of others located via that device, to let it get done (pp. 313f.).

Although categorial omni-relevance has been dealt with in analyses of interaction (e.g. Sacks 1995, Fitzgerald et al. 2008, McHoul and Rapley 2002), this notion can also be used in the case of non-interactive broadcasting formats. This can be demonstrated with the 'Peaceful and Stable Belarus' device. The fact that Belarusian news producers did not include anywhere in the news the Belarusian police attack on Belarusian citizens (which runs counter to the image of 'Peaceful and Stable Belarus') seems to show their orientation to this device, i.e. its omni-relevance, during the news production. Also, in Extract 1, when the interviewee reaches the point where she is speaking about the 'mess' caused by the West in the Ukraine (lines 35-37), she starts expressing envy for those who live in 'peaceful Belarus', i.e. peaceful not only during the elections (the main topic of the news item), but in general (lines 39-42). That is, when the 'Peaceful and Stable Belarus' device became contextually appropriate, it received priority. At the same time, the interviewee was not announcing as news that Belarus was peaceful and stable, but she was using the 'Peaceful and Stable Belarus' device as if it were an already available resource from a 'common stock of knowledge' (cf Fitzgerald et al. 2008: 5) in order to do something else (to express envy). In fact, it was not the interviewee but rather the news producers who used this device as omni-relevant. Namely, they did not edit the interviewee's statement about peaceful Belarus out, but, as the cut in line 39 (after the word 'Ukraine') shows, quite the opposite: they chose this statement to include it. This shows their orientation to this device. Similarly in Extract 2, the interviewee is not presented as describing or announcing how Belarus is peaceful and stable. Although in her turn alone she is doing this (lines 7-11), the news presenter and the narrator eventually contextualize her as just using this already available device to do something else (to say why she will vote for Belarus, lines 4f.). These editing practices suggest to us as viewers and analysts that the activity 'to be known to get done' (Sacks 1995) is to 'report on Belarus as "Peaceful and Stable Belarus"' and that this is an omni-relevant device here.

Extract 6 includes one or more devices that also seem to be treated/produced as omni-relevant. These are political devices which build on the 'Peaceful and Stable Belarus' device and amplify the contrast and opposition between Belarus and the West.

Extract 6 (BT Panorama 3 August 2005)

Displayed baseline text:
```
'Poland has not coped with the task of the American
     administration to stir up ethnic unrest in Belarus'
```
Sound:
```
1  PRESENTER: .hhh Poland has obviously not coped, with the USA's
2  task, to create an image of Belarus as a country, in which human
3  rights are violated. having observed the Polish government's
4  unsuccessful attempts, to stir up an ethnic conflict in Belarus,
5  the State Department of the USA has not resisted. (.) in its
6  absurdity in assessing the Belarusian situation, the State
7  Department again surpasses itself. this time, we cannot but
8  smile. from over the ocean, they call upon Minsk, to respect the
9  rights of the Belarusian citizens. .hhh this evidently means,
10 that in interfering in the internal affairs of sovereign Belarus,
11 and in trying to show the Belarusians how exactly they should
12 live, the United States respect the rights, of our citizens. (.)
13 NARRATOR: as a true teacher in front of a confused pupil, USA
14 sets Poland, on the right path. these words should be delivered
15 to the Poles on camera. our western neighbour, has not managed to
16 stir up the situation on the border. and, the elder brother, has
```

17 to intervene. (.) it showed up that the Americans. and not the
18 Poles on both sides of the border, understand the situation
19 better. one can see it better from over the ocean. it will not come
20 as a surprise, if after the State Department waves the flag, the
21 democratic government of Poland, plunges into inventing provocations,
22 undermining good neighbourly relations, with doubled force. after
23 all, an order for anti-Belarusian rhetoric, has already been placed.
24 and evidently, paid for. it is not surprising, that also Europe, which
25 ever more rarely manages to assert, its own interests, played the
26 second part with the Americans. the European Union, with a <u>profound</u>
27 concern, called upon Belarus to reconsider, its policy, towards,
28 ethnic communities. if this means, that the Belarusian government
29 has to <u>abandon</u> the policy of <u>tolerance</u>, and to stop providing
30 help to ethnic diasporas, our country, will definitely not comply.
31 the foreign-policy department, of our country, has condemned today
32 the USA's and EU's attempt to play an inter-ethnic game, on the
33 basis of the policy of double standards. Belarus does not violate
34 any single commitment, within the OSCE. and will <u>not</u> accept,
35 the rude interference, in the internal affairs, of a sovereign
36 country. states the announcement of the MFA's press-service. on
37 the other hand, stirring up inter-ethnic discord, contradicts the
38 policy of good neighbourly relations. which the EU declares. all
39 declarations remain, only on paper. at the same time, EU
40 officials, shut their eyes, to ethnic intolerance, <u>within</u> the
41 European Union. especially in its <u>new</u> members. it is always
42 easier to make use of any far-fetched pretence to exert pressure
43 on Belarus, than to solve one's own internal problems. anyway, a
44 a double standard is double, precisely to slander others, and
45 to look, white and fluffy. with a host of ethnic problems, behind
46 one's own, back.

With respect to omni-relevance, the passage in lines 26-30 is notable, where
the EU's political action ('calling upon Belarus to reconsider its policy towards
ethnic communities') is rejected as based on an incorrect assumption (such as:
something is wrong with Belarus' policy towards ethnic minorities). The 'policy
of tolerance' and 'providing help to ethnic diasporas' (a device which we can
call 'Good Ethnic Policy') is introduced instead. However, it is not announced
as news, but styled as retrieved from a 'common stock of knowledge' about
Belarus, as an already available, self-evident, device.

The use of omni-relevance and moral discrepancy for downgrading

This use of the 'Good Ethnic Policy' device – as well as of the 'Peaceful and Stable
Belarus' device discussed above – as omni-relevant allows opposing positions to be

discredited and disqualified explicitly. This is done by using several categorization devices, particularly the 'Moral Discrepancy' device. 'Moral Discrepancy' is a device for producing a normative breach by virtue of the fact that one of paired categories does not follow the other, e.g., when a declared intention is not followed by a normatively expected action, or when blame is not followed by punishment (Housley 2002, Housley and Fitzgerald 2003, this volume). The importance of this device for categorization work lies in the fact that, when an ascription of 'Moral Discrepancy' is successful, the resulting normative breach becomes a resource for ascribing further relevant categories, e.g. untrustworthiness, incompetence, lack of political skill or other attributes, to those responsible for this breach (Housley and Fitzgerald 2003, 4.1).

Extract 6 shows that 'Moral Discrepancy' can be used to produce such a normative breach not only when one of paired categories does not follow the other, but also when one of paired categories does follow the other, in spite of the fact that it 'should not'. In Extract 6, the presenter ascribes moral discrepancy to the US: they call upon 'Minsk' (Belarus) to 'respect the rights of the Belarusian citizens', but 'in trying to show the Belarusians how exactly they should live', the US themselves, as the presenter says ironically, do not respect these rights (lines 8-12). This discrepancy then becomes a resource or reason to meta-categorize the USA's categorization of Belarus ('a country in which human rights are violated', lines 2f.) as 'absurd' and the USA's action as an 'interference in the internal affairs of sovereign Belarus' (lines 5-10). A 'Moral Discrepancy' device is used one more time in this extract. Namely, 'Europe' (EU) is ascribed the use of 'double standards' of ethnic minority rights: it applies strict ones to Belarus, while overlooking ethnic problems 'behind one's back' (lines 39ff.). Because of this discrepant behaviour, the EU is not morally entitled to do such things as 'to call upon Belarus to reconsider its policy towards ethnic communities' (lines 26-28).

Other downgrading methods used against opponents

There are more devices in Extract 6 that downgrade the image and political competence of the three opponents of Belarus – the USA, the EU and Poland. The 'Geographical Distance' device is used with the USA, namely, it is not possible to assess correctly and to understand the situation in Belarus 'from over the ocean' (lines 17-19). General incompetence to assert its own interests politically downgrades 'Europe' (lines 24f.). Finally, Poland has been shown as a venal, immoral political actor, after the USA–Poland relationship was categorized as a relationship between the one who gave orders and money and the one who accepted them and did the job (lines 22f). The Belarusian Ministry of Foreign Affairs (MFA), in contrast, is the only political actor self-evidently legitimized to judge the situation (lines 30-36).

The disqualification of a policy carried out for money (the Venal Politics device) only featured briefly in this news item with 'Poland'. This topic was 'thickened' the next day by presenting 'facts that testify' that 'Poland has become one of the main bridgeheads of the West for interference in the internal affairs of Belarus', and that 'funds are established or activated' for this purpose (BT *Panorama* 4 August 2005). Legitimate political action is 'defined' here as a matter of creed and not of money – 'venal politics' (*prodazhnaya politika*) and 'venal politicians' (*prodazhnye politiki*) are morally disqualified. Belarusian TV news recursively applies this categorization to 'the opposition', thus disqualifying not only Poland but also the Belarusian opposition from legitimate political activities.

Category split and contrast as upgrading methods

An important step in the reporting on the Belarusian–Polish conflict came about when the category 'West' was split into 'the government' and 'the citizens'. This split became prominent when the TV news started to produce evidence that 'Polish citizens' expressed 'disapproval of their government's policy' and formulated 'support for the Belarusian government' (BT *Panorama* 4 August 2005). After Poland and the EU have become USA's allies (as in Extract 6 above), it is now Belarus which acquires allies among the western citizens.[2] Moreover, the news presented western citizens as being maltreated by their own governments. This move not only further strengthened the alliance between the western citizens and Belarus, but also made relevant the category 'government' within the 'Belarus' device and enabled to highlight the contrastingly good, caring approach of the Belarusian government to its citizens (cf Extract 3, lines 27-29; Extract 4, lines 17-20; Extract 6, lines 28-30). This categorization work thus allowed the practical purpose of the embellishment, legitimization and promotion of the Belarusian government's, and especially the president's, home policy. With respect to the showing of the West and 'the opposition' as inimical, incompetent, immoral and hence illegitimate political actors, it was also an act of their exclusion leading to the hegemony of the other side – of the current Belarusian president and his government – over any political activity in Belarus.

Styling Dialogue between Opposing Positions

The categorization work described above is oriented to 'external' hegemony in the political life outside the news discourse. The stylistics of opposing positions, however, also raises the question of what is their relationship inside the news discourse itself, i.e. how the dialogue between them looks like.

---

2   On recruiting allies through categorization, see also Leudar et al. (2004), Leudar and Nekvapil (2007).

Dialogue in media dialogical networks

As shown above, the selection and use of categories by news presenters, narrators and interviewees – as produced in the Belarusian news discourse – is in unison. To find opposing views, we had to abandon the dialogue in the sense of an exchange between two speakers in *hic et nunc* face-to-face interaction. Dialogue in the media can also take place even if its turns are distributed in time and space across several texts or discourse events, for example in a media dialogical network (Leudar and Nekvapil 2004, 2007, Nekvapil and Leudar 2002). Media dialogical networks concern the fact that media speakers/writers refer to what has been said or written elsewhere, or address a person who is absent from the present discursive event. It is this distributed form of dialogue that contains opposing voices in Belarusian TV news. Leudar and Nekvapil (2004) suggest that media dialogical networks are characteristic of societies in which public participation and debate are an important part of political culture (p. 264). The case of Belarusian TV news does not support this suggestion, since the data from Belarus with a different political culture has shown that explicit inter-textual references and orientation to past (or future) statements play an important part in structuring the news discourse (cf Extract 4 or 6). On the other hand, however, the character of media dialogical networks in Belarusian TV news differs from that described by Leudar and Nekvapil. In Belarusian TV news discourse, it is often not clear what statement or action the speaker is exactly responding to. For example, the intensive argumentation about good inter-ethnic relations in Belarus, as in Extract 3, was introduced as a response to something, but the initial action to which the news responded was not clearly recognizable at that moment: which action(s) does the phrase 'attempts from outside to play a political game' (lines 4f.) precisely refer to?[3] Constantly unavailable to the viewers was the action that initiated the proliferation of argumentation about the democratic character of the Belarusian 2004 referendum (had anyone disputed it?). This phenomenon of obscured or missing first parts of sequences in media dialogical networks relates to the overall style Belarusian television uses to produce opposing views.

Dialogue within utterances

As shown above, Belarusian TV news speakers, as a rule, advocate categorizations attributed to 'Belarus' and challenge those attributed to the 'West', creating thus a dialogue between them as between two opposing positions. 'Dialogue' is often understood only as an exchange between two speakers. However, our data invites us to use Bakhtin's (1963) concept of dialogue – a dialogue which takes place

---

3   Only if we also saw the news report on Euronews the day before (Extract 5), we would be able to infer that the Belarusian TV's response related to the fact that the Polish government turned to the EU for help in connection with the Belarusian police attack on the Polish minority organization.

between different 'voices', i.e. positions, evaluations, intentions or views, and not necessarily only between two speakers. In fact, a single utterance (discourse) is a site of micro-dialogue between the author's and another's 'voice'. The latter is not merely taken into account by the author, but is directly present in the authorial discourse and 'refracted' by it. Vološinov (1929) distinguishes two basic styles of representation (refraction) of another's 'voice' in authorial discourse: the 'linear' (or sequential) style consists of separating another's 'voice' from its authorial framing, in constructing clear-cut boundaries between the two, and ordering them linearly (sequentially) one after another. On the other hand, the 'pictorial' style is characterized by obliterating borders between the two 'voices', by infiltration and dispersion of another's 'voice' in the authorial discourse (Vološinov 1929: 142).

In TV news discourse, the author (news producer) produces others' 'voices' by means of editing, audio-video alignment, naming their physical voice or image, as well as categorization. To illustrate this point we can use Extract 2. The narrator's statement 'the Belarusians live better than the Moldovans' (lines 1f.) is explicitly attributed to another person ('this is the opinion of Alla Lopatyeva', lines 2f.), but the physical voice belongs to the narrator and the wording to the author (news producer). Later (in lines 7-11), in contrast, the 'voice' of Alla Lopatyeva is inserted in the TV news item 'linearly', i.e., separated from the preceding narrator's speech by the switch to Alla Lopatyeva's physical voice and synchronized with displaying her face (see Figure 8.2). In this latter part of the news item (lines 7-11), Alla Lopatyeva's 'voice' is stylistically less subjugated than in the former (lines 1-6).

Suppression of opposing 'voices'

A common feature of the Belarusian data is that the presenters and narrators position themselves as members of the category collection 'Belarus' – being on the Belarus' side, they speak on its behalf (Extract 4, in which the news presenter advocates Belarus arguing against Poland, is an exemplary case). Since this self-positioning equates the authorial position with the Belarus' position, the West becomes the Other, whose 'voice' is stylistically subjugated to the authorial discourse. We have seen this in the extracts above; however, a more striking example is a news item about the chairperson of the Union of Poles, Anżelika Borys (BT *Panorama* 30 July 2005), which showed her persona as a greedy and immoral climber who engages in 'dirty political games' against her country (Belarus) which she 'fiercely hates'. In this almost four-minute-long news item, Anżelika Borys was not given the chance to defend herself or express any position at all. She was not shown as a subject but a mere object of the news. Generally, representatives of those countries and organizations which are shown as accountable for 'anti-Belarusian' and other 'immoral' activities do not speak for themselves, are not given their own physical voice in Belarusian TV news.

Stylistic suppression of opposing 'voices' means producing hegemony. As Blommaert (2003) notes:

Hegemony may be what it is because there is a real price to be paid for being anti-hegemonic. The price may be that one is not understood, not heard, not recognised as a subject, but it may also be that one is ostracised, exiled, killed or jailed, made unemployable, or declared insane (p. 167).

This is the case of the 'voices' opposing the Belarusian government. They are not recognized as subjects of TV news (and outside the TV discourse, members of 'the opposition' are also made unemployable and jailed).

Promotion of the authorial 'voice'

In addition to suppressing others' opposing 'voices', promotion of the dominant authorial 'voice' also occurred. This is the case in Extract 7 from a report about the multi-religious town of Iwye, where the reporter posed a leading question (line 3). The interviewee provided a clearly 'preferred' answer[4] (see lines 4-6) which did not oppose but supported the authorial framing story that 'different peoples and world religions peacefully coexist on Belarusian soil'. However, as a rule, interviewers' questions are edited out in Belarusian TV news, so the extent to which Belarusian reporters use leading questions cannot be determined on the basis of the news discourse data alone.

Extract 7 (BT Panorama 14 October 2004)

```
1    'TATAR MUSLIM': we know our faith, we pray in our faith,
2    respect God, (      ).
3    REPORTER: you surely respect other confessions [too, don't you?
4    'TATAR MUSLIM':                                [of course! of
5    course! sure! we are happy, glad that people go even to the
6    Orthodox church, the Catholic churches,
```

Complementarily to the 'preferred' interviewees' responses which are in line with the position of presenters, narrators and reporters, also interviewees' hesitations to express an alternative view seem to contribute to the hegemonic practices of Belarusian TV news. This is suggested by 'dispreferred' designs of responses expressing alternative views. This point is elaborated upon below, however, at this moment it can be summed up that the Belarusian TV news produces hegemony within the news discourse through stylistic subjugation of opposing 'voices'. Moreover, the data suggests that the hegemony may also be stimulated by reporters' leading questions and by interviewees' hesitation

---

4 'Preferred' relates to the answer's design and delivery: it is a quick and direct response completing the initiating move without delay, hedges, pauses or similar phenomena which are characteristic of 'dispreferred' responses (cf Schegloff 2007).

to express views on television that are alternative or inconsistent with the dominant discourse.[5]

Styling Alternative Views as Non-Oppositional

Despite all the intensive category work against the views opposing the Belarusian government, the data contains less subjugated traces of alternative views concerning the West, particularly 'Europe'. For example, in a news item on a statue of Frantsisk Skaryna, 'the great Belarusian enlightener' of the 16th century, the narrator categorized Skaryna's great legacy as the *'European* conception of the human being' (BT *Panorama* 26 July 2005). As another example, the effective work of Minsk shop-assistants whose motto is 'to create pleasant conditions, to be able to demonstrate the product and to be always polite' was referred to as 'the *European* organization of business' (Lad *Naviny* 31 July 2005). Such predicates of Europe or the West in general as an ideal or model of economy, standards of living, culture and even democracy are, nevertheless, not 'thickened' in the news discourse and are rather scarce (only five occurrences in the recorded data).

Extract 8 shows an exceptionally extensive expression of an alternative view which does not feature 'Europe' or the 'West', but runs counter to the categorization of Belarus as an economically 'flourishing' country (the Flourishing Belarus device; cf Extract 2; Extract 3, line 31).

Extract 8 (ONT Nashi novosti 28 July 2005)

Displayed baseline text:
```
'Valentin Gurinovich, General Director of MAZ [the biggest
    truck producer in Belarus]'
```
Sound:
```
1     'GURINOVICH': there have appeared new cars from China. (.)
2     which, (.) it must be said, (.) surpass. today. our cars, in
3     terms of quality, .hh and in::: uh::: the durability of their
4     design, .hh well, they have su- sur- surpassed in t- us today
5     in technology already, (.) (well) and h- of course, it's very
6     difficult to compete with them.
7     NARRATOR: if we increase the rates of growth, the company
8     director says, then we will be facing the problem of sale
```

---

5   The ways of speaking on television shared in Belarusian society deserve further examination. Essays on Belarusian culture highlight 'Eurasian ideology', a form of collectivism in Soviet society (Florovskiy 1928), as a characteristic feature of Belarusian culture (Kuvayev 2006). It includes a high level of society members' orthopraxy in the public sphere, including the media.

```
9     permanently. the company's rates of growth are set by
10    the government. …
11    'GURINOVICH': I am obliged, as the director, to stick to the plan
12    on the one hand, (.) on the other hand, I am responsible for
13    the present work team, I am responsible for, .hh uh timely salary
14    payments, and if we s- produce and store the production,
15    in warehouses, the:n the company will not subsist long. …
16    NARRATOR: … virtually all producers of domestic machinery
17    and many other leading companies of other industries are
18    in such situation …
```

Although the director of the company states that their (Belarusian) products are uncompetitive, his first turn is tempered through 'dispreferred' design (pauses, hesitation sounds, recycled starts, discontinuous intonation), which suggests that the Flourishing Belarus device may be functioning as omni-relevant during the interview. A later fluent 'thickening' of the story by the narrator (lines 15-17) can be heard as a devastating critique of the government's economic policy. However, such episodic occurrences of alternative views do not seem to threaten the integrity of the dominant discourse. In Belarus, alternative views already exist in informal private communication, in what Vološinov (1929) terms the 'daily-life' ('behavioural') ideology, but their styling does not corrode the official, 'established', ideology. Namely, *alternative* views are not produced in Belarusian TV news as *opposing* views which would be in dialogue with the dominant view: they appear non-contrastively in separate news items, are not part of media dialogical networks, are scarce, and their design is minimized and tempering. In this way, the Belarusian TV news stylistics produces hegemony of the Belarusian government as its sociopolitical domination through discursive coercion and simulated consent.

Conclusion

Belarusian TV news discourse shows interviewees as sharing the same positions with each other as well as with news presenters and narrators. In this situation, it is seen to be suitable to understand 'dialogue' not as an interaction between two speakers, but between two contrasting positions. These can be encarnalized in two different speakers in social interaction, but can also be present within the utterance of a single speaker.

The latter is the case in Belarusian TV news which positions its speakers, especially presenters and narrators, as spokespersons of Belarus engaged in dialogue with other 'voices', such as those of the West and of 'the opposition'. These are not represented 'linearly', i.e., the physical voices, images and categorizations of members of these two categories are not inserted into the news discourse as they are, but 'pictorially', when the author (news producer) stylistically subjugates their physical voices, images and categorizations or edits them out altogether. As a result, the news discourse is one-directional, 'internally' hegemonic.

A most significant means of dialogue-building in this news is the contrasting of categories. Discursive representations of the two events include three main contrasts. The first is between Belarus as a country of peacefulness, stability and legitimate public policy, and the West as an inimical capital-driven aggressor with internal problems and moral defects. These polarizing categorizations correspond to what Wasburn and Burke (1997) describe as the 'cold-war news frame'. Thus, the Belarusian TV news producers have drawn on a cultural resource already available to them and their Belarusian viewers since Soviet times. Secondly, the contrast between Belarus and the West is recursively applied to the relationship between 'Belarus' and 'the opposition', the latter being produced as the weak enemy within, sold out to the strong enemy without (the West). A former Belarusian politician Pyatro Sadowski notes that this strategy resembles the Nazi propaganda rhetoric on the Doppelgänger (double) of the Urfeind (primordial enemy) (Sečkař et al. 2006: 9). This Double Enemy device, as well as some other devices presented in this chapter, were also amply used in East European communist media (cf Fidelius 1998, Pöppel 2007). The third contrast relates to the splitting up of the West into 'government' and 'citizens'. After producing the western citizens as Belarus' allies, the immoral western governments became a Contrastive Device for the embellishment, legitimization and promotion of the Belarus' president before the 2006 presidential election. These three category contrasts aim at 'external' hegemony – suppression of political opposition beyond the confines of the news discourse.

The analysis has suggested that categorial omni-relevance is another method of producing hegemony, namely, through producing/simulating certain knowledge as consensually shared by participants in the media communication. The 'omni-relevant categorization device' in TV news discourse of non-interactive format can be understood as a device which the news producer gives priority to when it becomes appropriate and invokes it, styled as an already available piece of shared knowledge, at various points in the news discourse. With such a device the news producer simulates some activities (such as reporting on the attributes of a 'Peaceful and Stable Belarus') as being known to be done in the TV news setting. Other participants, such as interviewees, are made (edited) to let these activities be done in the news discourse, or – as preferred/disprefferred designs of their responses suggest – they themselves let them be done when interviewed for television.

Whereas the focus on interactive broadcast formats of western media can suffice to 'illustrate and demonstrate how these settings can be understood to organize and present activities associated with the dissemination of information, public scrutiny, and accountability within democratic social forms' (Housley and Fitzgerald 2007: 189), this is not so in the case of Belarusian national television. Interactive broadcast formats are marginal there, and as we have seen above, contestation and opposition against the governmental policy are stylistically subjugated or excluded from the news. Bakhtin's conceptualization of discourse as a dialogue between different social positions proved to be useful for the analysis of Belarusian data in that it posed the general question of how news producers construct authorial vs. non-authorial views and the persons who take them.

Acknowledgements

I am grateful to my colleagues from Charles University, Prague, for discussions about the data and topic. The research for this chapter was supported by grant MSM002160828 of the Ministry of Education, Youth and Sports of the Czech Republic.

References

Bakhtin, M.M. 1963. *Проблемы поэтики Достоевского* [Problems of Dostoevsky's Poetics]. Moscow: Sovetskii pisatel.

Blommaert, J. 2005. *Discourse: A Critical Introduction*. Cambridge: Cambridge University Press.

Chloupek, J. and Nekvapil, J. 1993. *Studies in Functional Stylistics*. Amsterdam, Philadelphia, PA: John Benjamins.

Fidelius, P. 1998. *Řeč komunistické moci* [The Language of the Communist Power]. Praha: Triáda.

Fitzgerald, R., Housley, W. and Butler, C. 2008. Omni-relevance and interactional context. *Cardiff School of Social Sciences Working Paper 109* [Online]. http://www.cardiff.ac.uk/socsi/research/publications/workingpapers/paper-109.html.

Florovsky, G.V. 1928. Евразийский соблазн [The Eurasian temptation]. *Современные записки [Current Notes]*, 34, 312-346.

Housley, W. 2002. Moral discrepancy and 'fudging the issue' in a radio news interview. *Sociology*, 36 (1), 5-21.

Housley, W. and Fitzgerald, R. 2003. Moral discrepancy and political discourse: Accountability and the allocation of blame in a political news interview. *Sociological Research Online* [Online], 8 (2). http://www.socresonline.org.uk/8/2/housley.html.

Housley, W. and Fitzgerald, R. 2007. Categorisation, interaction, policy, and debate. *Critical Discourse Studies*, 4 (2), 187-206.

Hutchby, I. 2006. *Media Talk: Conversation Analysis and the Study of Broadcasting*. Maidenhead: Open University Press.

Ioffe, G. 2008. *Understanding Belarus and How Western Foreign Policy Misses the Mark*. Lanham, MD: Rowman & Littlefield Publishers.

IREX 2001-2008. *Media Sustainability Index 2001-2008: Development of Sustainable Independent Media in Europe and Eurasia: Belarus* [Online]. Available at: http://www.irex.org/programs/MSI_EUR/index.asp.

Kuvayev, A. 2006. Коммунизм и образование [Communism and education]. *Белорусы и рынок [Belarusians and the Market*, 4 and 18 September. Also available online at: http://www.br.minsk.by.

Leudar, I. and Nekvapil, J. 2004. Media dialogical networks and political argumentation. *Journal of Language and Politics*, 3 (2), 247-266.

Leudar, I. and Nekvapil, J. 2007. The war on terror and Muslim Briton's safety: A week in the life of a dialogical network. *Ethnographic Studies*, 9, 44-62.

Leudar, I., Marsland, V. and Nekvapil, J. 2004. On membership categorisation: 'Us', 'them' and 'doing violence' in political discourse. *Discourse and Society*, 15 (2 and 3), 243-266.

Marples, D. 2005. Europe's last dictatorship: The roots and perspectives of authoritarianism in 'White Russia'. *Europe-Asia Studies*, 57 (6), 895-908.

McHoul, A. and Rapley, M. 2002. 'Should we make a start then?': A strange case of (delayed) client-initiated psychological assessment. *Research on Language and Social Interaction*, 35 (1), 73-91.

Nekvapil, J. and Leudar, I. 2002. On dialogical networks: Arguments about the migration law in Czech mass media in 1993, in *Language, Interaction and National Identity: Studies in the Social Organisation of National Identity in Talk-in-Interaction*, edited by S. Hester and W. Housley. Aldershot: Ashgate, 60-101.

Pöppel, L. 2007. *The Rhetoric of 'Pravda' Editorials: A Diachronic Study of a Political Genre*. [Online]. Stockholm: University of Stockholm. Available at: http://urn.kb.se/resolve?urn=urn:nbn:se:su:diva-6765.

Sacks, H. 1995. *Lectures on Conversation*, edited by G. Jefferson. Oxford: Blackwell.

Schegloff, E.A. 2007. *Sequence Organization in Interaction: A Primer in Conversation Analysis I*. Cambridge: Cambridge University Press.

Sečkař, M. et al. 2006. Bez naděje a přece doufám: Otazníky a dilemata běloruské demokratické opozice [Without prospect I still hope: Questions and dilemmas of the Belarusian democratic opposition]. *Rozrazil*, 4, 3-19. Also available online at: http://www.vetrnemlyny.cz/rozrazil/index. php?action=archiv [accessed: 15 March 2009].

Thornborrow, J. and Fitzgerald, R. 2004. Storying the news through category, action, and reason. *The Communication Review*, 7 (4), 345-352.

Vološinov, V.N. 1929. *Марксизм и философия языка*. Ленинград: Прибой. [English translation: 1986. *Marxism and the Philosophy of Language*. Cambridge, London: Harvard University Press.]

Wasburn, P.C. and Burke, B.R. 1997. The symbolic construction of Russia and the United States on Russian national television. *The Sociological Quarterly*, 38 (4), 669-686.

Zhong, Y. 2002. Debating with muzzled mouths: a case analysis of how control works in a Chinese television debate used for educating youths. *Media, Culture and Society*, 24 (1), 27-47.

Chapter 9

Scandal and Dialogical Network: What Does Morality Do to Politics? About the Islamic Headscarf within the Egyptian Parliament

Baudouin Dupret, Enrique Klaus and Jean-Noël Ferrié

Introduction

This chapter aims to analyse the mechanisms specific to the birth, the swelling and the dying out of the particular public phenomenon of the scandal, as it can be observed within an Egyptian environment. Whilst normative assessments are made routinely, when aired in the public arena, these evaluations can create or reinforce reputations when positive, or undermine credibility when negative. In the public arena, the media constitute a means through which judgements concerning reputation can amplify and take the dimension of a scandal. Moreover, we recently examined how, together with the media, the Egyptian People's Assembly, the lower chamber of the Egyptian Parliament, can also be part of the broader dialogical network of a scandal, in this case ignited by a minister's statement, in what has been called the 'Fârûq Husnî case' (Klaus, Dupret and Ferrié 2008). In this chapter, we build on this research through an examination of the scandal as a dialogical network, analysed through its sequential organization and category work involving the protagonists and the audiences implicated in the unfolding of a news item of this type, which transformed into a scandal and even a public cause.

We proceed in three steps. First, we analyse the ordinary mechanisms of reputation and its breaches. We observe, in our material, how the structures of social and institutional life, like politeness, the protection of appearances, face preservation, but also their trial, like insults, humiliation and discredit, are achieved in action, through intertwined language games. Second, we describe how the mechanisms of ordinary reputation can be circumstantially mobilized to sustain, amplify and give credit to accusations and therefore contribute to a generalization process giving to a singular blame the generic status of a scandal. Third, we scrutinize the functioning of a phenomenon which, although it does not exhaust the scope of all possible modes of the unfolding of scandals, constitutes a recurring and important figure: the moral over-investment of politics. We conclude by describing how questions related to moral relevance can be treated as such by members, but can also aim, without using explicit terms, at objectives belonging to the political repertoire.

This affair has its starting point with the statement the Egyptian Minister of Culture Fârûq Husnî made to the *al-Misrî al-Yawm* newspaper on 16 November 2006, in which he presented the headscarf as a sign of the regression of Egyptian society. This statement provoked a controversy, with opposing protagonists coming from political, religious and artistic milieus. Shortly afterwards, it entered the precinct of the People's Assembly which was beginning its annual session. The parliamentary debate proved fierce. Within a couple of days, the press had amplified accounts of both the debate and diverse personalities' stakeouts. Without ever officially apologizing, the Minister proposed a conciliatory solution consisting in the creation of a religious commission at the Ministry of Culture. Little by little, the crisis dried up and, by mid-December, it was almost forgotten.

Good Press, Bad Press: Reputation in the Context of the Media and the Parliament

While potentially containing intimate elements of a biography, reputation nevertheless remains a thoroughly public phenomenon. Reputation is with regard to the tribunal of opinion what investigation is to the judicial court of justice. It is a kind of presumption about somebody else's identity with regard to a virtual public. Identity, in an interactional perspective, is the outcome of ascriptions and claims of ontological qualities ('I am', 'you are', 's/he is'), a game of being and seeming, a 'face' game, which is the object of constant negotiations. Pragmatic linguistics, concerned with this issue in situations of co-presence, treated 'face' as part of a politeness model (Brown and Levinson 1987). In the turmoil of social relations, people strive to preserve their face but in doing so they may threaten the other's face (face-threatening acts, FTA). Whilst for the most part face work

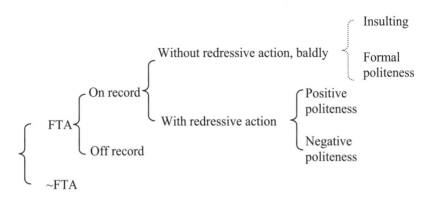

Figure 9.1   Brown and Levinson Model

involves mutual collaboration in the service of politeness, it can also have negative effects, although threatening, preserving and affecting face can still be seen as collaborative achievements. Brown and Levinson (1987: 69) summarize face-threatening strategies in Figure 9.1.

Figure 9.1 describes a situation where something threatens somebody else's face. One can choose to act in an implicit way, which has the benefit of not exposing oneself to the menace of discredit. One can also choose to act in an explicit way, in which case one might wish eventually to attenuate the damaging consequences for the other person or, on the contrary, not to care and to act in a blunt uncompromising way. If preserving someone else's face is at stake, one can also act so as to offer him/her a way out or not to make him/her risk ostracism. It seems to us that the Brown and Levinson model is excessively idealistic in omitting to consider situations where threatening someone else's face is a goal in itself, in which case insulting may be done in a more subtle manner and involve adopting a façade of politeness (stippled brackets in the figure). Such a strategy aims at maximizing discredit while preserving self-esteem; however, it may be more degrading for the formulator than for the addressee.

Although the Brown and Levinson model applies to face-to-face situations, it should not be discarded in situations where participants in the exchange are not physically gathered. Conversation analysis considers talk exchanges within a conversation as many speech-turns which are articulated to one another and therefore must be analysed in a sequential manner. The notion of speech-turns must be understood, in its most ordinary sense, as a statement formulated by one co-present participant responding to a preceding participant. The idea of a dialogical network (Nekvapil and Leudar 2002, Leudar and Nekvapil 2007, Leudar, Marsland and Nekvapil 2004) consists in extending the speech-turn system beyond situations of co-presence to all mediated exchanges. In other words, the parties to the exchange may not be physically gathered. Hence, the notion of a dialogical network allows stressing the networking of occurrences (press conferences, stakeouts, interviews) distant in time and space, mediatized and connected to each other thematically, interactively and argumentatively. We observe, through the analysis of our data on the Fârûq Husnî affair, in the press and in the parliamentary records, that the face-threatening and preserving mechanisms of the Brown and Levinson model remain effective in this type of network and can be applied to interactions separated in time and space.

The interlinked dialogical network of the affair that we concentrate on is rapidly set against the moral background of the Minister of Culture's reputation. This background is made up of biographical elements related either to his sexual intimacy or to the performance of his function. Even before the parliamentary session, the alleged homosexuality of the Minister can be read between the lines in the press, as in this statement by Hamdî Hasan: 'The Minister's ideas and his many provocative behaviours are something that his Lord only will judge' (*Nahdat Misr*, 18 November 2006). When suggesting Fârûq Husnî's indecency, his detractors open the possibility for inferential judgements stemming from the disjunctive categorial mechanism opposing a minister (whose perversity is 'well known') and the defenders of Islam (whose virtue is 'above suspicion'). The rationale of the accusation shows that it is not necessary to enter into the details of the reprobation in order to allow the latter to express itself forcefully. Moreover, the allusive character of a categorization and the amplitude of the inferential repertoire it opens prove most efficient. It is even more damaging for the stigmatized person that inferences to be drawn against a moral background discretely sketched can grow at the mercy of random communicational dynamics.

It is the possibility that his reputation as a homosexual affects his ministerial function that we can observe at the initial stage of this affair. So, Hamdî Hasan, continuing his declaration to *Nahdat Misr* (18 November 2006), adds: 'That he decides to make the Ministry of Culture adopt these principles and viewpoints, through his call to respectful work dedicated to keeping an open mind, this is what we oppose vigorously'. In this statement, it is the categorial pair of public–private which is mobilized to ground the Minister's illegitimacy and which then extends to his ministerial activity. This pair is embedded in an argumentative context aiming at separating the repertoires of action. In other argumentative contexts but in the same affair, it is exactly for converse purposes that the same pair can be invoked. This is the case, for instance, when the Minister is denied the right to make personal declarations for the reason that his responsibility as a public person cannot hide behind the personal character of some of his opinions.

In a more interactive way, the Minister's reputation is invoked and exploited throughout the parliamentary debates. It follows the same inferential scheme, starting with the questioning of the private person and ending with the denunciation of his public responsibilities. In the following extract, Sa'd 'Abbûd starts with a reminder of Fârûq Husnî's past declarations, in which he explained his reticence *vis-à-vis* marriage:

Extract 1: Parliamentary session, 20 November 2006 (verbatim)

```
The Hon. S.'A.'A.W. Qutb (Sa'd 'Abbûd)
494  Then, this way of behaving followed by this Minister has
495  antecedents, when he was publicly asked on the
496  television one day why he had married nobody and he
497  answered "He who wants a glass of milk buys a cow'. [These]
498  are words uttered by the Minister before. I understand them and
499  you understand them [as meaning that] he who wants to drink a
500  glass of milk has only to buy a cow. These words were used
501   before by this Minister's mouth […]
```

On many occasions, for example, during the TV episode referred to by the MP, the Minister's celibacy was cited as an incongruity asking for repair. Just focusing on this extract, we see how he justifies the reason for his celibacy with a kind of popular saying, but which leaves open a range of possible interpretations and potential inferences concerning his sexual permissiveness. With a specific lexicon and the language games it authorizes, and through the use of an intertextual technique embedding the Minister's voice to better document the authority of the damaging inference, Sa'd 'Abbûd builds a background nimbus grounding Fârûq Husnî's marginality. Equating the wife to the cow, and formulating the opinion that in sexual matters one has to look for what fits one's appetite, establishes an inferential moral substrate regarding the sexual orientations (heterosexual licentiousness, bisexual licentiousness, homosexuality) of the intended person.

Following up his intervention, the same speaker draws from the description of the Minister's intimacy conclusions as to his public activity:

Extract 2: Parliamentary session, 20 November 2006 (verbatim)

```
The Hon. S.'A.'A.W. Qutb (Sa'd 'Abbûd)
501 [...] by this Minister's mouth. Then the carrying out of
502 these declarations is a blow to this deeply Islamic country
503 on the Minister's behalf - fundamentally ...*. I require
504 that this minister resigns or that one fires this minister, for
505 what he sometimes blurts out, not regarding what is related to
506 the headscarf, but regarding what is related to his continuous
507 and provocative declarations through which he takes up
508 a way of behaving which contradicts our faith and our divine Law
509 (sharî'a). I repeat that this Minister's resignation is
510 compulsory and necessary now. Thank you.
*Indicates utterances which it was decided not to include.
```

As we stressed when addressing press discourse previously, the public–private distinction is used, but this time to refute the divide between the two pair parts. It clearly appears that the semantic dimension of categorizations cannot be understood outside the context of their usage, that is, outside their pragmatics.

Damaging somebody else's face is an action which presents serious risks for those who perform it, since participants' faces are mutually and collaboratively vulnerable during the exchange (Brown and Levinson 1987). Besides its deleterious character, insulting exposes its undertaker to a whole set of retaliatory measures stretching from recording this precedent in his/her moral profile to ostracism. This is how, in the press account of the parliamentary session, beyond the unexpected concord between majority MPs and Islamist minority MPs, journalists stress the breach made to the etiquette ruling parliamentary activities: 'What is new is the NDP's position[1] who slaughtered the Minister and offered [his remains] to the

---

1   National Democratic Party, that is to say, President Mubârak's ruling party, which used to always have a majority above two thirds of the two chambers' MPs.

[Muslim] Brothers[2] in their offending attack against him' (*al-Misrî al-Yawm*, 23 November 2006). Numerous commentaries and analyses depict scenes of lynching and killing to better express the virulence of Fârûq Husnî's discredit:

> The scene was scarry [sic] and frightening. They were
> all brandishing their unsheatered swords in the midst of
> crispation, outbursts of anger and uproar. It was like
> you could not hear but the cries: "Fârûq Husnî's head
> … Fârûq Husnî's head" … And actually the NDP's MPs made
> fall the Minister's head and brought it on an iron trail
> … to the Brothers (*Rûz al-Yûsif*, 22 November 2006).

Or even:

> And we decided to unwind on Fârûq Husnî, although it is
> known that he has clean hands and a fautless (*nazâha*)
> wealth, and that he was never, not even once, accused
> of corruption during his 20 years at the head of the
> Ministry of Culture. And this is not to defend Fârûq
> Husnî … (*al-Misrî al-Yawm*, 22 November 2006).

It appears from these journalistic metaphors that, because of the argumentative constraint exerted on participants, critique cannot address the substance of the debate and must limit itself to its form. In other words, since it is utterly difficult for participants in the debate to retract on a series of topics concerning what is 'Islamically correct' (what we called 'negative solidarity' in Ferrié 2004), unanimity can only be by-passed through a critique of the violation of basic forms of civility and by compensating the damage inflicted on one image by the showing of another image to its advantage. There is a more fundamental dividing line which is drawn beyond the Minister of Culture's reputation, which opposes the partisans of a contrasted normativity, despite the fact that it cannot enfold in all its nuances within a parliamentary precinct characterized by procedural constraints and negative-solidarity effects:

> "The Minister of Sins" as he is called by the Muslim
> Brotherhood, "the best Minister of Culture in Egypt's
> history" as he is described by leftist intellectuals,
> following the famous headscarf struggle. Here is the
> extreme contrast (*tabâyun*) between the Islamists'
> position and the leftist [personalities'], which grossly
> summarizes the fight which the Minister triggered among
> them (*al-Ahrâr*, 4 December 2006).

---

2 Muslim Brothers constitute the principal opposition force within the Egyptian People's Assembly, although the political party is not legally recognized.

From Discredit to Scandal

The mechanisms of reputation are revealed in action within the specific contexts of media and parliaments. However, damage inflicted on reputation usually remains confined within singular occurrences. It means that discredit rarely gets generalized. It is only occasionally that the ordinary-reputation mechanisms are mobilized to amplify accusations and to attempt shifting from a singular blame to the status of an affair as a 'scandalous' event. Three questions deserve special attention: first, we observe the use of words which, taken in context, share a family resemblance common to the language games of the scandal; second, we analyse how this language game structures itself in the practical grammar of a scandal process; third, we describe how, according to the satisfaction of some 'felicity conditions', a scandal process can be brought to a successful conclusion or, conversely and through various means, the generalization specific to this process can be impeded or inverted.

The Fârûq Husnî affair is certainly not systematically characterized as a scandal. Often, it is described as a controversy or a struggle. However, the terms used to speak of it share – to use Wittgenstein's expression (1965 and 1967) – a family resemblance, which make them belong to the language games pertaining to the scandal, that is (to give some minimalist definition of the word), to a process of publicly denouncing a breach of moral norms (cf also de Blic and Lemieux 2005: 10). But even so, the practical grammar of words related to scandal is complex: there is no undifferentiated, indifferent-to-enunciation-context, use of the word in its substantive (a scandal), predicative (a scandalous affair), verbal (to make a scandal), or adverbial (in a scandalous way) form. The words related to scandal have a major importance. On the one hand, an implicit and ordinary definition of the notion emerges from the family resemblance they share and the language games they allow. On the other hand, they function in a largely performative way: the use of these words create the break from the norm as much as they reflect it. In the Fârûq Husnî affair, the very quick characterization of the events as the 'struggle of the veil' (see Extract 3, line 1), and their insertion in the newspapers on the front page, achieve the dramatization of the facts and their tying-up to the scandal family, together with demands, relayed by the press, for the Minister's excuses and sacking:

Extract 3: al-Misrî al-yawm, front page, 18 November 2006

The Struggle (*ma'raka*) Of the Veil Between Fârûq Husnî, the Brothers and the Sheikhs
[Facsimile of the first article, caption:] Picture of *al-Misrî al-yawm*, yesterday's scoop article

```
1.    Yesterday, the struggle of the veil broke out between, on one
2.    side, Fârûq Husnî, Minister of Culture, and, on the other
```

3.   side, the sheikhs and the Muslim Brotherhood. Declarations
4.   made the day before by the Minister to al-Misrî al-Yawm on the
5.   topic of his rejection of the veil provoked various reactions.
6.   International press agencies reported, from al-Misrî al-Yawm,
7.   the Minister's declarations, which provoked a broad
8.   polemic on Islamic-oriented websites. Muslim Brothers
9.   launched a vast and forceful attack against the Minister.
10.   Husayn Ibrâhîm, the deputy president of the Brotherhood group
11.   at the People's Assembly, presented a memorandum to the
12.   Parliament, demanding from the President of the Republic the
13.   Minister's sacking ('uzl). At the same time, Dr Hamdî Hasan, the
14.   group's official spokesman, presented a request for urgent
15.   communication (bayân 'âjil) to the Prime Minister, in which he
16.   asks for the Minister's excuses (i'tizâr) and his sacking
17.   (iqâla). In parallel, intellectuals expressed their support to
18.   the Minister's opinion. They consider the veil as a Wahhabi
19.   phenomenon, [which] they describe as a seed planted by Sadat
20.   during the 1970s to achieve political goals. They claim that
21.   this is a "wahhabization" of the Egyptian culture. [...]

A categorization conflict follows between the Minister's defenders and denunciators, and even among the defenders themselves. We have already stressed that the use of categories 'allows members of a social group to produce inferences, judgements and justifiable ascriptions' (Dupret 2006: 399) concerning the social identity of things, people and actions (see also above). Knowledge is largely structured by categorizations, often organized in a paired way, to which types of activities, rights and duties are bound. In that sense, the choice of categorical descriptors has important consequences and is therefore the object of important conflicts. These conflicts often concern categorial pairs offering a morally consequential alternative to 'categorizers'. Thus, characterizing the veil as a 'Wahhabi phenomenon' or as a 'dress code' has huge consequences as to the identity of the person who characterized it so (e.g. intellectuals vs. Muslim Brothers), as to actions and commitments which can be expected from that person (e.g. supporting the Minister vs. bluntly attacking him), as to the right to take sides in the debate (e.g. illegitimate secularism vs. legitimate 'state Islamism'), and as to those on behalf of whom one claims to speak (e.g. non-representative minority vs. silent majority).

Beyond their organization in categorial pairs, the words of scandal have in common the concern for a moral norm and the denunciation of the breach made to it. This is why they present a family resemblance: they relate to an act of designating a normative contradiction which gives reasons to be scandalized (de Blic and Lemieux 2005: 20). So, in this case, the Minister's declarations are denounced as a 'permissive backwardness', 'irresponsible', contrary to the values of a 'pious people', at war against 'Islamic values', 'rejectionist', 'perverse', contrary to 'the Constitution and the *sharî'a*', immoral, opposed to 'the State's official religion' (*al-Misrî al-Yawm*, front-page article, 18 November 2006), indifferent to 'the sources of legislation in Islam' (*Nahdat Misr*, front-page article, 18 November 2006), inflammatory (*al-Karâma*, 21 November 2006), accommodating toward the West (*Nahdat Misr*, 21 November 2006), or even the emanation of a 'fifth column' (*Nahdat Misr*, 3 December).

The words of the scandal are articulated in a language game which is specific to the denunciation of the breach of the moral norm. This game is sensitive to context and, in this sense, it varies from one culture to another. De Blic and Lemieux (2005: 29) speak in that respect of a 'set of shared and evolutionary expectations related to procedures to respect in order to denounce, judge and sanction in public'. It means that language games are multiple and reflect forms of life which are culturally and praxiologically diverse, that is, they refer to communities of shared language and practices (Schulte 1992: 124-125). It is possible to describe the practical grammar and the usage conditions of these language games, that is to say, 'how language, action and enunciation circumstances articulate to each other' (Schulte 1992: 118). Quoting Jeff Coulter (1989: 49): 'Grammars reveal the manifold connections between kinds of expression and the sorts of circumstance within which and about which they may be used'.

Establishing the practical grammar of the scandal thus leads to the description of the sequential organization of the different elements of a 'scandal process'. As the expression indicates, this process has a necessarily public dimension: it takes place in public and it addresses a public audience. It starts with the designation of a moral contradiction which is given some publicity by denunciating the violation of a shared norm and justifying the right to be properly scandalized. This denunciation orients to an audience, although virtual, which it contributes to reflexively configure. Besides, by making visible the moral contradiction it supposes, the scandal process invites the sanction (always public) of the culprit. However, it does not mechanically produce the repair to the moral breach it supposes: fact characterization can be contested and the object of the scandal can resist. Moreover, in its sequential logic, the scandal process can go through high and low tides, but it always runs into a closing that could be either active (the sanction) or by default (the non-suit). Whatever the outcome, this process always concerns the identification and assessment of a collectivity's moral norms, therefore participating in their formation and transformation.

In this grammar of the scandal process, Garfinkel's discussion of degradation ceremonies (1956: 420-424) facilitates the analysis of morality-cognition mechanisms which are operating. Garfinkel defines status degradation as 'any communicative work between persons, whereby the public identity of an actor is transformed into something looked on as lower in the local scheme of social types' (ibid.: 420). It is a work of disqualification and re-qualification, the criteria of which are the motivations scheme that is socially ascribed to the denounced person to explicate his action. The public denunciation, which triggers the denounced person's degradation, aims at annihilating a social object in order to build another. Denunciation rhetoric often combines irony and the biographical re-examination of the denounced person. It also presents a number of features: (1) the event and the denounced person seem to be out of the ordinary; (2) the blamed thing and the denounced person are placed within a scheme of preferences between general types which are assessed by referring to a dialectical counterpart; (3) the denunciator behaves so that he appears as a public figure acting as such; (4) the denunciator makes salient the supra-personal values of the 'tribe' and achieves the denunciation in the name of these values; (5) the denunciator presents himself as invested of the right to speak in the name of these ultimate values; (6) the denunciator is perceived by witnesses as a supporter of these values; (7) the denunciator and the witnesses fix and perceive the distance that separates them from the denounced person; (8) the denounced person is ritually separated from the place he occupies in the legitimate order.

All these features are most explicitly found in the Fârûq Husnî affair: (1) the denounced person is a minister whose profile is marked and atypical, whose political longevity is outstanding, and whose public stakeouts are original and non-consensual; the wearing of the veil belongs to sensitive issues in today's Egypt – it is the object of recurring attritions, and challenging its religious-obligation dimension constitutes an exception to the ordinary mechanism of negative solidarity; (2) it is indeed an event of a general type – the breach to the principles of the 'True Religion' – which the denunciators make public; it is not only Fârûq Husnî who is under attack but, beyond his person, all the trend which is accused of despising religion and aping the West, even in its depraved values; the denounced event and person are not singularities, but are the expression of a generic though minority trend; they are systematically placed as a dialectical counterpart of virtuous principles and models; in other words, the features of the scandal object can be read as symmetrically opposite to the honest citizen's; the Egyptian citizen is not given alternatives within a range of moral possibilities, but is compelled to make the choice of the veil if s/he wants to warrant his/her respectability; (3) denunciators always present themselves as public figures acting in their quality and not as individuals, as the statutory guardians of morality and not as people acting for personal reasons (that is to say, as a sheikh, an MP, a Muslim Brother, a citizen, an upright journalist, a woman, an intellectual, a moral, or a religious authority and so on); (4) denunciators continually foreground the values common to Egyptians, among which, prominently, is piety; Fârûq Husnî's declaration is denounced in the name of the virtue of al-Azhar's country;[3] (5) when claiming their own virtue and their institutional quality, denunciators constantly stress their right to denounce; they even make it a duty, that is, an obligation proceeding from

---

3   Al-Azhar is a historic mosque in Cairo and the main Islamic university institution in Egypt.

the status they occupy; (6) journalists, when not themselves denunciators, act as witnesses to the fact that the denunciation finds its roots in these values which the denunciators are defending; (7) through the production of a distance between 'them' (those who, like Fârûq Husnî, are deviant) and 'us' (the virtuous people of Egypt and its representatives), denunciators draw a dividing line, the crossing of which looks impossible; (8) Fârûq Husnî is constantly presented as unworthy of his charge, all the more because culture is a fixation around which the debate on 're-Islamization' is largely crystallizing; this *de facto* indignity implies demanding his *de jure* resignation; the denunciation aims at stressing the distance which currently makes it impossible that the Minister keeps his position in the legitimate order.

The transgression which is denounced in the scandal process goes hand in hand with the call for the perpetrator's sanction and degradation. In the press, it can take the following shape: 'The Brothers demand the President of the Republic to fire Fârûq Husnî' (*al-Misrî al-Yawm*, front-page article, 18 November 2006). Within the People's Assembly, the conclusion of an 'Independent' MP's speech-turn constitutes another good example: 'It's necessary that this Minister resigns and if the government shows self-respect, it should fire the Minister of Culture' (excerpt 3, lines 343-344). The demand for sanctions does lead to a successful conclusion in an automatic manner. The transgressed-norm characterization does not proceed in a linear way, but is the object, as we have already seen, of contestations and attritions. Moreover, the scandal can, after having been made public, inflate or stagnate, according to the satisfaction of the denunciation felicity conditions. It is not so much about whether the denunciation is unanimous, but the denunciators' capacity to elevate the denounced thing and person to the rank of a social stake, to make it transform from a singular situation to a general case which can eventually achieve the status of a public cause. We shall be back to this issue, but for now it is enough to stress the contrasted nature of stakeouts in the 21 November 2006 edition of *Nahdat Misr*, or the amplification effect of the first parliamentary debate of 20 November 2006 (and its retake two days later). In other words, it is the dynamics specific to the dialogical network of the affair which explains its evolution. As for its close, it works in our case through the transition from confrontation to negotiation. People speak of 'defusing the crisis' and looking for 'intermediary solutions' (*Nahdat Misr*, 25 November 2006), of 'reconciliation operation' (*Akhbâr al-Yawm*, 25 November 2006), of 'a dialogue characterized by frankness and openness' (*al-Watan al-Yawm*, 28 November 2006). It is also notable that the moral norm, in the transgression of which the scandal originates, comes out strengthened from the process: the transaction does not concern its existence or its obligatory status, but the right of a minister to take personal positions and to have, as a norm, a discourse at the margins of the consensus which some morality entrepreneurs would like to promote. *Nahdat Misr* speaks of a minister who 'thinks about the formula proposed in the form of excuses for the evil that was caused by the [bad] interpretation of what he [said]' (3 December 2006); and of a crisis which 'ended without excuses', when the Muslim Brothers said they were satisfied with 'the Minister [expressing] his respect toward veiled women' (4 December 2006).

The scandal process may not produce the effects which were expected by its instigators. This is linked to the choice of the moral norm, the breach of which is denounced. In order for the process to succeed, such a norm must indeed be presented in a credible way as shared, even by those who do not adhere to it. In other words, it must be a norm propitious to the mechanism of negative solidarity which Jean-Noël Ferrié (2004: 122) defines as 'the adoption of a common behaviour [which] does not proceed from the unanimous choice of everybody, but from the difficulty for anybody to express his /her disagreement'. Such is the case in the Fârûq Husnî affair, in the sense that all the protagonists of the parliamentary debate – to confine ourselves to that setting – converge on the primacy of the religious reference:

```
Islamic religion is the religion of all civilisations.
And progress doesn't mean to depart from the
principles of Islam. Actually, progress means to
remain bound to Islamic principles (lines 150-153)
```

and on the infraction perpetrated by the Minister:

```
I adjure President Mubârak to come to the rescue of
Egypt's people and to fire the deviant Minister …* who
departed from what Islam requires, who departed from
the Egyptian people's consensus (lines 486-489).
```

Many participants posit the norm which is the object of the debate on the register of what is intangible:

```
The issue of the veil is not open to examination. It's
a question which has been settled for 1,400 years. It
isn't today that we'll examine the veil issue. The
veil issue isn't challengeable; it's an issue which is
closed (lines 479-482).
```

Obviously, this intangibility and the negative solidarity it creates are no matters of fact, but an achievement, the outcome of an argumentative endeavour of normalization which progressively shrinks the space allowed for nuance and forces the expression of a façade consensus. Many excerpts of the parliamentary debate could be used to illustrate how any deviance *vis-à-vis* the axiological norm promoted by the denouncers is sanctioned by an interruption which places the speaker on the defensive and compels them to progressively get in line with the position of those doing the interrupting. In a dynamic of successive sanctions imposing step by step the shrinking of the range of options open to the speaker, denouncers succeed in having the latter restrict themselves to minimum consensus, the content of which fits the moral axiology promoted by the entrepreneurs of the scandal process because s/he had to step back in order to save his/her face.

The scandal process can also come to an end without the suggested sanction being implemented. The fact that Fârûq Husnî neither resigned nor was sacked does not mean in any way that the scandal process he went through failed. As Beaumarchais' quote goes, 'if you speak ill of somebody, there will always remain something'. Indeed, some effects of the scandal process related to the wearing of the veil continue; the scandal is the object of retakes, in the same way that it itself leant on the retake of former affairs which can be traced back to different points of the dialogical network enfolding. It is as much from the accumulation of processes of this type as from the violence or the acuity of one of them that some effect can proceed, be it expected originally or not. In Jon Elster's terms, one can speak of the indirect effects of actions undertaken for other purposes (Elster 1987). It is not sure that the entrepreneurs of the scandal process against Fârûq Husnî had really considered the possibility of his sacking. It appears that the sanction which was demanded by the denouncers did not necessarily constitute the goal of the scandal process they triggered or fed. The call for sanction is part of the grammar of the 'scandalization', the end of which, in any case contingent and contextual, proceeds from a will of political participation that must be accounted for.

The Moral Over-investment of Politics

Although the political dimension of its trigger element is not initially obvious, the Fârûq Husnî dialogical network proves thoroughly political. The political tone goes through the whole network and it is mainly the participants in the network who give it this political dimension, in their quality of politicians for some of them, but also through the mobilization of this repertoire when intervening in Parliament and in the press. The political repertoire indexing is indeed noticeable in the institutional inferences the participants in the debate mobilize, as for this MP who calls upon the government's responsibility and demands it collectively takes a position:

```
Now, a Muslim Minister of the Egyptian government
comes and attacks the veil. He must withdraw from
the opinion he formulated. There must be a statement
of the government and the Party against the Minister
(lines 267-269).
```

Journalists and chief editors similarly pick on the Prime Minister and stress his delay in taking a position in this affair, some two weeks after its ignition. For some of them, the government was expected to take a stance with regards to the scandal, as it has been invested with so many political implications:

> The Prime Minister, Dr Ahmad Nazîf, criticized the violent
> attack to which the artist Minister Fârûq Husnî was
> exposed. He repeated – two weeks after the veil affair
> broke out, in the calm after the storm of attacks against
> Husnî – that public personalities may give personal
> opinions in questions which do not pertain to their work
> (*al-Misrî al-Yawm*, 30 November 2006).

It is mainly via institutional inferences that participants can speak of a crisis and of lack of balance between the legislative and executive powers. Hence, when Fârûq Husnî's absence is noticed at the time of the parliamentary debate, it is the whole institutional system which is questioned and specifically the Assembly's right to control the government's activities, both in Parliament and in the press:

> But when a Minister of Culture is opposed to the veil and the
> Islamic costume, without being accurate, then he is responsible
> in front of the People's Assembly [Applause] (lines 255-257).

> The People's Assembly was effectively exerting its
> original competence when interrogating the ministers. If
> ministers cannot be interrogated anymore, it would reflect
> the decline of one of the most important means of the
> People's Assembly and the MPs' loss of their right [to
> exert their prerogatives] (*al-Jamâhîr*, 29 November 2006).

It becomes obvious that, since protagonists and contexts are characterized in political terms, the stakes of the affair are presented as specifically political. This is why we can observe participants concurring to impose their definition of these stakes, starting with the question of the official or unofficial character of the Minister's declarations. For some people, the blamed declarations have *ab initio* a political dimension and reflect a more general trend of the government *vis-à-vis* Islam: 'This is not a Minister's [stance], but we know this is the State's [stance] against the veil and against Islam's principles' (lines 702-704). For other people, it is a question of preserving appearances and not compromising the regime: 'The National Party expresses its opinion and condemns these declarations' (lines 406-407). Originally, the characterization of the declaration as personal corresponded to the Minister's attempt at taming the damaging consequences of his statements being made public. In the same attempt at deflating the affair, NDP big shots tried to sort out issues according to their political importance and to relegate the 'struggle of the veil' to the background:

> This is why I ask the Honourable President and the
> honourable brothers and sisters members of the People's
> Assembly not to give this topic more importance than
> it deserves. Because we have questions of an extreme
> importance (lines 102-105).

In this context, even President Mubârak's announcement of constitutional amendments was evoked by the Minister for Parliamentary Affairs:

> How painful it is for me [to see] that our first working
> session [takes place] in this extreme tension. This,
> after we heard yesterday the important talk of Mister the
> President of the Republic. We're accomplishing a serious
> and critical work concerning the constitutional amendments
> and the laws (lines 923-927).

Others worry about the negative consequences of the Fârûq Husnî affair on the political agenda:

> Some ministers warned against the fact that, if we don't
> contain the crisis rapidly, it'll lead to a critical
> deterioration of the government's position *vis-à-vis*
> public opinion, and the Brothers will get in considerable
> gain at a critical time before discussing constitutional
> amendments (*Nahdat Misr*, 19 November 2006).

Finally, among the political stakes of the affair as defined by the commentators, one finds numerous interpretations re-actualizing the issue of the Muslim Brothers' call for the building of an Islamic State:

> It is not about the veil affair, it is about the future
> of the civilian State, of civilisation, of history, of
> the acceptation of the other, of the necessity for Egypt,
> in the course of life, to remain itself (*Nahdat Misr*, 22
> November 2006).

We see through these statements that the specific dispute which started with Fârûq Husnî's declaration amplified and eventually became something like the 'Fârûq Husnî affair'. Egyptian public life frequently witnesses this type of incident. In the judicial context, we analysed many similar situations where a banal event crystallized and became publicly notorious (Dupret and Ferrié 1997). In this sense, an affair means the taking by a singular and ordinary fact of a public and media-geared dimension. In turn, the affair takes a particular shape when, transcending the singular and personal dimension of the case, it is mobilized to sustain a cause of general concern.

Elisabeth Claverie (1994) shows how, in the Calas affair, Voltaire did not confer importance to Calas *per se*, but to the cause which made him incarnate, that is to say, the cause of humanity. The cause is thus the mobilization of general concern, above and outside particular interests, for the sake of 'public good'. It is a procedure taking the pretext of a singular question projected into the public space to serve in supporting the claim and defence of a certain conception of society's general ordering. Through a work of 'denunciatory displaying' or 'critical exhibiting' (Claverie 1994: 85), 'entrepreneurs of morality' seek to inflect the substantial definition of the public, while using different institutional resources which are available to them and staying formally within the scope of sense and reference authorized by the authorities. In a certain way, the cause is thus the projection of a conception of society, public good and general interest, around which one seeks to proceed to a moral and normative mobilization. As for the affair, it is the starting point of a generalizing process and the opportunity of a generic positioning.

The dialogical network of the Fârûq Husnî affair is scattered with speech turns exhibiting its use for the purposes of a public cause, that is to say, the cause of Islam and of its status within Egyptian state and society. During the parliamentary debate, Egypt's Islamic character is not laid down in terms of confession or religious belonging *stricto sensu*. It is presented as a positioning or a commitment performatively taken when formulating the following assertions:

> Yes, we're an Islamic State. Yes, our Constitution
> stipulates that *sharî'a* is the principal source of
> legislation. Yes, we're all Muslims. Yes, we all value
> Islamic religion, Islamic predication (*da'wâ*), and Islam's
> principles. For all of us, our relationship to God – be He
> praised and exalted! – is the relationship of any zealous
> Muslim individual to his religion (lines 127-133).

Still during the parliamentary debate, Egypt's Islamic character is equally presented in opposition to a non-Islamic otherness or externality:

> *Sharî'a* stipulates it, Islam stipulates it, and all
> Islamic countries confirm [the necessity] of the veil. Must
> I do myself as Europe or France which forbad the veil?!
> (lines 333-336)
> What is attributed to the Minister is therefore external
> to al-Azhar's Egypt, to Islamic Egypt, to the Islamic
> world (lines 482-484).

As soon as this virtuous Islamicity is put forward, the cause of the defence of Islam steps in as a category-bound activity. The fact that defending Islam unfolds within the precinct of the People's Assembly has direct consequences on the way it is defended. MPs calling for Islam's defence orient to the rules of the institutional game:

```
I urge the State's President to be the President of the
Islamic State, that is, a Muslim President in al-Azhar's
land, as well as I ask him to fire this Minister (lines
571-574).
```

It was all the more necessary to elevate this singular dispute to the status of a cause, that the adverse camp (that is to say, the camp that did not lean on this particular case to defend Islam) saw in the Islamic generalizing process the ground for a counter-cause. Although it would be wrong to oppose the Parliament to the press in this case, it is mainly, because of the pragmatic aligning of positions in the former and because of the argumentative constraint exerted on its members in the column of the latter, that one can track the formulation of the counter-cause:

```
It is not the affair of the veil, it is this of tolerance.
[...] It is not the affair of the veil, it is this of
political Islam in Egypt (al-Misrî al-Yawm, 24 November
2006)
```

For the proponents of these counter-readings of the affair, the veil issue was perceived as a prerequisite, a first step before the advent of a political system wholly dominated by the Islamic reference. So, we see that, beyond the issue of the chastity of the female dress, moral stakes eventually become political.

Considering the explicit character of this affair, we find here another confirmation that participating in politics means striving for the definition of norms (Dupret and Ferrié 1997). One of the means which is used to participate in power consists of appropriating a pre-existing normative form, to substantiate it and thus to instate rules fixing normalcy and deviance. According to Howard Becker, this morality enterprise is grounded on three constitutive elements: initiative, publicity and interest.

```
Firstly, there must be somebody taking the initiative
to make punish the supposed culprit; to implement a
norm supposes thus a spirit of enterprise and implies
an entrepreneur. Secondly, these who wish the norm to
be implemented must draw the attention of others on
the infraction; when made public, the latter cannot be
neglected. In other words, there must be somebody shouting
theft. Thirdly, in order to shout theft, there must be an
```

```
advantage: it is personal interest which pushes to take
this initiative (Becker 1963: 145-146).
```

In this context, the invention of the Islamic normative tradition is embedded in a double move of power exercise and normative claim which, if analytically distinct, remains nevertheless phenomenologically indissociable.

Extract 8: Parliamentary session, 20 November 2006 (verbatim)

```
The Hon. K.H.M. Hasan (Karam al-Hifyân)
721   [...] What Mister the Minister of Culture
722   declared constitutes a
723   flagrant attack against sharî'a and against the Constitution and
724   it constitutes a deviance from Islam and Islamic principles.
725   The legal rule (fiqhiyya) stipulates that there's no
726   interpretation of a clear text. As soon as the text has a
727   clear affiliation, one can't interpret it, either through
728   a personal opinion or a non-personal opinion.
729   The question of the veil belongs to the Islamic
730   principles which were stipulated in the Koran, the established
731   Tradition and the consensus of jurists (fuqahâ') and imams.
732   This is why I consider it a great honour for Mister
733   the leader and the chief Muhammad Husnî Mubârak, for the
734   majority's MPs and for the National Party to condemn
735   and to ask for the resignation of the Minister of
736   Culture. It'll strengthen the trust in the Egyptian
737   legislature, the government and the National Party
738   majority.
```

Prefacing his turn, the speaker characterizes the Minister's deviance regarding Islam, its principles and the Egyptian constitution which refers to them. Then, in one and the same token, the MP actualizes the authority of the norm and its substantiation by relating the veil to four normative bodies, that is to say, the legal rule, the Koran and the principles it stipulates, the Prophet's Tradition and the consensus among jurists and imams on this issue. In the same extract, one finds the three features identified by Becker in his definition of morality enterprise: publicity, through the debate which took place in the Parliament and in which the MP participated; the initiative 'to condemn and to ask for the resignation of the Minister' (lines 734-5); and the interest, both honorific ('a great honour' – line 732) and political, since, according to the speaker, achieving this initiative will 'strengthen the trust in the Egyptian legislature, the government and the National Party majority' (lines 736-8). One can also notice the specifically political character of the interest derived from this morality enterprise. In this case, we stress the MP's granting of the morality-enterprise retribution to different instances of the ruling authorities: the President of the Republic (though silent in this affair), the MPs of the majority and the ruling party. The same double claim of power exercise and norm ediction can be found in the speech of the Minister for Parliamentary Affairs:

> At every step, in each of its legislations and decisions, the government sticks (*multazima*) to the precepts of our religion, considering that *sharî'a*, according to Article 2 of the Constitution, is the main source of legislation. All respect and all consideration (*ijlâl*) [are due] to the precepts of the Islamic religion, the main source of our legislation (lines 938-943).

Submitting to the norm appears as a governmental principle, a commitment (which is one of the possible translations of the term *multazima*) and an institutional constraint (according to Article 2 of the Constitution).

When the norm of reference is imposed, it often becomes impossible to contest its primacy, because of the mechanism of negative solidarity explained above. Contrary to classical sociology which relates the plurality of values to the plurality of groups, we contend that we should better insist on the idea of persons embedded within the same space of references and playing, simultaneously, alternatively or concurrently, with values they share in common (Boltanski 1990: 81). Such lack of concurrence about norms of reference frequently initiates reflection about the substantiation of norms and thus on their implementation. It is exactly in these terms that the press reacts the day after the parliamentary session dealing with the Fârûq Husnî affair. Whereas NDP and Muslim Brothers MPs are known as political opponents, their will to fall into line with a virtual public opinion goes through moral overbidding:

> History has nothing to do with Fârûq Husnî's opinion – and we disagree with him on this issue – but it concerns the phenomenon of ruling politics which bends over all storms and raises religious slogans (*Nahdat Misr*, 21 November 2006).

The ruling party's MPs come to circumstantially espouse the opposition's themes in order to secure their individual popularity (necessary in the Egyptian electoral system) and to allow the party to which they belong to escape the disgrace ignited by one, important though marginal, of its members' declarations. Moreover, one should not totally ignore personal resentment among MPs, albeit from the NDP, *vis-à-vis* a minister whose stances do not belong to the normalcy we formerly alluded to.

Although the scandal is triggered for itself, that is, in reaction to something considered as outrageous, it has the capacity to transform into a resource for political action, moral normativity being given the status of a major political stake. In a relatively closed system like in Egypt, where there is no pluralism sorting out explicit political antagonisms, the many members share both rhetoric and values, and struggle for the monopoly of their promulgation and implementation. Therefore, there is no concurrence on the conception of normativity, but on its performing.[4] As we have previously discussed elsewhere about the Abu Zayd affair (Dupret and Ferrié 1997), the people who desire to participate in power must posit themselves in a controlled political locus, and seek to profit from and exploit some potentialities by maximizing the opportunities it offers. This is what we mean by the moral over-investment of politics.

In the whole range of political action, this is a specific form (over)investing the repertoire of morality. Often, this form of action operates through the scandal. The detailed analysis of the Fârûq Husnî affair shows how, in Egypt, the moral repertoire can be largely invested by political actors who seek, by so doing, to bypass the fencing of public life. At the institutional level, this fencing is instantiated by the rulers' capacity to dodge any sanction of their action and management of public affairs, for example, by cheating the polls. This fencing is observable in the fact that Egyptian political life finds its way within a double constraint: some channels which are explicitly political (like the alternation of rulers) are clogged; other channels are hardly practicable and are expensive for those who, individually or collectively, take them.

Because of these constraints and fencing, morality, which is already heavily invested in all political regimes, becomes particularly solicited. Its accessibility, its relative efficacy, and its cheaper cost belong to the explicative factors of this preponderance. Its accessibility is even stronger because of the domination of one reference, that is to say, Islam, the monopoly of which is constantly disputed by the political protagonists. As for the efficacy of the moral repertoire and henceforth its cheaper political cost, it proceeds from both the centrality of the reference to Islam in Egyptian public life and the specific tendency of morality to take the shape of Islamic normativity. Mobilizing the repertoire of Islamic normativity allows the person who uses it to be assimilated with the 'good' part of the contrastive and antithetical pair moral–immoral, relegating his/her detractors to the categorial otherness of moral deviance. Let us remind ourselves in that respect that it is proper in any statutory degradation ceremony, and thus of any political action using the repertoire of morality, to make salient the group's supra-personal values, to initiate the denunciation in the name of these values, to ascribe oneself the status of proponent and defender of these values, and to claim to be invested of the legitimate right to talk in their name.

---

4   Note that it is not very different in an open system in which the ostentatious foregrounding of difference cannot hide the fact that it is often only a variation on the same theme.

Concluding Remarks

At least three figures of the moral investment of politics are observable in the Fârûq Husnî affair and testify to the equivocal character of the relations between politics and morals. The first figure is the moralization of politics, by which we aim at these situations where some protagonists benefit from their position within the political game to denounce what they consider to be outrageous. In this case, although it is difficult or even impossible to document the participants' sincerity (which does not mean that one should doubt this sincerity *a priori*), the moral norm is exploited in itself and for itself, in order to secure its respect. In other words, politics is used to promote morality. In the two other figures, the equation is inverted: morality is used to better invest the field of politics, and the moral repertoire becomes a repertoire of political action. These two inverted figures must be related to the fencing of public life as to the complicated use of some specifically political channels. It corresponds either to a cautious dodging of politics or to its re-characterization in non-directly oppositional terms. In the first case, one seeks to spare the cost of a direct political action. It is in that direction that heads the editor-in-chief of an opposition newspaper when noting that 'it is easy to grip the government when entangled in a vice scandal, but harder to grip it in a corruption scandal' (*al-Fajr*, 27 November 2006). The second case corresponds to those situations in which one seeks the full retributive and electoral profit of the use of the moral repertoire in politics. This is the meaning of one political commentator's remarks:

> How to explain the NDP MPs' position? […] I do not think that the NDP has a religious stance in that respect. Then, does the NDP MPs' revolution express personal positions regarding a personal opinion or does it [constitute] some political exaggerating of the kind which allows to become popular in the street? Answer: Generally, such is the position of NDP MPs. But how to explain this coordination which clearly appeared in the room of the People's Assembly among NDP MPs? This, it cannot be explained. Maybe does it proceed from the will of some people to make Fârûq Husnî fall and to use him as a scapegoat. Politics, as everybody knows, has no morals (*al-Misrî al-Yawm*, 23 November 2006).

However, the two latter figures cannot be considered separately from the former in the enfolding of a scandal. The equivocal character of morals in politics stems from this.

The moral investment of politics is not the simple political use of morals. To say that the use of morals is part of strategies which can be documented, either in the parliamentary precinct or beyond, in the dialogical network that the Minister of Culture's declarations ignited, does not mean that morals are just a means. It cannot be deduced from the opponents' investment in the building of a scandal that they use it in a simply manipulative way. Actually, the use of strategic resources does not implicate that the cause for which one uses them is itself a resource for other purposes. Parliamentary life and, more broadly, political life are so ordered that the game is played in a certain way and with certain resources. As stressed by Riker (1986), political life is an art of manipulation, but this is only a *technical* feature and not a cynical assessment of the manipulating people's beliefs and goals. It is possible to be a manipulator and to believe; to methodically and strategically proceed to establishing a fact and conducting a demonstration and to be nevertheless committed *vis-à-vis* this fact and the object of the demonstration, according to a conviction and not to an interest. The same holds true with strategy. To put it in a nutshell, means which are used for a political cause do not constitute a cause transformed into a political means. Besides, public interventions of MPs elected on a programme of Islamic normativity conform so well to this programme that it seems unnecessary to ascribe this conformity any cause but the programme itself. Of course, some people among the promoters of the scandal may just consider it as a political means serving political interests. It could be the case of members of the majority wishing to 'go popular'. However, opportunist people are, by nature, secondary people and not promoters. Moreover, although they do not themselves believe in the values they defend, they believe that others believe in them and, in that sense, they believe in the efficacy of those values. Any staging, even strictly utilitarian, of these values contributes to increase this efficacy and to force the respect of those who believe in them only partly.

We have henceforth good reasons to think that opportunist promoters and users of the scandal act in this way, not because they have no other choice due to the political regime's nature, but mainly because the use of this repertoire of action directly proceeds from the reasons of their engagement in politics and from the analysis they make of the 'public's' expectations. In that sense, they would do the same in a democratic context, since their motivation is moral and not strategic, and since, when it proves strategic, it is grounded on the fact that they believe *a minima* that others have moral values and that they value their respect by the rulers. Thus, the moral repertoire is not initially selected because it allows doing politics indirectly in a context which does not permit it; it is foremost chosen for itself and indissociably for what it represents for the people. Nevertheless, it seems to fit the context, meaning that the rulers can hardly censor any public expression founded on it, because they cannot retract from values they proclaim themselves, and because they believe, like their opponents and probably for the same reasons, that these values are largely shared. That the regime authorizes the expression of one type of values while censoring another does not implicate logically that the former was chosen *ex ante* because of this specificity. However, the evidence of its efficacy can further encourage *ex post* political actors to use it. Strategy is here the heir of morals.

References

Becker, H. 1963. *Outsiders*. Glencoe, IL: The Free Press.

de Blic, D. and Lemieux, C. 2005. Le scandale comme épreuve: éléments de sociologie pragmatique. *Politix*, 71 (18), 9-38.

Boltanski, L. 1990. *L'Amour et la Justice comme compétences*. Paris: Métaillé.

Brown, P. and Levinson, S.C. 1987. *Politeness. Some Universals in Language Usage*. Cambridge: Cambridge University Press.

Claverie, E. 1994. Procès, affaire, cause. Voltaire et l'innovation critique. *Politix*, 26 (7), 76-85.

Coulter, J. 1989. *Mind In Action*. Atlantic Highlands, NJ: Humanities Press International.

Dupret, B. 2006. *Le jugement en action: Ethnométhodologie du droit, de la morale et de la justice en Égypte*. Geneva: Droz.

Dupret, B. and Ferrié, J.-N. 1997. Participer au pouvoir, c'est imposer la norme: sur l'affaire Abu Zayd (Égypte, 1992-1996). *Revue Française de Science Politique*, 47 (6), 762-775.

Dupret, B. and Ferrié, J.-N. 2007. The audience they assign themselves: Three Arab channels and their 'self-presentation' (al-Jazeera, al-Manar, al-Hurra). *Ethnographic Studies*, 9 (1), 63-80.

Dupret, B. and Ferrié, J.-N. 2008. News headlines: Stating in brief what is relevant in today's world (al-Arabiya, al-Jazeera, al-Manar, BBC World). *Ethnographic Studies*, 10 (1), 49-68.

Elster, J. 1987. *Le Laboureur et ses enfants. Deux essais sur les limites de la Rationalité*. Paris: Minuit.

Ferrié, J.-N. 2004. *Le régime de la civilité. Public et réislamisation en Égypte*. Paris: Presses du CNRS.

Ferrié, J.-N. and Dupret, B. 2007. La danseuse du ventre et son double: scandale et jeux de catégorisation en Égypte. *Quaderni*, 63 (30), 97-108.

Garfinkel, H. 1956. Conditions of successful degradation ceremonies. *American Journal of Sociology*, 61 (5), 420-424.

Klaus, E., Dupret, B. and Ferrié, J.-N. 2008. Derrière le voile. Analyse d'un réseau dialogique égyptien. *Droits et Sociétés*, 68, 153-179.

Leudar, I. and Nekvapil, J. 2004. Media networks and political argumentation. *Journal of Language and Politics*, 3 (2), 247-266.

Leudar, I. and Nekvapil, J. 2007. The war on terror and Muslim Britons' safety: A week in the life of a dialogical network. *Ethnographic Studies*, 9 (1), 44-62.

Leudar, I., Marsland, V. and Nekvapil, J. 2004. On Membership Categorization: 'Us', 'them' and 'doing violence' in political discourse. *Discourse and Society*, 15 (2-3), 243-266.

Nekvapil, J. and Leudar, I. 2002. On dialogical networks: Arguments about the migration law in Czech mass media in 1993, in *Language, Interaction and National Identity*, edited by S. Hester and W. Housley. Aldershot: Ashgate, 60-101.

Riker, W. 1986. *The Art of Political Manipulation*. New Haven, CT: Yale University
   Press.

Sacks, H. 1995. *Lectures on Conversation*. Oxford: Blackwell.

Schulte, J. 1992. *Lire Wittgenstein. Dire et montrer* (translated by Charrière, M.
   and Cometti, J.-P.). Combas: Éditions de l'éclat.

Wittgenstein, L. 1965. *Le Cahier bleu et le Cahier brun* (translated by Durand,
   G.). Paris: Gallimard.

Wittgenstein, L. 1967. *Philosophical Investigations* (translated by Anscombe, G.).
   Oxford and Cambridge: Blackwell.

Chapter 10

Moving Teachers: Public Texts and Institutional Power

Susan Bridges and Brendan Bartlett

Introduction

In 2000, teachers in the Hong Kong Special Administrative Region (HKSAR) were asked by their Government and employing body to 'move'. The resulting movement was both figurative and literal in intent. Teachers were asked (a) to rethink their professional standing, and (b) to choose professional retraining options. For some, the latter required a 'movement' of mindset (from teacher to learner), of life paths (from recreation to professional development), and of location (from Hong Kong to overseas institutions). For Hong Kong's teachers, these types of movement formed social imperatives linked to professional gatekeeping – one's position as a language teacher would be lost if language 'benchmarks' were not met.

A multi-layered analysis of one institutional text provides a basis for examining part of the public mechanism that Hong Kong instituted to promote the achievement of this movement. As an artefact within the Language Proficiency Requirement (LPR) policy phenomenon, the text had strong repercussions for organising patterns of life (Geertz 1973) as it directed certain teachers to undertake formal in-service training under the Chinese and English language syllabus specifications. The form of this public text was an open letter to teachers (see Appendix). As such, it was an institutional document that was purposefully crafted by the then Secretary for the Hong Kong Education and Manpower Bureau (EMB). It was issued in September 2000 to all serving primary and secondary teachers in the Hong Kong Special Administrative Region (HKSAR) and was accompanied by a government press release (Information Services Department HKSAR 2000). The open letter was distributed in response to teachers' industrial action after circulation of the LPR and language proficiency syllabus specifications. Its purpose was to displace initial negative reaction to the syllabus requirements with a more understanding and compliant response. In effect, it asked teachers to 'move'. The aim of this chapter is to investigate the machinery by which this purpose is realised within one text.

Three analytical approaches are applied in the document analysis. First, historical, social and intertextual contexts are described to situate the document within the dominant discourse. Second, membership categorisation analysis (MCA) (Freebody 2003, Sacks 1972, Sacks, Schegloff, and Jefferson 1974, Silverman 1998) is used to explore the organisation of social relations in the creation of a virtual reality. Third, linguistic analysis is applied to identify the purposeful and creative applications of language in the service of achieving institutional aims. The blending of these approaches proves useful in establishing how teachers of English from Hong Kong had decided to undertake their professional training and accreditation at approved local or overseas institutions.

Sociolinguistic and sociocultural dimensions are delineated as part of the analysis. Thus, the text's content, and also its purpose and deployment in a particular social circumstance, are subject to analysis. This facilitates an understanding of the socio-political background that had generated the LPR phenomenon. Our approach to such an analysis of textual and intertextual features was framed by Smith's (1990) orientation to texts:

> The realities to which action and decision are oriented are *virtual* (original emphasis) realities vested in texts and accomplished in distinctive practices of reading and writing (p. 62).

In order to define the 'virtual reality' inherent in a reading of this document, we selected methods for textual analyses for two major purposes. These were (a) to interpret the interactive power of texts, and (b) to identify how participants accounted for reality. This dual approach reflects Freebody's (2003) use as a method for reading texts as sociocultural data. The analysis presented here reflects this duality of purpose. First, it works to situate the social context of the text within the dominant discourse. Second, it works to understand the interactive power of such a public text. The aim is to show how the machinery of the text worked to motivate teachers to 'move'. A blended approach is adopted within a multi-layered analysis.

In the first layer, the social reality of this text is explored. The socio-cultural context of the open letter is briefly recounted through tracing the historical and social factors that situate it within the domain of English language acquisition in Hong Kong at the end of the 20th century. This approach builds from Smith's (1987, 1990), Gee's (1990) and Freebody's (2003: 181) approaches to texts 'as objects that reflect and construct accounts of realities'. Our institutional text is analysed as an artefact which worked to construct a new social reality. An exploration of its intertextual features situates it further within the institutional discourse available at the time in Hong Kong's educational system. The underlying premise of this level of analysis is that such a public text lives in reference to other policy-related documents. As such, it is part of an intertextual web promoting a new social 'reality'. For teachers in Hong Kong, this reality was the Language Proficiency Requirement (LPR).

The second layer of analysis adopts Freebody's (2003) approach to Harvey Sacks' original work on (MCA) (Sacks 1972, Sacks et al. 1974, Silverman, 1998) as an analytic tool for examining 'members' identified in the text and 'attributions' ascribed to them. Such an approach can support investigations of how power is enacted through a public text. Gee's (1990) stance is that sociolinguistic analysis of a text becomes a moral matter, as an analyst using an analytical tool deconstructs the ideologies underpinning the action of the text. He defined such ideologies as 'tacit views of what counts as the right stance' (p. 130). In applying analytical tools such as Sacks' MCA to the open letter, the underpinning ideologies – the 'right stance' taken by the producer of a text – are explored and identified. MCA assists in highlighting the producer's explicit or implicit articulation of moral stance. As researchers utilising MCA, we aim to validate interpretations through a transparent and well explicated analysis of the text.

In the final layer of analysis, linguistic features of the text are identified. A particular interest of ours is how different lexical choices worked to promote ideologies of the text and its surrounding discourse.

Thus, the blended analysis permits us to examine a single text through three different lenses from the field of applied language research. The multi-method approach to analysis supports a rigorous investigation of the machinery by which a publicly-mediated text asked teachers to 'move'.

Framing Textual Analysis

Texts are defined in this chapter as 'crafted communications – visual, graphic and electronic representations of language and objects' (Freebody 2003: 174). Educational sociologists have built upon earlier ethnographic and discourse analytic traditions to argue for the centrality of textual analysis in research in educational policy in order to provide:

> ... a critical understanding of cultural practice and social organisation [which] depends fundamentally on an understanding of how texts operate. This is because societies are made possible by the production and exchange of written, oral, electronic and visual textual material (p. 178).

Early theorising in ethnographic research saw cultural artefacts as situated within 'webs of significance' that could be made subject to an 'interpretive... search of meaning' Geertz (1973: 5). The cultural analysis movement in the 1970s integrated academic thought:

> from diverse intellectual sources in anthropology, microsociology, textual analysis, social and cultural history, and psychoanalysis: and through its own hybrid practices, generated new and distinctive syntheses (Murdock 1997: 181).

From here, discourse analysts established texts as culturally and ideologically bound – thereby contributing to the construction of social reality (Smith 1990, Gee 1990). Policy analysis then becomes a deconstructive process providing specific tools through which the researcher can lay bare the mechanisms of social organisation as produced within and through policy texts. Building from ethnomethodological traditions, Housley and Fitzgerald (2007) posited that discursive analysis can:

> examine how methods of social organization and situated machinery for invoking and processing members' knowledge are used to represent, explore, and promote specific world views and configure the manner in which the public is given voice in relation to government policy. This form of life, this interactional milieu, is suffused with practical methods of reasoning (pp. 202-203).

The interests of this chapter are therefore inherently sociological and discursive. If one is to follow Freebody's definition of text as representations, then a framework for analysis must consider how such representations are constructed. In examining policy texts, in particular, one must consider the multiple aspects of textual deconstruction for analysis. The ensuing three layers of analysis aim both to expose the situated machinery of a public text and to explore how reasoning appears to have been invoked to promote moral order. The blending of these layers of analysis works to answer macro-sociological questions related to the policy in social context while also addressing micro-sociological questions as to how these can be examined within the situated machinery of a constructed text. In taking a blended approach to analysis we argue that while each of the three layers provides specific and separate mechanisms for textual analysis, their combination as complementary, unfolding layers adds to a 'whole' analysis, offering more to a situated analysis than the sum of the parts.

Key to the analytic frame adopted are questions developed from Sacks and colleagues' pioneering work in ethnomethodology, particularly in terms of organisation interaction. While Sacks may have been seen as taking a 'basic' approach to research in analysing the social organisation of a text for its relevance to the text itself rather than to solving practical issues external to it (Silverman 1998: 40), his approach recognised that in the process of understanding how texts are operationalised and rendered understandable one is addressing fundamental sociological questions. Sacks' colleague, Emmanuel Schegloff remained focussed on his research on analysis of naturally-occurring talk as data. However, in a primer on conversation analysis (CA) he posited important sociological questions that are relevant to both branches of ethnomethodology – CA and MCA. Particularly cogent to the framing of analysis in this chapter and resonating with Geertz's (1973) 'webs of significance' analogy is his question:

> What is the web of practices that serves as the infrastructure of social institutions in the same way that a system of transportation serves as the infrastructure for an economy, that is so transparent that it is opaque, whose omnipresence and centrality make it *a* – if not *the* – core root of sociality itself? (Schegloff 2007: xiii)

Indeed, the foundational frame for the analysis presented here is to make obvious that which otherwise may seem 'so transparent for the producers and readers of texts that it is opaque'. We take the stance that a policy text is part of 'the web of practices' of a particular 'social institution'. By adopting a blended approach and by drawing on branches of discourse analysis and MCA together, we try to uncover some of the complexities involved in *how* a text works in a social context to make unnatural and observable that which is accepted as natural and assumed. We have adopted Sacks' stance to examine the 'everyday skills all of us (including Durkheim) are using to *see* a norm together and to know that we saw the same thing (*LC*1: 93)' (Silverman 1998: 45).

As Silverman (1998) noted, Sacks' sociological vision was not political but rather aesthetic (p. 57). Sacks saw the artistic construction of social life in the detail. By drawing on the notion of craftsmanship in Freebody's definition of texts as 'crafted communication' we echo this belief in the aesthetic. In using a blended approach to analysis, we seek to examine the social artistry of its construction. However, as the subject of analysis is a policy text, we depart from Sacks' aesthetic vision to recognise that such texts are inherently political and their artistic crafting can serve political ends. Thus, a blending of discursive analysis with MCA may serve to show how *the aesthetic* is crafted to support *the political*.

Layer 1: Texts and Social Reality

Situating one public text

As noted in the introduction, the public text that is the focus of our discursive analysis in this chapter is an open letter issued in September 2000 to all serving primary and secondary teachers in the HKSAR from a government body (see Appendix. Before engaging in a micro-analysis of the text itself, this first layer of analysis aims to situate the document historically, socially and intertextually within an evolving discourse.

Historical context

The open letter and its relationship to requirements teachers in Hong Kong must meet for language proficiency are framed within historical developments of language policy in a post-colonial setting. The language proficiency requirement evolved as policy during the two years immediately following the 1997 'handover' from British to Chinese rule under the 'one country – two systems policy' and the establishment of Hong Kong's special status as a Special Administrative Region (SAR). Linked to this early post-colonial period was an official change in focus from English as a Medium of Instruction (EMI) to first language education or Chinese as a medium of instruction (CMI) (Tsui 2004). Concerns were raised within many government and public spheres regarding sufficiency in the skills and resources currently available in the education system to implement the new

HKSAR language policy of trilingualism (Cantonese, Mandarin, English) and biliteracy (Chinese and English) (Bray and Koo 2004). One response to these concerns was the instigation of the LPR as government policy.

Social context

Educational reform in Hong Kong at this time was focused on the twin needs of educational innovation (Pennington 1995, Cooke 2000), and language proficiency (Tsui 2004). The government's questioning of the adequacy of teachers' pedagogic skills was made public. It moved to secure systemic innovation in education through Education Commission reports and reviews (Education Commission 1994, 1996, 1999) and departmental documents such as *Learning to Learn: General Studies for Primary Schools* (Curriculum Development Council 2000).

Reviews highlighted a lack of formal teacher training for many who were currently practising in the profession. Language teachers' linguistic competence was questioned in public forums such as newspapers, television and parliamentary debates. A response within the government's educational system to these concerns and to documents and debates that had arisen about them was the establishment of the Standing Committee on Language Education and Research (SCOLAR) in November 2000 with the role of advising the government on language education.

Intertextual context

In 2001, SCOLAR began its review of language education in Hong Kong. Its final report, *Action Plan to Raise Language Standards in Hong Kong* (2003) was presented at policy-making levels (Legislative Council Panel on Education (LP), Education Commission (EC), Curriculum Development Council (EDC), etc) and to all other stakeholders in language education from universities to schools to parents. Its major aims were:

> Point 1.8 '... to introduce concrete, concerted and well-targeted measures to raise the language standards of the population to match the ever-increasing demand for students and workers with good language skills'.

> Point 1.9 '... specifying a clear and realistic set of expected language competencies to reflect the current and future needs of our society ...';

> Point 1.10 '... creating a more motivating language learning environment for our students and workforce'. (p. 5)

The revised syllabus, *Language Proficiency Assessment for Teachers (English Language)* (LPATE[1]) (HKSAR, November 2000), was one of several education reform initiatives linked to language proficiency and teacher education proposed by the Education Commission (1994) and endorsed by SCOLAR (2003) in its final report.

Other important institutional documents complemented the texts from SCOLAR, reflecting the building discourse at government level regarding the post-handover focus on teacher training, professional qualifications, and language proficiency. In 1999, the then Hong Kong Education Department (HKED) disseminated a report stating that the proportion of trained secondary teachers serving in schools in 1998 was 79 percent (HKED, 1999). In his 1999 Policy Address, the Chief Executive at the time, Mr Tung Chee-Hwa, outlined a program for 'upgrading all pre-service training courses ... by 2004 ... to degree level' (Tung 1999: 23).

Resulting changes to teacher qualifications and accreditation meant that the number of primary school teachers with formally-accredited teacher training rose from 73.6 percent in 1992/1993 to 86.6 percent in 2001/02 and for secondary teachers from 76.9 percent to 83.5 percent (Education and Manpower Bureau 2003). Figures published in 2007 placed the level of teacher accreditation at 93.9 percent for secondary teachers and 95 percent for primary teachers (Education Bureau, 2007a, 2007b). These long-term increases reflect both qualifications undertaken and attained as well as some attrition as untrained teachers left the workforce.

Related to publication of these documents was the growing imperative for Hong Kong's teaching profession to address concerns about levels of teachers' language proficiency. The then Secretary's open letter to serving teachers (Appendix A) was a direct response to another government text published first in April then revised in November 2000 – the LPATE syllabus specifications (HKSAR, 2000). The 'action' of the earlier text was the proficiency assessment process (commonly known as 'benchmarking') that had drawn heated reaction from practising teachers. This had led to a highly active process of political lobbying from the Hong Kong Professional Teachers' Union (PTU), which staged mass rallies and protests in the streets of Hong Kong (PTU 2000). The letter sent by the Secretary was grounded in an institutional discourse determined by specific historical and social forces. These forces gave warrant for the content, publication and dissemination of this and related texts. The purpose was to perpetuate a specific type of action within the dominant discourse – the continuation of the LPR policy – and to quell

---

1   The Syllabus Specifiactions for the Language Proficiency Assessment for Teachers (English Language) (HKSAR November 2000) included a set of four language proficiency papers administered by the Hong Kong Examinations Authority (HKEA) and two Classroom Language Assessments (CLA) administered by the then Hong Kong Education and Manpower Bureau (EMB) with the aim of 'benchmarking' English skills. The assessment scale ranged from 1 to 5 with a score of 5 reflecting near-native speaker ability. All serving teachers were required to pass the LPATE by the end of the 2005/2006 school year.

opposing discourses. The text is about power wielded in support of the dominant discourse.

Moving teachers

Further intertextual links can be made to teachers' reflective accounts in-situ after serving teachers had 'moved' in response to the LPR policy and to the open letter – the latter calling for teachers' compliance with the initiative to raise levels of language proficiency among teachers of English and Mandarin. For teachers of English, there were a variety of options for completion of LPATE syllabus requirements. One was to take an overseas in-service education and training course (INSET) using the immersion model (Bridges 2007). Participants G and H (below) were teachers who had 'moved' by taking this option, and in particular to participating in a specific instance of INSET that provided their professional development in Australia. This INSET was an intensive 6-week program, delivered and assessed in English. As such, the participatory experience required a 'movement' of mindset (from teacher to learner), of life paths (from recreation to professional development), and of location (from Hong Kong to Australia).

"As being a teacher is a hard job in HK, we have no working hours. Every day, when we open our eyes, we work until close our eyes. So, taking in-service courses is another hard job to me. With no support from our principal, we feel disappointed because the society forces all teachers to bear the bad outcome of all students. However, when the outcome is good, no praise for any teacher from the society. So, in this situation, if teachers continue to take more courses to broaden their knowledge, I think they are great and I hope they can withstand the courses comfortably."	"In-service courses give non-native English teachers a chance to observe how other teachers teach, share ideas about education with other participants and practice their own English. Both English proficiency and pedagogical knowledge are crucial for effective English teaching. Learning English should be a life-long process. English teachers should keep on taking in-service courses regularly but no formal assessments should be imposed on the participants to ruin the joy of learning."
Participant G, Group 1	**Participant H, Group 2**

The two reflective accounts reproduced above were written on the last day of one immersion INSET. Both indicate a 'bittersweet' reaction to in-service programs in general with Participant G more obviously concerned about the demanding working conditions for teachers and the fact that professional development programs themselves play a role in this relentless grind. She hoped that teachers could endure the added workload that such in-service programs were perceived as imposing. She wrote of long working hours and of lack of support, both institutionally and socially. She added to these problems the issues of strenuous working conditions as *we work until close our eyes*, and negative perceptions of in-service programs themselves added to the bitterness, as they are *another hard job*. Participant H, while more circumspect, reminded the readers that (for teachers) *learning English should be a life-long process*. Both teachers portrayed in-service in terms of demands and hardship especially in relationship to assessment. The message of both reflections is that in-service is onerous with Participant G hoping *they can withstand the courses comfortably*.

However, both Participants G and H indicated professional benefits from the program. These ranged from a perceived increase in language proficiency and pedagogical learning to networking with Hong Kong colleagues and Australian teachers. Participant G ends with the positive assertion that in this situation, *if teachers continue to take more courses to broaden their knowledge, I think they are great and I hope they can withstand the courses comfortably.* Participant H qualifies her assessment of INSET in general noting their benefits but also recognising the devaluing of the experience imposed by assessment: *English teachers should keep on taking in-service courses regularly but no formal assessments should be imposed on the participants to ruin the joy of learning.*

A sense of ambivalence is evident in these two vignettes. Both entries indicate different levels of hardship but the participants also wrote that there were many positive aspects to INSET in general. The purpose of this chapter is to present results from a textual analysis that depicts an investigation of this move as a social imperative.

Layer 2: Texts, Membership Categorisation and Moral Stance

Policy texts as social organisation

The brief overview above situates the LPR phenomenon and the specific text for analysis socio-politically by framing its relationship to historical, social and intertextual contexts. It is now appropriate to examine in detail, the machinery whereby it accomplishes the work of social organisation. As noted above, the textual analysis focuses on excerpts from an institutional document purposefully crafted by the Secretary for the Hong Kong Education and Manpower Bureau (EMB) as an open letter to teachers (see Appendix). The letter was issued to all serving primary and secondary teachers in the HKSAR in September 2000. As an institutional document, the letter reflected Smith's (1990) 'action and decision' categorisation of a text (p. 62). As such, it features an identifiable sender (the Secretary, EMB), recipients (principals and teachers), place (HKSAR) and time (September 2000).

If we consider Smith's notions of institutional texts as 'virtual reality', the work of the policy text in the Appendix is to support the shaping of a 'truth', a new reality. This is consistent with Gee's (1990) argument that texts and ideologies are inextricably linked in promoting a right stance. The task for analysis is to define the 'truth' that the Secretary conveyed and to analyse the means by which this was accomplished. A new government policy had been instituted and reactions from the teaching profession were strong. Smith's (1987) analysis of institutional discourse led her to believe that, 'institutional forms of discourse create relations between subjects appearing as a body of knowledge existing in its own right' (p. 214). The letter served to convey the 'truth' that the proficiency requirement would proceed and the text projected itself as a 'body of knowledge' (see Appendix). This text was also the site whereby as an institutional representative, the author constructed the text to 'organise relations among subjects active in the discourse' (Smith 1987: 214).

In order to define the 'virtual reality' inherent in a reading of this policy text, we employ MCA. The methodological aim is to examine the "situated articulation and promotion of world views' (Housley and Fitzgerald 2007) and to open for analysis the machinery whereby this is accomplished. This assists in revealing the process of promulgating a dominant institutional ideology resulting in individual action. Membership categorisation attempts to operationalise relations between members represented in a text such as the Secretary's letter, and permits its sociological 'reality' to be explored. In his later biographical work on Sacks, Silverman (1998) interpreted the aim of Sacks' membership categorisation as:

> to try to understand when and how members do descriptions, seeking thereby
> to describe the apparatus through which members' descriptions are properly
> produced (p. 76)

The MCA approach focuses on members (people referred to) and activities associated with them (attributions). For Sacks (1972), a membership categorisation device constituted the collection of membership categories onto which rules were applied 'for the pairing of at least a population member and a categorisation device member' making the device 'a collection plus rules of application' (Silverman 1998: 79). 'Role partners' can be developed in terms of paired associations or as 'standard relational pairs (SRP)' (Silverman 1993: 88). This procedure makes MCA a useful tool for analysis of social constructs within the texts including interpretation of the representations of identities in the 'said' and 'unsaid' of the text.

This analysis departs, however, from Sacks' original work on spoken texts and employs these principles in analysis of a written text. The closest that Sacks came to analysis of a written text was his work with a *New York Times* article about a navy pilot. His analysis, however, remained fixed on the categorisation work of the pilot's direct speech as reported in the article (Silverman 1998: 90-93). Elsewhere, MCA work on newspaper headlines was undertaken by Lee (1984) and Hester and Eglin (1992). Later, Eglin and Hester (1999) employed MCA across multiple texts related to the 'Montreal Massacre' to examine the machinery of moral reasoning. This use by Eglin and Hester is important in that it was a methodological step beyond the traditional ethnomethodological focus on naturally-occurring talk

Table 10.1   MCA of opening and closing paragraphs in text – 'Language Proficiency Letter'

Categorisation	Attributions	Substantiation procedures
• Students	• language proficiency	
	• Motivation	• factor in students' proficiency
	• Learning	• effectiveness improved
• Hong Kong community • community at large	• grave concern • different view	
• Family	• Support	• factor in students' proficiency
• teachers • language teachers	• language proficiency • overall proficiency expected	• factor in students' proficiency
	• helping language teachers	• to improve their language proficiency and professional skills
• some quarters of the teaching profession • serving teachers	• reacted strongly to the announcement in April	
 • you	• registered status	• not affected by the outcome of the language proficiency training or assessment
	• committed teacher • will support lifelong learning	• will see the holistic approach • improve your effectiveness in facilitating student learning
• the Administration	• announced the introduction of benchmarking in April	• drew strong reactions
• parents	• different view	
• education bodies	• different view	
• We	• have reviewed comments received	• discussed with key stakeholders
• Key stakeholders	• discussed	
•I	• announce	• revised arrangements for language proficiency • complementary measures to improve the teaching of languages in schools
	• wish to re-emphasise	• by no means 're-licensing'
	• trust	• committed teacher will support lifelong learning • further effectiveness in facilitating student learning

to one where written texts are used as a data source. In addition to drawing on newspapers' reported direct speech by the 'killer' and eyewitnesses (as per Sacks' navy pilot analysis), they included analysis of the killer's recovered suicide letter. In what follows, we build on this shift in data for MCA to include an analysis of a letter constructed within an institutional context.

A second departure from traditional MCA is our employment of Freebody's (2003) tabular approach for the first analytic pass. Such a process can provide an effective schematic of the categories established within a text and their attributions and substantiation procedures. As Freebody reiterates, MCA posits that members hold commonsense, shared understandings of social structures through, in part, their understanding of categorisations (pp. 158-159). By employing Sacks' rules of application and analysis of membership categorisation under Freebody's tabular approach (see Table 10.1), we can uncover the production of members' descriptions in key sections of the open letter and the motives for making them. As categorisations are constructed in the opening and closing paragraphs of the open letter (see Appendix 1), it is these sections that have been selected for detailed analysis. Table 10.1 therefore represents only those categorisations established in these key paragraphs. An associated press release (Information Services Department HKSAR 2000) further outlined the package of measures'

In his economy rule Sacks stated that, 'a single category from any membership categorisation device can be referentially adequate' (cited in Silverman 1998: 79). By applying the economy rule to this text, single categories as *you* are referentially tied to collections such as *language teachers* and *teachers*. *Teachers* are established in the text as having a number of standard relational pairs (SRPs): *language teachers*; *some quarters of the teaching profession*; *serving teachers*; and *you*. Within these SRPs, there is a binary contrast at work establishing *some quarters of the teaching profession* in a paradigmatic opposition to *language teachers*; *serving teachers*; and *you*. How and why this binary is established becomes clearer through examination of the attributions for those membership category devices.

To explore how the various members are positioned within the category of *teachers*, Sacks' *positioned categories maxim* may be applied. The maxim is that 'a collection has positioned categories where one member can be said to be higher or lower than another' (Silverman 1998: 84). The attributions listed in Table 10.1 assist in identifying the positions of members. *Language teachers* are ascribed the attribution of *language proficiency* followed by *overall proficiency expected*. These attributions are linked with such category-bound relationships as *factor in students' proficiency* and *to improve their language proficiency and professional skills*. The category-bound activities of teachers who follow the directives in language skilling are *professional* and contributing to their *students' proficiency*. *Serving teachers* are attributed with a *registered status* that is *not affected by the outcome of the language proficiency training or assessment*. The positioned category, *you*, has attributions of *committed teacher* who *will support lifelong learning* with the substantiation procedure established as *will see the holistic approach and improve your effectiveness in facilitating student learning*.

These category-bound activities are dominantly positive and equate to a high moral position. The membership category *some quarters of the teaching profession* contrasts strongly. It is given the negative attribution of *reacted strongly to the announcement in April*. The positioned category of *some quarters of the teaching profession* is lower.

The 'unsaid' of the text is also interesting in terms of positioned categories. While all the other categories of *teacher* have a stated substantiation procedure (see Table 10.1), the membership category *some quarters of the teaching profession* does not. With the positive cause and effects stacked on the *teacher'* side of the binary, the 'unsaid' cause and effect of *some quarters of the teaching profession* can be read as a negative, especially when considered in relation to the discourse surrounding this text. These various attributions, cause and effects and category-bound activities for *teachers* are used purposefully to isolate opponents and to quell dissension in order to perpetuate the ideology of the dominant discourse – the continued enforcement of the language proficiency measures.

Applying Sack's consistency rule is useful also in exploring the perpetuation of ideology in this text. This rule argues that:

> if some category from a device's collection has been used to categorize a first member of the population, then that category ... may be used to categorize further members of the population (Silverman 1998: 80).

In the letter, the consistency rule is employed to enforce a newly-defined social reality and to isolate those who reject the dominant discourse. The text works to weaken the discourse of opponents of language skilling by setting up another strong binary contrast. It does this by placing *some quarters of the teaching profession* with their attribute of *reacted strongly to the announcement in April* in opposition to *the community at large* that is attributed with a *different view.*

The *community at large* is positioned in a SRP with the *Hong Kong community* whose attribute is *grave concern*. Thus, *some quarters of the teaching profession* are placed in opposition to the *Hong Kong community*. By applying the consistency rule, 'a few agitating teachers' is placed in opposition to 'the rest of Hong Kong'. The position of the opponents is greatly weakened in the text. The attribution of *different view* is given to *parents* and *education bodies* as well as to the *community at large*. This aligns these members within the binary in opposition to *some quarters of the teaching profession*. The extension further weakens the opponents' position in the contrast.

The application of category-bound activities in combination with the economy and consistency rules enables the moral stance and virtual reality of the text to be paraphrased: 'If you are a committed teacher who is interested in supporting the language development of your students and professional development as the parents, education bodies and whole Hong Kong community wishes, then you will follow the revised arrangements without dissension'.

Layer 3: Texts, Language and Ideology

The language of power

Examination of linguistic properties within the letter also adds to the analysis of this text. Different lexical choices have been made purposefully in order to promote ideology and its surrounding discourse. In institutional texts, the common nominal structure is the application of the agent-less passive. In this text, however, there are three instances where the then Secretary has used the first person singular in order to position the writer in relation to the readers/employees and to facilitate a particular reality (see Appendix A). The application of the genre of 'open letter' also supports a personalised position and lends itself generically to these usages of the first person.

The first instance is in the second paragraph *I announced revised arrangements*. In this line, the author is positioned as:

1. The person of power who is authorised to make such an announcement;
2. The harbinger of news about change; and
3. The mediator who has listened to *key stakeholders*.

Whilst reinforcing power and status, linguistic choices in this section of the text establish a tone of reason and arbitration so as to 'soften' the power relations. This purposefully positions the author within the text as both as reasonable and personable in order to weaken the stance of opponents who *reacted strongly*. These are contrastively emotive lexical choices. Indeed, as the text is in the target language of English, its linguistic worth (error-free with appropriate usage) also reinforces the position and argument of the writer – the Secretary is communicating effectively in the target language to principals and teaching staff, thereby modelling an appropriate level of proficiency.

Second and third usages of first person occur in the closing paragraph. The Secretary added personal weight to the reassurance that *the registered status of serving teachers will not be affected by the outcome of the language proficiency training or assessment*. The position here might be described as paternalistic as the text allays fears by applying a strongly reassuring proposition.

The third and most explicitly powerful usage of the first person is employed in the closing line: *I also trust that as a committed teacher, you will support lifelong learning to improve further your effectiveness in facilitating student learning*. As an attribution to a category of teacher, the text reinforces the Secretary's position of power enabling the positioning of the reader as a *committed teacher* with the attribution of *will support lifelong learning* and, by association, the LPAT directive. The employment of an upwardly sliding list of attributes creates a logical chain of arguments (Freebody 2003). In turn, this leads to justification of the proficiency requirement measures. If the readers (who are employees) wish to be viewed as *committed* by their employer, they will need *to support lifelong learning* and *improve further ... effectiveness in facilitating student learning.* Within the discourse of this text, the causal link is made between the proficiency requirement measures that have been announced and individuals' commitment and dedication to their profession. Participant H's reflection at the beginning of the chapter aligns strongly with these notions of lifelong learning and the need for proficiency in both linguistic and pedagogic skills. However, this teacher resisted endorsing the language proficiency requirement in her assertion that *no formal assessments should be imposed on the participants to ruin the joy of learning.* The text works to address this area of resistance.

Foucault (1984) posited this conceptualisation of power:

> What makes power hold good, what makes it accepted, is simply the fact that it doesn't weigh as a force that says no but that it traverses and produces things, it induces pleasure, forms knowledge, produces discourse. It needs to be considered as a productive network which runs through the whole social body, much more than as a negative insistence whose function is repression (p. 61).

Foucault's notion of power as creative contrasts with the Marxian model of power as repressive and has interesting applications for this text. Certainly, the 'unsaid' of the text acts repressively as a definite 'no' to public protests and to further agitation as was seen in the membership category analysis. At the textual level, however, the 'said' of the text acts in Foucault's sense as an empowering instrument delivered by the most senior official of the employing department in order to inspire teachers to be 'productive'. The use of the first person is indicative of a highly proactive and productive application of power. It reinforces the author's position as the wielder of productive power.

Conclusion

In his recent work on textual analysis in qualitative research, Peräkylä (2005) made the initial distinction between discourse analytic approaches, influenced largely by the work of Foucault, and MCA with the former 'concerned about the assumptions that underlie *what* is (and what is not said) in the text' and the latter 'concerned about the *descriptive apparatus* that makes it possible to say whatever is said' (p. 872). However, his later commentary on Eglin and Hester's work on the 'Montreal Massacre' acknowledged that 'categories are not however, neutral resources of description' and that 'the analysis of categorisation gives the researcher access to the cultural worlds and moral orders on which the text hinges' (p. 874). He concluded that 'at the end of the day, membership categorisation analysis invites the qualitative researcher to explore the conditions of action of description in itself' (ibid).

By adopting a blended approach in this chapter, we have taken up this invitation to explore both the 'conditions' and 'action' of the letter. We have drawn upon three traditions to examine the underlying ideological and moral *what* of this letter and the mechanisms for *how* this was constructed. We believe that the three layers of analysis presented here support Gee's (1990) view that 'language is inherently ideological, that is, that any use of the language is both an assessment and expression, in both form and function, of ideology' (p. 131). As a sample of institutional discourse, this text organises social relations in order to create the virtual reality of the language proficiency measures as the dominant ideology or 'right stance' (Gee 1990). The historical, social and intertextual contexts first situated the text within the dominant discourse of the times. The MCA then explored the organisation of the social relations in the creation of a virtual reality. The linguistic analysis explored the purposeful and creative applications of language within the text identifying its aims as:

1. To wield institutionalised power; and
2. To promote language proficiency measures as the 'right stance'.

Textual analysis of the Secretary's letter has identified the social machinery at work in this text in creating a logic that contributed to the construction of a virtual reality that had to be taken up by classroom teachers in Hong Kong. Teachers were asked to 'move' both figuratively in terms of mindset, and literally in terms of location and life paths. For some, accepting the productive power of the new reality of the LPAT imperative constituted undertaking an immersion INSET abroad to complete the training and assessment. As a policy text, this work was accomplished in and through its interactional machinery. Linguistically and categorically, the text was 'suffused with practical methods of reasoning' (Housley and Fitzgerald 2007: 202-203) that supported the promulgation of the new reality of the Hong Kong Language Proficiency Requirement policy.

References

Bray, M. and Koo, R. 2004. Postcolonial patterns and paradoxes: Language and education in Hong Kong and Macao. *Comparative Education*, 40 (2), 226-238.

Bridges, S. 2007. Learner perceptions of a professional development immersion course. *Prospect*, 22 (2), 39-60.

Cooke, B. 2000. Hong Kong, in *Teacher Education in the Asia-Pacific Region: A Comparative Study*, edited by P. Morris and J. Williamson. New York: Falmer, 33-74.

Curriculum Development Council. 2000. *Learning to Learn: General Studies for Primary Schools* (Consultation document). Hong Kong: HKSAR.

Education Bureau. 2007a. *Key Statistics – Primary Education*. Accessed March 2008 at http://www.edb.gov.hk/index.aspx?langno=1&nodeid=1038.

Education Bureau. 2007b. *Key Statistics – Secondary Education*. Accessed March 2008 at http://www.edb.gov.hk/index.aspx?langno=1&nodeid=1039.

Education and Manpower Bureau. 2003. *Education Statistics*. Hong Kong: HKSAR.

Education Commission. 1994. *Report on the Working Group on Language Proficiency*. Hong Kong: Government Printer.

Education Commission. 1996. *Report (No. 6)*. Hong Kong: Government Printer.

Education Commission. 1999. *Review of Education System: Framework for Education Reform – Learning for Life*. Hong Kong: HKSAR.

Eglin, P. and Hester, S. 1999. 'You're all a bunch of feminists:' Categorization and the politics of terror in the Montreal Massacre. *Human Studies*, 22 (2), 253-272.

Foucault, M. 1984. Truth and power, in *The Foucault Reader*, edited by M. Foucault and P. Rabinow. New York, NY: Pantheon, 51-75.

Freebody, P. 2003. *Qualitative Research in Education: Interaction and Practice*. London: Sage.

Gee, J.P. 1990. *Sociolinguistics and Literacies: Ideology in Discourses*. London: Falmer Press.

Geertz, C. 1973. *The Interpretation of Cultures: Selected Essays*. New York, NY: Basic Books.

Government of the Hong Kong Special Administrative Region (HKSAR). November 2000. *Syllabus Specifications for the Language Proficiency Assessment for Teachers (English Language)*. Hong Kong: HKSAR.

Hester, S. and Eglin, P. 1992. *A Sociology of Crime*. London: Routledge.

Hong Kong Professional Teachers' Union. 2000. *Extracts From Minutes of Four Seminars on Benchmark Exam For Principals and Teachers*. PTU News, 29, 1-2.

Housley, W. and Fitzgerald, R. 2007. Categorization, interaction, policy, and debate. *Critical Discourse Studies*, 4 (2), 187-206.

Information Services Department HKSAR. (2000, September 25). Revised arrangements help teachers attain language benchmarks. Retrieved May 6, 2008 from http://www.info.gov.hk/gia/general/200009/25/0925249.htm.

Lee, J. 1984. Innocent victims and evil-doers. *Women's Studies International Forum*, 7 (1), 69-73.

Murdock, G. 1997. Cultural studies at the crossroads, in *Studying Culture: An Introductory Reader* (2nd ed.), edited by A. Gray and J. McGuigan. London: Arnold, 80-90.

Peräkylä, A. 2005. Analyzing talk and text, in *The Sage Handbook of Qualitative Research* (3rd ed.), edited by N.K. Denzin and Y.S. Lincoln. Thousand Oaks, CA: Sage, 869-886.

Pennington, M.C. 1995. *Research Monograph 5: Modeling Teacher Change: Relating Input to Output*. Hong Kong: English Department, City University of Hong Kong.

Sacks, H. 1972. On the analyzability of stories by children, in *Directions in Sociolinguistics: The Ethnography of Communication*, edited by J. J. Gumperez and D. Hymes. New York, NY: Rinehart and Winston, 325-345.

Sacks, H., Schegloff, E.A. and Jefferson, G. 1974. A simplest systematics for the organisation of turn taking for conversation. *Language*, 50, 696-735.

Schegloff, E.A. 2007. *Sequence Organization in Interaction: A Primer in Conversation Analysis 1*. Cambridge: Cambridge University Press.

Silverman, D. 1993. *Interpreting Qualitative Data: Methods for Analysing Talk, Text and Interaction*. London: Sage.

Silverman, D. 1998. *Harvey Sacks – Social Science and Conversation Analysis*. New York, NY: Oxford University Press.

Smith, D. 1987. *The Everyday World as Problematic: A Feminist Sociology*. Boston, NJ: Northeastern University Press.

Smith, D. 1990. The *Conceptual Practices of Power: A Feminist Sociology of Knowledge*. Boston: Northeastern University Press.

Standing Committee on Language Education and Research. 2003. *Final Report of Language Education Review*. Hong Kong: Printing Department of the HKSAR.

Tsui, A.B.M. 2004. Medium of instruction in Hong Kong: One country, two systems, whose language?, in *Medium of Instruction Policies: Which Agenda? Whose Agenda?*, edited by J.W. Tollefson and A.B.M. Tsui. Mahwah, NJ: Lawrence Erlbaum Associates, 97-116.

Tung, C.H. 1999. *Quality People Quality Home: Positioning Hong Kong for the 21st Century*. Hong Kong: HKSAR Information Services Department.

Appendix: Excerpts 'Language Proficiency'

Sept 25, 2000

Dear Principal/Teacher,

Language Proficiency

The language proficiency of students has been a matter of grave concern to the Hong Kong community. It depends on the interplay of many factors, e.g. the language environment, family support, student motivation, and the language proficiency of teachers. Much has been done over the years to address these issues. One of the elements in the overall strategy is the introduction of language benchmarks which set the standards for overall proficiency expected of language teachers.

When the Administration announced the introduction of language benchmarking in April, it drew strong reactions from some quarters of the teaching profession and different views from parents, education bodies and the community at large. We have reviewed the comments received and discussed with the key stakeholders.

Today, I announced revised arrangements for enhancing the language proficiency of teachers and complementary measures to improve the teaching of languages in school. A document setting out the revised arrangements is attached.

You will see that we have taken a more holistic approach in helping language teachers to improve their language proficiency and professional skills. The ultimate objective is to improve the effectiveness of student learning. The salient features of the revised package of measures are as follows:

[...]

I wish to re-emphasise that language benchmarking is by no means 're-licensing'; the registered status of serving teachers will not be affected by the outcome of the language proficiency training or assessment. I also trust that as a committed teacher, you will support lifelong learning to improve further your effectiveness in facilitating student learning.

Yours sincerely

Secretary for Education and Manpower

Chapter 11

Newspapers on Education Policy: Constructing an Authoritative Public Voice on Education

Sue Thomas

Introduction

In 2006, one Australian newspaper, *The Australian*, published a series of items on education. *The Australian*, published by Rupert Murdoch's News Ltd, is the biggest-selling national newspaper in Australia. Established in the sixties as a left-liberal newspaper, it has increasingly moved to the right. More recently, Murdoch has used *The Australian* to push economic liberalism onto the political agenda of many governments (Hobbs, 2007). Indeed, Hobbs (2007) notes that *The Australian* 'abandoned all pretence to critical, balanced journalism during 2003, and, instead, use the editorial and opinion pages of its Australian titles to further arguments calling for Australia's involvement in the 2003 invasion of Iraq' (266).

Similar campaigns have been conducted on industrial relations (cf.Buchanan 2008) and on education (2002-2008) (cf.Freesmith 2006, McLeod and Yates 2006, Snyder 2008), as senior members in the then Federal Government and their supporters in the Murdoch press created public controversies designed to propagate their ideology and to defend their policies (Buchanan 2008). Indeed in late 2007, '*The Australian* was informally known among some in the media and policy circles at the time as "the Government Gazette"' (Buchanan 2008: 34).

The series of items published in *The Australian* in 2006 was part of one such campaign that worked to construct an authoritative public voice on education that questioned the quality of Australian schooling and teachers. Teacher quality was an important element of the then Federal Government's education policy as evidenced by the Australian Government Quality Teacher Programme (AGQTP). This chapter analyses the ways in which the newspaper constructed a particular version of what good teachers should be within the policy context of the Australian Quality Teacher Programme. That is, it explores the interrelationships between the public debates on teacher quality in the media and the policies on teacher quality that formed the basis of the AGQTP. The chapter then examines the contribution of senior members of the Federal government to these debates. In so doing, the chapter shows how critical discourse analysis can provide a framework for understanding, and exploring, the interface between government, media and education policy.

The chapter first outlines a framework that conceptualises media and policy texts as public discourses, that is, of discourses in the public sphere, and of the public sphere as discursive space. It argues that such a conceptualisation enables investigations into the interface, or conjunctures, between discourses in the public sphere. Critical discourse analysis (CDA) is identified as a suitable means for analysing these discourses (Thomas 2006). Next, the chapter traces the discourses on quality constructed in both the education policies of the AQTP and in items about education in *The Australian*. The analysis shows how policy and media texts in public debates on quality in Australia constructed three discourses on teacher quality and standards. They were discourses of quality assurance, of quality improvement and of commonsense (Sachs 2003).

A critical discourse analysis of these texts shows how discourses of quality assurance and of quality improvement were constructed in the education policies in the AQTP. However, the analysis of the newspaper items traces the construction of an alternative, commonsense discourse on teacher quality that rejected these policy discourses. This commonsense discourse on teacher quality presented an authoritative public voice on teacher quality. The analysis then shows how this commonsense discourse was reinforced by the contributions of senior members of government to the media debates on quality schooling. The chapter concludes with comments on the ideological nature of public discourses on education. It shows how such discourses work within the public sphere to define educational policies and identities in particular ways.

Media and Education Policy as Public Discourses

Media texts and educational policies can be understood as discourses, that is, as social practices that represent social realities in particular ways, and construct particular social positions (Thomas 2006). Such an understanding recognises the importance of language and text in contemporary society, for as Luke (2002) argues, 'text, language and discourse have become the principal modes of social relations, civic and political life, economic behaviour and activity, where means of production and modes of information become intertwined in analytically complex ways' (98). Understanding media and policy as discourse draws on the Foucauldian theory of discourse as the conjunction of power and knowledge (cf Foucault 1976). Discourses are manifestations of power (Harvey 1996) in that they are sites of struggle over understandings of reality. Discursive struggles construct a preferred discourse that presents an hegemonic, common-sense version of the world (Allan 1998, A. Luke 1995/1996), an 'authorial voice' that suppresses differences and masks the socially constructed nature of the discourse (Gardiner 1992: 192).

Media and policy discourses work within discursive struggle to define not only what can be said and thought about education, but also to define who can speak, where, when and with what authority. Media texts are forms of public, institutional discourse embedded in relations of power and resistance (cf Bell and Garrett 1998, Fairclough 1995, Falk 1994, Higgins 1991, van Dijk 1988a, 1988b). As Allan (1998) notes, news discourse works to inscribe a preferred map of social reality in which certain definitions of reality are aligned with commonsense, thus naturalizing a preferred range of truth claims.

Similarly, educational policy can be understood as discursive practices and educational policies can be examined as discourse-related problems (cf Bacchi 2000, Ball 1993, Gale 2003, Taylor 2004, Thomas 2005). Policy documents are discursively produced 'within particular contexts whose parameters and particulars have been temporarily (and strategically) settled by discourse(s) in dominance' (Gale 1999: 405). The policy process, therefore, is a matter of discursive and textual practices (Jones, Lee, and Poynton 1998: 146). It is a site of discursive struggle between competing but unequal interests (Ball 1993, Gale 2003, Taylor, Rizvi, Lingard, and Henry 1997).

Both media and policy discourses may be described as public discourses that work to influence public opinion. In this chapter, the term 'public' does not refer to the state (government) or to private commodity-and service-producing organisations. Rather, the public is concerned with communal well-being and community interests (Sholar 1994). That is, publicness is the principle that corresponds to the public sphere, to that sphere in which public opinion is formed (Habermas 1996). It constitutes the 'social spaces and social practices in which people as citizens dialogue on issues' (Chouliaraki and Fairclough 1999: 137). However, the Habermasian (1989/1962, 1996) public sphere has been critiqued for its universalistic nature and its failure to address the plurality and fragmentation of contemporary social life (Benhabib 1996, Calhoun 1992, Fraser, 1992, Hunter, 2001).

The possibilities for critical, rational deliberation in contemporary media-saturated society have been questioned also (Gerstl-Pepin 2007, Lunt and Stenner 2005). Further, as Rundle (2007) notes,

> the structural and psychological changes created by the new media, global markets, and image cultures have utterly reconstructed the public sphere in which national political conversations were hitherto based and that, barring a huge global developmental reversal, it is not returning (p. 28).

These changes, together with the criticisms noted above, have led to work that has reconceptualised the public sphere as discursive space, that is, as a complex arena of discursive relations (McLaughlin 1994, Thomas 2004). Such an understanding of the public sphere recognises the fluid, dynamic structure of the public sphere and enables an analysis of the discursive connections made across local sites. The following analysis is informed by this understanding as it traces media and policy discourses that were constructed in public debates on education.

The public sphere is a media saturated one, producing and disseminating descriptions of the social order and social identities (Barker 1999, Gerstl-Pepin, 2007). Media discourses, while produced within privately owned organisations (Cunningham and Turner 2002) are intended to influence the public sphere and thus shape social relations (Falk 1994, Marginson 1993). Indeed, media discourses are the means by which government policy is interpreted for, as Falk (1994) has shown, 'the newspaper medium selects, develops and presents for public consumption what the discursive themes of policy will be' (p. 11). That is, media collude with government to construct particular versions of what public policy should be (Anderson 2007, C. Luke 2007), acting as conduits for policy agendas (Collins, Abelson, Pyman, and Lavis 2006). Policy documents can be described as the public expression of the intent of government (Marginson 1993) and as the constitution of the official discourse of the state (Codd 1988). However, as the state has responded to the demands of increasingly more assertive interest groups, they have become the bureaucratic instruments that administer public expectations (Taylor et al. 1997), and as such, constitute discourses directed to the public sphere. Thus, despite being produced in either the private or the government sectors, both policy and media discourses can be conceptualised as discourses of the public sphere, that is, as sites where power is exercised by contesting groups in discursive struggles over the construction of a public authoritative voice, in this case, on education.

CDA has been shown to be a valuable tool for investigating both media and educational policy discourses, and for investigating the links between these public discourses (cf Thomas 2004, 2006). CDA is a transdisciplinary method of analysis that draws on an ensemble of social science techniques. As such it provides a flexible means to analyse the discursive interrelationships inherent in complex social processes, including the interrelationships between media and policy discourses. It is employed in the following analysis to trace the discourses on quality and standards constructed both in education policy and in *The Australian*. Of principal concern is the discursive construction of an authorial, public voice on teachers.

The Australian Government Quality Teacher Programme

The Australian Commonwealth Government established the Australian Government Quality Teacher Program (AGQTP) in 1999. The programme was outlined in two reports: *Teachers for the 21st Century* (Department of Employment Education Training and Youth Affairs 2000) and *Australia's Teachers: Australia's Future* (Department of Education Science and Training 2003). Together these reports mapped out a national project that had two objectives: 'to update and improve teachers' skills and understanding in priority areas' and 'to enhance the status of teaching in government and non-government schools' (Australian Government Department of Education 2005: 1). The evaluation of the programme recommended that the AGQTP be continued for another four years, that is until 2009 and focus on the one objective, 'to increase teacher and school leader skills and understanding' (Australian Government Department of Education 2005: ix). Thus, the policy discourses constructed in these two reports continued to guide Australian Government policy in 2006, the period in which *The Australian* published a number of items on teacher quality.

These two policies constructed two discourses on quality and standards, both of which emphasised the importance of professional standards. However, each discourse advocated the development of standards through different means and for different purposes. *Teachers for the 21st Century* constructed a discourse that emphasised the link between national productivity and quality schooling, and in particular, teacher quality. It noted that

> education of the highest quality is the foundation of all our futures. It is education which empowers us to rise to the challenges of social, cultural, economic and technological change that we confront today ... education of the highest quality requires teachers of the highest quality. (Department of Employment Education Training and Youth Affairs 2000: 3)

The policy outlined a program designed to improve teacher quality and to increase the effectiveness of schools. The following extract contains the description of the program.

> *Teachers for the 21st Century* will improve teacher quality and increase the number of highly effective Australian schools in order to maximise student learning outcomes. It will do so by:
>
> * lifting the quality of teaching through targeted professional development and enhancing professional standards;
> * developing the skills of school leaders;
> * supporting quality school management; and
> * recognising and rewarding quality schools, school leaders and teachers.
>
> (Department of Employment Education Training and Youth Affairs, 2000: 3, 5, 13).

This description was repeated word for word three times throughout the policy: in the introduction by the then Federal Minister for Education, in the Executive Summary, and in the body of the report when outlining the central purpose of the program, to construct a deficit discourse of teachers and schools.

The discursive importance of repetition stems from the repetitive use of words to constitute 'a particular way of dividing up some aspect of reality which is built upon a particular ideological representation of that reality' (Fairclough 2001: 96) that works to privilege certain meanings over others as commonsense and uncontestable. The use of repetition in *Teachers for the 21st Century* constructed a deficit discourse of teachers and schools. This discourse painted a picture of low educational standards in Australian schools and repeatedly stressed the need to raise these standards (Department of Employment Education Training and Youth Affairs 2000: 12). The quality of the teaching profession was identified as being both the cause of these low standards and as the means by which educational standards will be raised. Teachers were required to

> work together within their school communities to identify goals, define standards and expectations, review and refine teaching practices and prioritise areas for action and improvement. They [were to] accept responsibility for assessing the impact of their teaching on student outcomes and report on and [were to be] accountable for these outcomes (Department of Employment Education Training and Youth Affairs 2000: 11).

In this way, standards were explicitly linked to student outcomes and to teacher accountability. Teachers were 'the primary means by which educational standards will be raised' (p. 12). However, teachers were depicted as needing external assistance to set professional standards. Indeed, standards were to be developed 'by working with and through the teaching profession' (p. 12) in 'a cooperative effort from the Commonwealth Government, State and Territory government and non-government education providers, schools, principals, professional associations and parents' (p. 12). That is, the teaching profession was not granted autonomy to develop standards and determine the norms of professional practice that would lead to improved student outcomes, but rather were to be guided by government.

Teachers for the 21st Century constructed a preferred discourse of quality assurance (Sachs 2003), one that emphasised regulation and certification through standards. Standards 'were the means of improving the quality of teaching and enhancing the professional standing of teachers' (Department of Employment Education Training and Youth Affairs 2000: 17). That is, it was a regulatory discourse of quality in which teachers were positioned as needing to improve their skills. The focus of such a discourse was on the attainment of standards that would lead to improved performance.

Rather than focusing on a lack of skills and the need for regulation through the introduction of national standards, the second policy document, *Australia's Teachers: Australia's Future*, constructed a discourse on quality teachers and schools that focused on innovation. Quality schooling was seen to be necessary to sustain innovation, and was defined in terms of the renewal of cultures of continuous innovation. Unlike *Teachers for the 21st Century*, quality was not seen to be problematic, although complacency about standards was to be avoided.

Australia has a comprehensive and inclusive education system which performs very well in international comparisons, meeting standards for a well-educated citizenry and workforce. Average standards are high and the best students and schools are amongst the best anywhere, but there is no cause for complacency. (Department of Education Science and Training 2003: xvii)

The report therefore, emphasised not the raising of standards, but the 'energising [of] schools for innovation' (Department of Education Science and Training 2003: 217). Teachers were positioned by this discourse as 'the key to mobilising schools for innovation' (Department of Education Science and Training 2003: xvii) as the discourse emphasised the role of standards in teacher development through professional learning.

The preferred discourse constructed in *Australia's Teachers, Australia's Future* was a discourse of quality improvement through standards (Sachs 2003). Such a discourse promotes a developmental approach to standards in the context of teacher professional development, learning and career advancement. It identifies the development of standards as a means of making explicit the norms of professional practice to which pupils are entitled and of which the wider public has a legitimate right to be assured. This discourse advocates transparency regarding the social and professional expectations and obligations of teachers. Professional standards developed in this context signal a democratic form of professionalism (Ingvarson 1998) and are most likely to be in the best interests of the profession (Sachs 2003).

Thus, the discourses on teacher quality constructed in the education policies that form the basis of the AGQTP both emphasised the introduction of professional standards. The preferred discourse constructed in the first policy was a discourse of quality assurance, focusing on the use of standards to improve performance. The preferred discourse in the second policy was a discourse of quality improvement that focused on the use of standards as a basis of reforming the profession. While the two discourses could be distinguished on the basis of varying degrees of professional autonomy over the control and ownership of the development and monitoring of the standards, both discourses are concerned with the processes of ensuring teacher quality. In contrast, as the following analysis demonstrates, the preferred media discourse constructed in *The Australian* in 2006 was a commonsense discourse on quality that measures teacher quality in terms of a product, student outcomes.

The 2006 Campaign on Education in *The Australian*

In 2006, *The Australian* published a large number (141) items on education. These items raised concerns about the standard of education in Australian schools. They were part of a long-standing campaign on education that targeted:

the alleged transgressions of progressive literacy teachers and educators. The newspaper's explicit intention has been to change the literacy curriculum. The Coalition government has also played an active role in the campaign, aiming to assume greater centralised control of literacy education via a national curriculum (Snyder 2008: 214).

The items published in 2006 covered five broad themes: the teaching of English/ literacy, science/mathematics teaching, outcomes-based education (OBE), the history curriculum and the quality of teachers. Fifteen items focused specifically on the quality of teaching and will form the basis of the following analysis. Teacher quality was raised as a concern in many of the items that focused on the other themes also. For example, an article (Box 2006: 8) that dealt with the teaching of literature was headed 'Writer backs PM attack on teaching' and repeated the Prime Minister's comments on contemporary teaching practices in literature as 'rubbish' and on outcomes-based education as 'gobbledegook'.

Of the 15 items on quality teaching, seven, or almost half, were published in the months of July and August when the number of articles on Education peaked. Items that covered the lead up to, the reporting on, and the aftermath of, a national summit on the History curriculum held in mid-August 2007 dominated the news coverage in these months. Significantly, three articles on the quality of teaching were published in the last three days of August following the summit. Two, headed 'Teachers are not so clever any more' (Ferrari 2006a: 1) and 'A failure to make the grade' (Leigh and Ryan 2006: 8), raised questions about the quality of teachers, and so led the reader to question teachers' abilities to make decisions about appropriate History curricula.

Declarative sentences are a characteristic feature of most media texts, including newspaper items. Making statements involves the exchange of knowledge or what Fairclough (2003) calls epistemic modality. Epistemic modality refers to the authors' commitment to the truth. Assertions or statements of fact realise strong commitments to truth. Evaluation refers to the ways in which authors commit themselves to values and concerns the authors' commitment to desirability (Fairclough 2003). Of particular interest to the following analysis are evaluative statements about desirability and undesirability, about what is good and what is bad. Thus, analyses of modality and evaluation involve analyses of how the world is represented, of the desirability or undesirability of these representations, and of how an authoritative voice on such realities is constructed.

This was certainly the case in the 15 items under analysis. However, several of these items also included questions. A total of eight questions were raised in the 15 items on teacher quality. The eight questions, listed in chronological order, were:

1. The question at the forefront of every parent's mind must therefore be: how

    trustworthy are those hands? (Auty 2006: 14)

2. Did someone mention that dreaded T-word – testing? (Auty 2006: 14)
3. What can be done to make teaching more family friendly? (Donnelly 2006c: 24)
4. Why not free schools to reward better-performing teachers, especially women, instead of having a centralised, lock-step salary scale? (Donnelly 2006c: 24)
5. So what is the best way to reward better performing teachers? (Donnelly, 2006b: 14)
6. Should we worry if the literacy and numeracy of new teachers has fallen? (Leigh and Ryan 2006: 8)
7. Why have schools been powerless to sack bad teachers, child abusers and thieves? (Wheeldon 2006: 29)
8. What other issues might be on the agenda? (Donnelly 2006a: 17)

These questions were found in the feature articles, guest columns written by political, social, religious or academic leaders (Harriss, Leiter, and Johnson 1992: 468), which did not report an event but, rather, commented on a particular issue. The nature of such columns privileged the writer as an authority on the issue under discussion. The use of questions in the feature articles was significant as asking questions indicates a knowledge exchange where the (authoritative) author elicits the reader's commitment to truth (Fairclough 2003). An analysis of the questions raised in the features on teacher quality, therefore, highlights those features evaluated as desirable or undesirable by authoritative voices on education, features to which the reader's commitment is sought. The eight questions listed above highlighted features that raised concerns about the trustworthiness of teachers, including their ability to make decisions about assessment and curriculum; the falling standard, or quality, of teachers, including the notion of better-performing teachers, and by presupposition bad teachers; and an agenda on education that should be taken to address teacher quality. That is, these features worked together to construct a preferred media discourse on schools and teachers.

The Trustworthiness of Teachers

The first item that explicitly looked at the quality of teachers was a feature item published in February (Auty 2006). This item was the first to question the trustworthiness of teachers.

> Whether we like it or not the future character of Australia lies fairly and squarely in the hands of our educators. The question at the forefront of every parent's mind must therefore be: how trustworthy are those hands? (Auty 2006: 14).

As the following quote shows, the item depicted teachers in an unfavourable light, as 'educational brainwashers' and as 'habitual liars', and questioned their teaching of the curriculum, especially the history curriculum.

> My belief is that, like habitual liars, deliberate educational brainwashers are quick to see their own habits mirrored in the actions of others. According to such people and their international mentors no one ever acted dispassionately even when making every effort to do so... Indeed this precise argument is used regularly nowadays as a justification for the deliberation fabrication of history. (Auty 2006: 14)

These constructions were to be repeated throughout the year. For example, Wheeldon (2006) explicitly raised the question of the loss of trust in teachers and its leading to the undervaluation of teachers in an item published in December.

An anonymous item, anonymous in that there was no byline, published in March described teachers as 'Know nothings' who 'make a mockery of education' (MATP 2006: 13). That item went on to establish an opposition between 'hard-Left cadre of theoreticians and educrats who believe that the worst things kids can be exposed to are competition, memorisation and John Howard' (MATP 2006: 13) and individual teachers doing 'excellent, even heroic, jobs in the classrooms' (MATP 2006: 13). Binary oppositions construct a relationship between a preferred version of reality on the one hand and the description of a behaviour or event on the other. The relationship is constructed in such a way that the event or behaviour does not fit the rules or categories of preferred version of reality. The effect is to construct 'a binary opposition of the permitted and the forbidden' (Foucault 1977: 183). The use of binary oppositions enables the Other to be identified as the source of problems (Apple 1989, van Leeuwen 1996). Thus, in the opposition noted above, 'good, heroic' teachers were valued positively over 'Left cadre theoreticians and educrats' who fight parents and governments as they refuse to adopt a uniform A-E report card system. As Auty (2006: 14) asked, 'did someone mention that dreaded T-word – testing?' (p. 14).

Auty also used an opposition to identify undesirable and desirable teaching practices. Reflecting the opposition between the heroic teacher and the Left educrat, this opposition contrasted radicalism with 'anything established or traditional or – worst of all – conservative' (Auty 2006: 14). Radicalism is found in 'the methods and emphases employed by newer generations of teachers' (Auty 2006: 14). Radicalism was seen to be undesirable for it politicises the classroom and

> the basis for such a belief [in radicalism] rests almost always on rhetorical cliché rather than empirical evidence does nothing to lesson its self-righteous force. The phenomena I describe as the rhetoric of radicalism is ubiquitious in education and the arts where it creates untold damage through causing a too-ready abandonment of tested principles. (Auty 2006: 14).

These items depicted undesirable teachers as radical, left-leaning 'educrats' who fight with parents and governments, who avoid testing, who fabricate history, and most importantly are not to be trusted. They were the Other, the source of problems in education.

The Falling Standards of Teachers

Not only are untrustworthy teachers constructed as the source of problems in education, but teacher standards were depicted as falling. One item (Ferrari 2006a) states that 'teachers are not as smart as they were 20 years ago, an Australian-first study concludes in a finding that will reinforce concerns over declining classroom standards' (p. 1). The study conducted by two economists compared the literacy and numeracy standards of new teachers over a 20 year period and found that 'the standards of new teachers has fallen substantially' (Leigh and Ryan 2006: 8), particularly the standards of women teachers. This latter finding echoed the theme of an earlier item that sent 'an urgent call to schoolmarms' (Donnelly 2006c: 24) and outlined the desirability of the recruitment and retaining of high-achieving women as teachers.

Other items presented an alternative view on the standards of teachers. For example, an item, published on the day after the two items noting the declining standards of new teachers, claimed that 'Uni's top students choose teaching' (Ferrari 2006b: 7) because 'more than half the students starting a teaching degree at one of the nation's leading universities chose a teaching career, despite having the marks to study engineering, arts, science or medicine' (Ferrari 2006b: 7). New teacher education students at this university were high-achievers. Another item reported on a conference of educators that 'defended the 'impressive record' of Australia's school teachers' (Illing 2006: 2). However, these views on the standards of teachers and teaching were given little credence in the feature articles that focused on the quality of teachers, although recognition was given to 'better performing teachers' (Donnelly 2006b, 2006c) in discussions of what should be done to address the problem of quality in Australian schools.

Looking Ahead to What Should be Done

The solution to improving teacher quality was seen to lie in freeing schools 'to reward better-performing teachers, especially women, instead of having a centralised, lock-step salary scale' (Donnelly 2006c: 24). Wheeldon (2006) encapsulated this solution best when she stated that

> loss of trust in a handful of teachers leads to undervaluation of them all. This undervaluation becomes a short-sighted excuse for a depression of salaries, which of course lowers the quality of intake of new teachers, and so the spiral

goes on. Now we do not have enough teachers to teach our children, largely
because of our inability to terminate those who have lost our confidence. Sack
the bad ones, pay the good ones professional salaries. Give teachers respect.
Then stand back and watch intelligent people, including men, line up for a very
rewarding career (p. 29).

Such a solution constructed an opposition between teachers, that of better-
performing, good teachers and bad teachers, who were likened to child abusers
and thieves (Wheeldon 2006: 29). Better-performing teachers were identified
as teachers who 'are more successful in improving students' results, especially
in hard-to-staff schools in disadvantaged areas' (Donnelly 2006b: 14). That is,
judgements about good teachers are linked to students' results and accountability
(Donnelly 2006a). Good teachers should be rewarded, bad or underperforming
teachers on the other hand, should be dealt with, fired (Donnelly 2006a), sacked
(Hannan 2006, Wheeldon 2006).

In the final feature article on education, published in the final edition of *The
Australian* for the year, Donnelly outlined an agenda for school education the
'burning issue that will only get hotter in 2007' (Donnelly 2006a: 17). In that
item, Donnelly reiterated the issues identified above, issues that together worked
to construct a preferred discourse on schools and teachers. The discourse identified
'the widespread concerns about falling standards and academic rigour in the
curriculum' (Donnelly 2006a: 17). Teachers, described as untrustworthy, radical,
'know nothings' with lower standards in literacy and numeracy, were depicted as
a key factor in these concerns. Consequently, increased accountability was needed
in order to reward better-performing, good teachers and deal with bad teachers.
Judgements on teacher performance should be made on the basis of students'
results.

Such a discourse was a discourse on standards as commonsense (Sachs 2003).
It constructed a view of teacher standards and quality that saw a regulatory,
framework that controlled teachers and teaching as commonsense, 'sack the bad
ones, pay the good ones professional salaries' (Wheeldon 2006: 29). It presented
an uncritical view of standards as benchmarks to be imposed on the profession,
benchmarks measured against students' results in literacy and numeracy.

Government Contributions to the Debate

It was noted earlier in this chapter that the news coverage of the issue of teacher
quality peaked in the months of July and August, that is in the time of the national
summit on the History curriculum held in mid-August 2007. Three items directly
attributed to senior members of the Australian government, specifically the Prime
Minister of Australia, John Howard, and the Minister for Education, Julie Bishop,
were included in this coverage. These items differed from the previously noted item
that reported on statements by the then Prime Minister, John Howard, statements

that described current teaching practices as 'rubbish' and 'gobbledegook'. Rather than reporting on statements made by the Prime Minister and the Education Minister, the items contained extracts of speeches given by these senior members of the government. As the following analysis will show, the speeches of both the Minister and the Prime Minister constructed a discourse of poor teaching that endorsed the commonsense discourse traced in *The Australian*.

This government discourse was characterised by declarative sentences that asserted strong commitments to the truth about history teaching. The discourse constructed the teaching of history as being problematic. Specifically, there were

> two glaring problems with regard to the teaching of Australian history: the quantitative problem and the qualitative problem. Not enough students are learning Australian history; and there is too much political bias and not enough pivotal facts and dates being taught (Bishop 2006c: 12).

The solution to this problem was a renaissance in the teaching of history that focused on big themes, such as the Enlightenment and the British inheritance, and that developed 'a body of knowledge that is rich in dates, facts and events' (Bishop 2006c: 12). The truth of this construction was established by the repeated use of the adjective *proper* as in 'I don't think you can have a proper teaching and comprehension of Australian history' (Howard 2006: 15) and the modal adverb *obviously* as in 'we obviously have to see Australia as heavily influenced by the Western intellectual position, the Enlightenment and all that's associated with it' (Howard 2006: 15). The evaluation of history teaching in the discourse constructed by senior member of the Australian government worked to establish current practices in the teaching of history as being undesirable. While this discourse specifically refers to History teaching, the questioning of the current teaching practices presupposes a questioning of teacher quality. Indeed, this is apparent in the full speech given by the Minister for Education, where reference is made to 'unqualified or scarcely-qualified teachers' (Bishop 2006a).

Further, as noted earlier, statements of desirability and undesirability position the speakers, in this case, the Minister for Education and the Prime Minister, as the authoritative voices on the teaching of History. Such a positioning is evidenced also in the Minister and Prime Minister's use of the deictic categories *I*, *we* and *our* throughout their speeches. For example, the Minister for Education claims that

> we have a rich and unique national story. We have to ask ourselves why so few of our children know it. Whatever the reasons, the situation is not good enough. I see this is an issue of national importance. I believe it's time to fix it (Bishop 2006b: 11).

The reason for the problem and the solution can be found in the Prime Minister's statement that 'we want to bring about a renaissance of both interest in and understanding of Australian history, and that this must involve a greater focus on disciplined teaching and understanding of history in Australian schools' (Howard 2006: 15).

In both these extracts, the use of deictic categories encouraged the hearer/reader to identify with the interests outlined in the truth claims constructed in the discourse (Allan 1998). That is, it positioned the hearer/reader of the speech to agree with the construction of History teaching and teachers as problematic. At the same time, others who did not agree with these evaluations, specifically teachers, were positioned outside the discourse. Thus, the speeches of the two senior members of the Australian government constructed a commonsense discourse of teaching and teacher quality. This discourse positioned the Minister and the Prime Minister as the authoritative public voice on, and excluded teachers from, the debate (see also Bridges and Bartlett (this volume) for another example of the 'truth' of institutional discourse). Further, this discourse focused on poor student outcomes, that is, on students' lack of knowledge of the facts of Australian history. As such, it such echoed and reinforced the commonsense discourse on teacher quality constructed in The Australian newspaper items analysed above

A Shared Authoritative Public Voice on Education

The above analysis has shown how *The Australian* and senior members of the then Federal Government conducted a campaign on teacher quality. The campaign was characterised by the use of right wing columnists writing in the opinion pages, attacks on the credibility of teachers and the intervention of senior members of the Government. The campaign resulted in the construction of a commonsense discourse on teaching and teachers in Australian schools. This discourse worked to naturalise, or reify, commonsense understandings of teachers in schools, privileging a decisive definition of low teacher quality that results in poor student outcomes. This privileged version of teacher quality is at odds with that constructed in the policy documents, which emphasised the development of professional standards.

Indeed, the notion of a professional body that will 'identify standards that are associated with best practice and certify how well teachers meet the criteria' (Donnelly 2006b: 14) was seen to be flawed as such standards can be politicised or be 'so vacuous as to appear useless' (Donnelly 2006b: 14). This was seen to be 'highly likely given that the board of Teaching Australia [the body established by the Australian Government 'as the national body for the teaching profession, to be conducted by teachers and school leaders' (Teaching Australia 2006)] consists of the usual education suspects' (Donnelly 2006b: 14). At the time, such attacks on the credibility of persons who were perceived to be at odds with Government policy was a 'standard operating procedure for the Howard [the then Federal] Government' (Buchanan 2008: 37).

Thus, policy discourses on teacher quality, discourses that emphasised professional standards, and identified teachers as stakeholders in the introduction of these standards, were rejected in favour of a commonsense discourse on teacher quality. Such a discourse was characterised by statements that evaluated teachers as untrustworthy; as teaching inappropriate curriculum; as of a lower quality that teachers of previous generations; and who were responsible for falling standards and poor student outcomes in Australian schools. The discourse called for increased accountability for teachers, who were to be judged in terms of student outcomes and sacked if they were found wanting. Rather than focusing on the process of ensuring quality through professional standards, the focus was on a measurable product, thus simplifying, and so reducing the complexity of, the issue of quality teaching. In this way, the commonsense discourse on quality established an authoritative public voice on education and teacher quality.

The critical discourse analysis outlined in this chapter illustrated how discourses work to naturalise, or reify, commonsense understandings of issues in public debates on education. In so doing, it demonstrated the ideological nature of public discourses in debates about teachers and education. That is, it showed how discourses constructed an hegemonic equilibrium that constituted particular realities through discursive practices in a complex process of contestation and negotiation, and in the making of discursive links across the sites of media, government and education policy. The analysis illustrated the complexity of the interrelationships between media and policy discourses.

Rather than a bridge between contexts of policy-making (Ball 1990, Wallace 1994) or an unseen hand guiding the policy-making process (Wallace 1993), it showed that the media is best described as an integral part of the proliferation of discourses that constitute public debates on education policies. That is, it demonstrated how the media acted as a conduit, colluding with government to generate debate on public policy in such a way that it constructed an authoritative public version of teacher quality. Finally, the analysis established that media discourses are essential to the construction of discursive threads within the complex web of contested meanings that characterise policy-making processes, working within the public sphere to construct an authoritative public voice that defines educational policies and identities in particular ways.

References

Allan, S. 1998. News from nowhere: Televisual news discourse and the construction of hegemony, in *Approaches to Media Discourse* edited by A. Bell and P. Garrett. Oxford: Blackwell Publishers, 105-141.

Anderson, G.L. 2007. Media's impact on educational policies and practices: Political spectacle and social control. *Peabody Journal of Education*, 82 (1), 103-120.

Apple, M.W. 1989. Critical introduction: Ideology and the state in education policy, in *The State and Education Policy* edited by R. Dale. Milton Keynes: Open University Press, 1-20.

Australian Government Department of Education, S.a.T. 2005. *An Evaluation of the Australian Government Quality Teacher Programme 1999 to 2004*. Canberra: Commonwealth of Australia.

Auty, G. 2006, Friday 3 February 2006. Teaching is failing the test. *The Australian:* 14.

Bacchi, C. 2000. Policy as discourse: what does it mean? Where does it get us? *Discourse: Studies in the Cultural Politics of Education*, 21 (1), 45-57.

Ball, S.J. 1990. *Politics and Policy Making in Education: Explorations in Policy Sociology*. London: Routledge.

Ball, S.J. 1993. What is policy? Texts, trajectories and toolboxes. *Discourse: The Australian Journal of Educational Studies*, 13 (2), 10-17.

Barker, C. 1999. *Television, Globalization and Cultural Identities*. Buckingham: Open University Press.

Bell, A. and Garrett, P. (eds). 1998. *Approaches to Media Discourse*. Oxford: Blackwell Publishers.

Benhabib, S. 1996. Toward a deliberative model of democratic legitimacy, in *Democracy and Difference: Contesting the Boundaries of the Political*, edited by S. Benhabib. Princeton, NJ: Princeton University Press, 67-94.

Bishop, J. 2006a. Forgetting our past, failing our future: The teaching of Australian history [Electronic Version]. Retrieved 26 May 2008 from http://www.dest. gov.au/Ministers/Media/Bishop/2006/08/b001170806.asp.

Bishop, J. 2006b, Thursday 17 August 2006. If we forget our nation's past, we will fail our future. *The Australian*, 11.

Bishop, J. 2006c, Thursday, 6 July 2006. Our classrooms need to make a date with the facts. *The Australian*, 12.

Box, D. 2006, Saturday, 22 April 2006. Writer backs PM on teaching. *The Australian*, 8.

Buchanan, J. 2008. Values, research and industrial relations policy: Recent controversies and implications for the future. *Dialogue (Academy of the Social Sciences in Australia)*, 27 (1), 30-39.

Calhoun, C. (ed.). 1992. *Habermas and the Public Sphere*. Cambridge, MA: The MIT Press.

Chouliaraki, L., and Fairclough, N. 1999. *Discourse in Late Modernity Rethinking Critical Discourse Analysis*. Edinburgh: Edinburgh University Press.

Codd, J. 1988. The construction and deconstruction of educational policy documents. *Journal of Education Policy*, 3 (3), 235-247.

Collins, P.A., Abelson, J., Pyman, H. and Lavis, J.N. 2006. Are we expecting too much from print media? An analysis of newspaper coverage of the 2002 Canadian healthcare reform debate. *Social Science and Medicine*, 63, 89-102.

Cunningham, S. and Turner, G. 2002. *The Media and Communications in Australia* (2nd ed.). St. Leonards, N.S.W.: Allen & Unwin.

Department of Education Science and Training. (2003). Australia's teachers, Australia's future: Advancing innovation, science, technology and mathematics.

Retrieved 19 September, 2004, from http://dest.gov.au/schools/teachingreview/documents/Main-Report.pdf.

Department of Employment Education Training and Youth Affairs. 2000. *Teachers for the 21st Century: Making the Difference*. Canberra: Commonwealth of Australia.

Donnelly, K. 2006a, Saturday 30 December 2006. Gloves off for rumble in the blackboard jungle. *The Australian*, 17.

Donnelly, K. 2006b, Friday 14 July 2006. Right criteria for rewards. *The Australian*, 14.

Donnelly, K. 2006c, Saturday 6 May 2006. Sounding an urgent call to schoolmarms. *The Australian*, 24.

Fairclough, N. 1995. *Critical Discourse Analysis: The Critical Study of Language*. London and New York: Longman.

Fairclough, N. 2001. *Language and Power* (2nd ed.). Harlow: Longman.

Fairclough, N. 2003. *Analysing Discourse and Text: Textual Analysis for Social Research*. London: Routledge.

Falk, I. 1994. The making of policy: Media discourse conversations. *Discourse: Studies in the Cultural Politics of Education*, 15 (2), 1-12.

Ferrari, J. 2006a, Monday 28 August 2006. Teachers are not so clever any more. *The Australian*, 1.

Ferrari, J. 2006b, Tuesday 29 August 2006. Uni's top students chooose teaching. *The Australian*, 7.

Foucault, M. 1976. Politics and the study of discourse. *Ideology and Consciousness*, 3, 7-26.

Foucault, M. 1977. *Discipline and Punish* (A. Sheridan, trans.). London: Penguin Books.

Fraser, N. 1992. Rethinking the public sphere: A contribution to the critique of actually existing democracy, in *Habermas and the Public Sphere* edited by C. Calhoun. Cambridge, Massachusetts: The MIT Press, 109-142.

Freesmith, D. 2006. The politics of the English curriculum: Ideology in the campaign against critical literacy in *The Australian*. *English in Australia*, 41 (1), 25-30.

Gale, T. 1999. Policy Trajectories: treading the discursive path of policy analysis. *Discourse: Studies in the Cultural Politics of Education*, 20 (3), 393-407.

Gale, T. 2003. Realising Policy: the who and how of policy production. *Discourse: Studies in the Cultural Politics of Education*, 24 (1), 51-65.

Gardiner, M. 1992. *The Dialogics of Critique: M.M. Bakhtin and the Theory of Ideology*. London: Routledge.

Gerstl-Pepin, C. 2007. Introduction to the special issue on the media, democracy, and the politics of education. *Peabody Journal of Education*, 82 (1), 1-9.

Habermas, J. 1989/1962. *The Structural Transformation of the Public Sphere: An Inquiry into a Category of Bourgeois Society* (T.W. Burger and F. Lawrence, trans.). Cambridge, MA: MIT Press.

Habermas, J. 1996. The public sphere, in *Media Studies: A Reader* edited by P. Marris and S. Thornham. Edinburgh: Edinburgh University Press, 55-59.

Hannan, E. 2006, Friday 3 March 2006. Update or face sack, teachers told. *The Australian*, 7.

Harriss, J., Leiter, K. and Johnson, S. 1992. *The Complete Reporter: Fundamentals of News Gathering, Writing, Editing* (Sixth ed.). New York: Macmillan.

Harvey, D. 1996. *Justice, Nature and the Geography of Difference*. Oxford: Blackwell Publishers.

Higgins, C. 1991. Broadcast news: a linguistic mode of analysis. *Continuum: The Australian Journal of Media and Culture*, 5 (1), 149-165.

Hobbs, M. 2007. 'More paper than physical': The reincorporation of News Corp and its representation in the Australian press. *Journal of Sociology*, 43 (3), 263-281.

Howard, J. 2006, Friday 18 August 2006. Let's understand our Western institutional heritage. *The Australian*, 15.

Hunter, N.D. 2001. Accommodating the public sphere: Beyond the market model. *Minnesota Law Review*, 85 (6), 1591-1637.

Illing, D. 2006, Monday 18 December 2006. Teachers defend their 'impressive record'. *The Australian*, 2.

Ingvarson, L. 1998. Teaching standards: foundations for professional development reform, in *International Handbook of Educational Change* edited by A. Hargreaves, A. Lieberman, M. Fullan and D. Hopkins. Amsterdam: Kluwer.

Jones, G., Lee, A. and Poynton, C. 1998. Discourse analysis and policy activism: readings and rewritings of Australian university research policy, in *Activism and the Policy Process* edited by A. Yeatman. St Leonards, NSW: Allen & Unwin, 146-170.

Leigh, A. and Ryan, C. 2006, Monday 28 August 2006. A failure to make the grade. *The Australian,* 8.

Luke, A. 1995/1996. Text and discourse: An introduction to critical discourse analysis, in *Review of Research in Education* edited by M.W. Apple. 21 1995-1996 Washington, DC: American Educational Research Association, 3-48.

Luke, A. 2002. Beyond science and ideology critique: Developments in critical discourse analysis. *Annual Review of Applied Linguistics*, 22, 96-110.

Luke, C. 2007. As seen on TV or was that my phone? New media literacy. *Policy Futures in Education*, 5 (1), 50-58.

Lunt, P. and Stenner, P. 2005. The Jerry Springer Show as an emotional public sphere. *Media, Culture and Society*, 27 (1), 59-81.

Marginson, S. 1993. *Education and Public Policy in Australia*. Sydney: Cambridge University Press.

MATP. 2006, Wednesday 1 March 2006. KNOW NOTHINGS – NSW teachers make a mockery of education. *The Australian*, 13.

McLaughlin, L. 1994. Introduction: Critical Media Pedagogy and the Public Sphere. *Journal of Communication Inquiry*, 18 (2), 5-7.

McLeod, J. and Yates, L. 2006. *Making Modern Lives Subjectivity, Schooling, and Social Change*. Albany, NY: State University of New York Press.

Rundle, G. 2007. Power Intellectuals in the Howard era. *Arena Magazine*, 91, 25-31.

Sachs, J. 2003. *The Activist Teaching Profession*. Buckingham: Open University Press.

Sholar, S.E. 1994. Habermas, Marx and Gramsci: Investigating the public sphere in organisational communication and public relations courses. *Journal of Communication Inquiry*, 18 (2), 77-92.

Snyder, I. 2008. *The Literacy Wars: Why Teaching Children to Read and Write is a Battleground in Australia*. Crow's Nest, NSW: Allen & Unwin.

Taylor, S. 2004. Researching educational policy and change in 'new times': using critical discourse analysis. *Journal of Education Policy*, 19 (4), 433-451.

Taylor, S., Rizvi, F., Lingard, B. and Henry, M. 1997. *Educational Policy and the Politics of Change*. London: Routledge.

Teaching Australia. 2006. Strategic Plan 2006-2009. Retrieved 18 December 2008 from http://www.teachingaustralia.edu.au/ta/webdav/site/tasite/shared/Publica tions%20and%20Covers/Our%20Plan:%202006-2009.pdf.

Thomas, S. 2004. Reconfiguring the Public Sphere: implications for analyses of educational policy. *British Journal of Educational Studies*, 52 (3), 228-248.

Thomas, S. 2005. The construction of teacher identities in educational policy documents: a Critical Discourse Analysis. *Melbourne Studies in Education*, 46 (1), 25-44.

Thomas, S. 2006. *Education Policy in the Media: Public Discourses on Education*. Tenerife: Post Pressed.

van Dijk, T.A. 1988a. *News Analysis*. Hillsdale, NJ: Lawrence Erlbaum Associates.

van Dijk, T.A. 1988b. *News as Discourse*. Hillsdale, NJ: Lawrence Erlbaum Associates.

van Leeuwen, T. 1996. The representation of social actors, in *Texts and Practices Readings in Critical Discourse Analysis* edited by C.R. Caldas-Coulthard M. Coulthard. London: Routledge, 32-70.

Wallace, M. 1993. Discourse of derision: the role of the mass media within the education policy process. *Journal of Education Policy*, 8 (4), 321-337.

Wallace, M. 1994, 4-8 April, 1994. *The Contribution of the Mass Media to the Education Policy Process*. Paper presented at the Annual Meeting of the American Educational Research Association, New Orleans.

Wheeldon, J. 2006, Saturday 2 December 2006. Blackboard bungle. *The Australian*, 29.

Index